Fear, greed
and panic

Fear, greed and panic

The psychology of the stock market

DAVID COHEN

JOHN WILEY & SONS, LTD

Chichester · New York · Weinheim · Brisbane · Singapore · Toronto

Published in 2001 by John Wiley & Sons Ltd,
Baffins Lane, Chichester
West Sussex PO19 1UD, England

National   01243 779777
International (+44) 1243 779777
e-mail (for orders and customer service enquiries):
cs-books@wiley.co.uk
Visit our Home Page on http://www.wiley.co.uk

Other Wiley Editorial Offices

John Wiley & Sons, Inc., 605 Third Avenue,
New York, NY 10158-0012, USA

WILEY-VCH Verlag GmbH, Pappelallee 3,
D-69469 Weinheim, Germany

John Wiley & Sons Australia Ltd, 33 Park Road, Milton,
Queensland 4064, Australia

John Wiley & Sons (Asia) Pte Ltd, 2 Clementi Loop #02-01,
Jin Xing Distripark, Singapore 129809

John Wiley & Sons (Canada) Ltd, 22 Worcester Road,
Rexdale, Ontario M9W 1L1, Canada

British Library Cataloguing in Publication Data
A catalogue record for this book is available from the British Library

Library of Congress Cataloging-in-Publication Data
Cohen, David, 1946–
    Fear, greed and panic : the psychology of the stock market / David Cohen.
        p. cm.
    Includes index.
    ISBN 0-471-48659-0 (paper)
    1. Investments—Psychological aspects.   2. Stocks—Psychological aspects.
    I. Title
HG4515.15 .C64 2001
332.63'22'019—dc21

2001024909

ISBN 0-471-48659-0

Project management by Originator, Gt Yarmouth, Norfolk (typeset in 10/12 Palatino)
Printed and bound in Great Britain by Biddles Ltd, Guildford and King's Lynn.
This book is printed on acid-free paper responsibly manufactured from sustainable
forestation, in which at least two trees are planted for each one used for paper
production.

In memory of two men
who loved – and hated –
the stock market:

William I. La Tourette (1925–1975)
Benjamin Cohen (1908–1994)

Contents

Contents _____

Contents

About the author

David Cohen is a psychologist, writer and film-maker. He has reported on mental health, immigration, why people make false confessions, sex, marketing to children, cults, finance, cigars and pirates for outlets as diverse as Channel 4, *Sunday Business*, Discovery, *Harpers and Queens*, ITV and the *New Scientist*. Recent films include one on Grace Kelly for Channel 4, the award winning *The Madness of Children* and *The Nuclear Game*. His books include *Psychologists on Psychology*, *The Development of Play*, the best selling *How to Succeed in Psychometric Tests* and *Bears and Bulls*. He hopes one day to write a good poem.

Acknowledgements

This book is an expanded and updated version of *Bears and Bulls* which was published early in 2000 by Metro Books. The stock market has changed mightily since and so the text needed many changes though the main thrust – that psychology has much to offer investors and market professionals – remains true.

I should like to thank Adrian Furnham and Bob Cumber for their comments. Bryce Cottrell, Matthew Orr, Hugh Priestley, Paul O'Donnell, André Giraud, Charles Clark, Roger Yates and Andrew Smithers were most generous with their time as were staff at The City Business Library. I am also grateful to Dr Vivien Ward at John Wiley for her support in making this edition happen – and to Bruce Shuttlewood at Originator for his care in editing this version.

Introduction

At the start of 2001, stock-market analysts were bewildered by the volatility of share prices. When the results for the Christmas trading season were announced in the UK, the share price of a number of stores plunged dramatically. Great Universal Stores, owners of up-market Burberrys and less than upmarket Argos, dropped 20 per cent in value on 11 January. The Body Shop fell 25 per cent; the discount retailer Matalan fell even more drastically. Did these stores do so badly at Christmas that hardly anyone bought Fragrance of Oil of Dewberry or the Lara Croft electronic toaster or an old Burberry mac?

Eh ... well ... no ... all these stores reported increased sales but sales had not increased as much as stock-market analysts hoped for. Many commentators gloom that the markets have gone mad – probably due to holes in the ozone layer over Wall Street – because in the good old days, stocks were stable, investors were sensible and the old-boy brolly network controlled the casino, sorry, stock market. The old-style brokers may have been sexist, racist and often drunk on a three-martini lunch but they were sound, bless them. Finance like most disciplines has its myth of golden times.

Think back nearly 200 years. On 18 June the future of Europe hinged on the Battle of Waterloo. At dawn on 20 June, hours after the battle ended, the financier Nathan Rothschild met one of his couriers at Folkestone harbour. The courier had just crossed the Channel from Ostend and had the first report of the battle. Hours before anyone in London, Rothschild knew Napoleon had lost.

Moments later Nathan was racing to London. His first call was on the Prime Minister, who had just heard of the English defeat at

Quatre Bras. The government was convinced that Nathan had got it wrong and that the Battle of Waterloo was lost. Nathan, however, had no doubt about the accuracy of his information. He drove from the Prime Minister straight on to the Stock Exchange.

The market was anxious. The price of Consols, the main government stock, was already low. The stock would rise, however, the moment people knew Napoleon had been defeated. Nathan leant against his favourite pillar at the Exchange, looked impassive and started selling. He sold Consols by the thousands. The price fell. He sold more. The price fell more. He sold more. Everyone followed his lead. If Nathan Rothschild who had the best networks of agents and information in Europe was selling, he must know what had happened and it could only mean Napoleon had won.

Then, when the price hit rock bottom, Nathan placed one huge order for Consols. It was perfect timing. A few minutes later, the truth was out. Napoleon had been defeated. The price of Consols soared. Nathan had shown cold cunning and a perfect reading of market psychology; he had made sharp use of his information advantage. This coup made him famous throughout Europe.

Two points emerge from this. Markets have always been volatile though it may be true that we are living through a period of unusual volatility. Political analysts point out that the voters in countries like Britain and the USA are more volatile than ever before and, perhaps, there is some connexion. The second point is that in his dealings Rothschild had shown the kind of psychological insight more often associated with the psychoanalyst Sigmund Freud. For the Freud family – not to mention the Freud theory – money sometimes caused surprising problems.

In 1866, when he was 10 years old, Sigmund Freud's Uncle Josef was arrested for forging 18,000 Russian roubles. The police suspected that the forgery was the tip of the iceberg and that the 'real source of the counterfeit money was England'. When they searched Josef Freud's home, the police found two suspicious letters from cousins of Sigmund who were living in Manchester. One boasted that 'fortune will not fail to smile on us'; in the second, the cousins asked Uncle Josef to 'find a bank for the merchandise where the turnover will be larger, faster and more profitable'. The last especially was read as proof of guilt and Josef Freud was sentenced to 10 years in jail.

In *Questions for Freud*, two American historians of psychiatry (Rand and Torok 1997) argue that the experience of seeing his uncle arrested scarred Sigmund Freud for life. Some 30 years later he was still having nightmares about Uncle Josef. It affected not only his attitudes to money – Freud refused to marry until he was sure he could support his wife – but also his attitudes to scientific research. The full details of the crime and its impact on Sigmund Freud allegedly can be found in papers deposited in the Library of Congress, which are embargoed until 2010. It seems, however, that Freud was ashamed that his much loved uncle was so obsessed with wealth – and that affected his psychoanalytic ideas about money, as I shall show.

Greed can make us believe in the truly bizarre. For 30 years a newsletter in the USA offered subscribers advice given by J.P. Morgan, the great financier. In fact, J.P. was long dead and the newsletter claimed to be communicating with his ghost, who could not stop thinking about the stock market and handed out supernatural share tips. In 1948 *Time* magazine exposed the scam. Subscribers to the newsletter were furious: J.P.'s ghost had given good tips.

Time's subscribers may have been furious, but they did not storm the editorial offices. Today – perhaps a sign of extreme volatility – there have been some cases of investors extracting the ultimate revenge. One in Atlanta in 1998 made world headlines.

Isolated explosive disorder – or being a bad loser

Mark Barton was a 44-year-old chemist who collected $600,000 insurance when his first wife was killed in 1993. He then became a day trader, an investor who deals for himself without a broker and who tries to buy and sell shares within a day making small profits on many quick trades. Barton, however, was a day trader who kept on losing. On Thursday 29 July 1998 he killed his second wife, their two children and nine workers in Atlanta brokerage houses. Hours later he put two guns to his head – and shot himself.

Mark Barton may be a one-off case but his actions may also suggest changes in the operations of markets are having an impact. Certainly there never seems to have been a case like it before. Bill Campbell, the mayor of Atlanta, said that one of Barton's many suicide notes expressed 'some concern about market losses'. Campbell insisted the killings weren't just a reaction to market fluctuations.

American psychiatrists never short of a label – and a dire pun – say Barton suffered from 'isolated explosive disorder'. But Barton chose the firms he attacked with grisly care.

In his lethal rampage he killed four people at All Tech and five at Momentum Securities. Both firms were zealots for day trading. Harvey Houtkin of All Tech calls himself the father of electronic trading; James Lee of Momentum Securities is president of the Electronic Traders Association.

I will return to the case of Barton and what it reveals about the illusions of being in control that investors can have.

These stories illustrate the fact that behaviours around money and investment are very much matters of psychology. However, traditionally economists deny this. According to Paul Ormerod (1997) in his *Butterfly Economics*, economists have been fixated for over 250 years on the theory of the rational man (and woman). This theory assumes it is natural to be rational about money and that human beings are by nature calculating machines who can analyse the risks and rewards of investments perfectly. This view flatters investment professionals who like to believe their decisions are based on rational assessment of evidence; they do not want clients to imagine that they place millions of money as a result of tips, fantasies, hunches gossiped up over sushi and champers at lunch. (The role of alcohol and cocaine in stock-market analysts' work, now there's a rich PhD ground for someone.)

The last 9 months of 2000 saw remarkable swings in the stock market especially in the NASDAQ index for high-tech shares and the Japanese Nikkei which fell from 20,000-odd in late 1998 to 13,100 in January 2001. The 8th of January 2001 saw the largest ever fall in the Dow Jones index and also in the NASDAQ index of high-technology shares.

In his influential book *Irrational Exuberance* (2000), Robert Shiller argues the American Dow Jones average tripled between 1994 and 1999 for a number of non-economic reasons; he lists the arrival of the

Internet, a new faith in technology, the baby-boomers and the behaviour of the growing number of day traders. I am not sure Shiller has nailed all the causes. In Britain the social and cultural context has been rather different. Up to 1999 there were few day traders; the Internet came to the UK later and there has never been quite the same faith in technology. Yet in Britain the FT-SE Index also rose from around 2,700 in 1994 to 6,500 in 2000. James Urquhart Stewart of Barclays Stockbrokers told me he was appalled by fellow City types who weren't happy just to make a sound profit but who were surfing the markets looking for a 'ten banger', a share which went up 10 times – i.e. a 1,000 per cent profit – in a matter of weeks. That was gambling, not investment, and certainly not the behaviour of a rational economic man.

Shekels, loot, lolly, dosh, moolah, the green stuff, ponies, monkeys, readies – there are as many slang words for money as for sex – are too important, however, for us to be easily rational about them. Money represents status, power, freedom. Most of us complain that we never have enough. It has been estimated that 23 per cent of daydreams concern money; the only two subjects we daydream about more are food and sex.

While governments insist we are going to have to save more for our old age, it is actually getting less easy to be rational about investment decisions because the small investor is faced with more and more choices and pressures.

Should you assume that you are going to live to the age of 90 and save for that, denying yourself reasonable treats like that holiday in Thailand? After all, you don't want to end up in the workhouse. But perhaps you need Thailand, the beaches, the strip clubs and the casinos, because you need to recharge. Or perhaps you should compromise and go to Corfu. Perhaps you need a variable holiday with a commodity-linked pension scheme. Help!

Money taboos

First, many people do not like thinking about investments or the risks they involve. People used to rely on the advice of bank managers they had known for years, but most British clearing banks no longer have old-style managers you can have a chat with. Evidence from the Basic Skills Agency and Department of Education and Employment suggests the majority of adults in Britain are mathematically incompetent; many are uncomfortable about their lack of skill and alarmed by the fact that to assess investment risks involves looking at, and thinking about, numbers.

Second, we have certain taboos about money. How much you earn, how much you have, is private. Nowadays one partner often doesn't know what the other partner is earning. I may know what will make you wildly excited in bed but I don't know how much you've got in the building society. Everyone talks about sex but dosh ... that's very confidential.

Third, money often causes personal conflict. In their books about arguments Deborah Tannen (1997) and Elisabeth Mapstone (1998) both show that a third of rows are about money, with partners accusing each other of being irresponsible and irrational about finance.

Fourth, we find it hard to analyse our own attitudes to risk, and our attitudes are affected by personality and past experiences. The research also shows our attitudes depend on what psychologists call our locus of control.

Rational economic man is not subject to mood swings, highs and lows, personality quirks or hunches. He can calculate decisions about spending, investment and risk with perfect accuracy. Risk to reward ratios are mother's milk to him. I shall argue, however, that rational economic man is a fantasy being.

According to Andrew Smithers of Smithers & Co., who provide economic data to investment funds, even market professionals find it hard to assess accurately the risks they take. 'In the City it's all about other people's money,' Smithers told me. And that influences how people see – and deal with – risk.

The first example of investment advice is to be found in the *Talmud*. The rabbis recommended – and they were interpreting the word of God – that we should keep a third in merchandise, a third in real estate and a third in cash. God probably got it right. He certainly got it more right than many earthbound investment advisers.

Smithers also believes that investment experts are influenced by peer pressure. If all your competitors are putting money in tracker funds (which invest only in the shares of the 100 largest companies on the London Stock Exchange, the shares that make up the FT-SE or Footsie 100 Index), you have to be very brave to do something different, even if you suspect that what everyone else is doing is not particularly rational.

The problem is made worse by the sheer volume of information that investors need to analyse. Today's share trader has access to computer systems which offer 28 real-time screen windows that show share prices from all over the world. The global exchange never sleeps. There are more financial markets than ever before, trading more shares, bonds, options, convertible bonds, derivatives, silver, gold, invertebrates, warrants, commodities, junk bonds and index trades. The effect is information overload.

Information overload has been studied experimentally. (You've just been a victim of it if you didn't shake your head at 'invertebrates' in the list above. There isn't yet an insect exchange but give City professionals time. You want to buy Future Ants – no problem.) In a classic experiment on information overload, a subject sits in front of an array of screens, and has the task of spotting when a Red Intruder invades and when a Blue Intruder invades. As the number of variables to watch for is increased, subjects suffer stress and make errors they would not normally make. They miss the Blue Invader. Today investors and investment experts have, like such subjects, to keep track of constantly changing movements.

One form of this information are performance measures which allow investors to compare how funds, share sectors and indices perform against each other. Critics have always complained of the short-termism in the City; now the sheer flow of information is making the short term even shorter. Many of those I interviewed for this book talked about the 'time horizon', which sounds like a phrase from *Star Trek*. The time horizon now is the blink of an index. The Footsie Index changes from minute to minute and so your performance as a fund manager can be measured from minute to minute. It doesn't matter if you had a good six months before; if your performance at 1.12 p.m. on 7 July is 1.7 per cent down against the Index, you are in trouble.

One of the oldest laws in psychology is the Yerkes Dodson law. Based on work by Robert Yerkes and J.D. Dodson, it claims that subjects perform best in a variety of experiments when they were under some pressure. Too much pressure, however, damaged performance. A series of studies such as Kahn and Cooper's (1993) *Stress in the Dealing Room* suggest many City professionals feel under great pressure – and that pressure is getting worse, as today financial markets are changing fast.

There is a long literature on how workers respond to changing work cultures. And the City was one of the most traditional work environments until Big Bang in 1986. Since then change has been very rapid. Major firms like IBM spend large budgets on getting their employees used to change because change causes anxiety. Few financial firms seem to have invested in similar programmes, however.

One of the anxieties City professionals have but rarely voice is that soon investors will not need their skills and will not be willing to pay their fees, especially as research shows brokers and analysts are very poor at predicting how the market will move. The Internet is also changing the investment business. Charles Schwab, the American brokers who execute deals, say that 75 per cent of their business is now done on the Internet. Clients no longer telephone to talk to a broker: the work is all done screen to screen.

Surveying recent issues of the *Journal of Portfolio Management*, the *Financial Analysts Journal* and the *Journal of Finance*, the leading academic journals in this area, it becomes clear more work than ever before is being done on how analysts perform. William Cabot, a leading American fund manager, wrote recently in the *Financial Analysts Journal* (Cabot 1998) that 'many if not all managers are frustrated that they cannot beat it (the market) on any consistent basis.' He admitted to being 'as nervous and uneasy' as anyone else about how badly his fund has done compared to the market as a whole. He also outlined some of the tricks brokers and funds use to make their figures look better.

The sad saga of Equitable Life shows the lengths to which managers of pension funds will go to attract new business. Equitable Life guaranteed high levels of annuities to new clients in the 1970s and 1980s when inflation was high; as a result the company had to stop writing new business at the end of 2000 after the House of Lords ruled the Equitable could not renege on guarantees given to 90,000 investors. Lower inflation had made the guarantees very expensive to honour.

Private investors are also having to adapt to these changes in markets. Private investors' attitudes have been, we shall see, studied remarkably little. There has been far more research into why people buy washing up liquid than into why they buy shares. The largest published surveys of why people invest in shares have been carried out on samples of about 500, so it is a little hard to be certain. In this book, I rely not just on these surveys but on interviews to try and establish some facts.

The Poseidon adventure

I have never been a consistent investor but I have been interested in the markets since I left university. When I was 22 I had a big break. I was hired by James Mason to write a film script of the novel *Jane Eyre*. I was paid the then fabulous sum of £1,000. I decided to buy shares with some of this money. I invested in a company called Poseidon, which had found gold in Australia. I was so excited that I often bought three editions of the *Evening Standard* in one day to keep my eye on share-price movements. I still remember the small thrill of pleasure when the price was going up. Needless to say, when I was calculating my profits, I did not deduct the extra I had spent on endless copies of the *Evening Standard*.

A few months later I sold my shares and made a nice profit, which paid for part of the deposit on my first flat. I was rather sad at having to sell, because the news was that Poseidon would soon find gold and the shares would rocket; but I was just married, we needed a place to live and my then wife, Aileen, insisted I sell.

I was lucky. Or Aileen was wise. Soon after I sold the truth about Poseidon came out. Its mines turned out not to have gold but to be a big black hole in the Australian hills. If I had waited for a few more weeks, I would have lost most of my *Jane Eyre* money. Before and after leaving university I also worked for my father, the late Dr Benjamin Cohen, who was a company doctor. I saw at first hand how investors in high-risk situations behaved when they lost their money.

In this book I do not offer a guide to family finances or tips as to what shares to buy. Rather, I argue that to understand how markets work and to make the most of our opportunities we need to understand the relevant psychology. Commentators tend to rattle off the view that the psychology of the market is dominated by greed, fear and the herd instinct. I try to analyse this notion and I argue that current psychological research can shed light on a number of important and specific questions involving financial markets – questions such as:

- How emotional are investors and how does that affect their judgement?
- How do the mechanisms of greed, fear and panic work? Is everyone susceptible to the same extent and in the same way?
- Do shares have emotional associations and, if they do, what is the impact of these associations on the value of shares? In Chapter 9, I develop the idea of wet (emotionally laden) and dry (emotionally neutral) shares and suggest interesting differences in their performance.
- Why do analysts often ignore key pieces of information?
- Why do investors and even professional brokers find it so hard to sell shares even when they know they ought to sell?
- What affects our attitudes to risk? Why does one person see a particular risk as crazy while another person sees it as a good bet?
- How do the people who make financial decisions for us – brokers and dealers – operate?
- How does the pressured, competitive environment in which they work affect their decision making. Your money is in their hands – how does this affect your chances of making a profit?

In Britain few books have looked in detail at the psychology of financial markets. In America there has been a little more work in this area though the overwhelming number of texts on investment are based on accountancy principles. Benjamin Graham who was a great guru from the 1940s onwards still is a dominant presence and he argued we should look for shares which have hidden value. Warren Buffett, reckoned to be the world's greatest investor, is very much a disciple. Some American investment gurus like Tom Basso have been more influenced by psychology but most of Basso's work offers investors rather simplistic advice on their psychology.

He warns, for example, of the dangers of letting your ego interfere with your investments.

The bottom line or a matter of 'posterior overconfidence'

Most market analysts still seem to feel psychology can offer little to investors. A review of the last 5 years' issues of the *Journal of Portfolio Management*, the *Journal of Finance*, the *Journal of Financial Markets* and the *Financial Analysts Journal* shows there are countless studies of how the markets work.

Few studies, however, look at how people behave when it comes to investment. I was delighted when I found an article on aggressive investment in the *Journal of International Financial Markets*. Benos (1999) wrote: 'We study an extreme form of posterior overconfidence where some risk neutral investors overestimate the precision of their private information.' Benos went on to outline how 'the unconscious committment to aggressive trading' affected their dealing.

It was only when I read his methodology, however, that it became clear he had not talked to one investor. He had no subject who suffered from the delightfully named problem of posterior overconfidence. Benos's paper was entirely based on modelling what he thought an overconfident investor might think.

For a psychologist such a lack of rigorous methodology is like being transported back to the 1890s when armchair psychology was popular. Then, intense Germans and Americans tried to work out a theory of consciousness by thinking about what they were thinking. Total reliance on introspection led to a dead end and eventually psychologists had to propel themselves out of their armchairs to get real data on real people.

One amusing but hardly rigorous recent development in America has been to bring the insights of martial arts to the investment scene. I have skimmed through some wonderful titles such as *Zen and the Art of Investment*, *Trading Like a Warrior* and *The Art of War and Trading*, and I am looking forward to *The Seven Samurai Take Wall Street by Storm*.

In Britain psychology is still a little distrusted. One press officer for a large investment house was blunt. 'The stock market has no psychology. It's a building,' said Jean Diment of Capel Cure Sharp. Many of the City professionals I talked to, however, were intrigued by the idea that psychology might have some influence on stock-market dealings but psychology was not the kind of stuff they read or thought about. Sometimes, as I interviewed them, I had the feeling that they were doing a spot of introspection to please me. It was as if they had never before thought about what made them buy shares or the feelings good or bad deals aroused.

Academic psychology has also tended to ignore financial markets until very recently. Exceptions are projects at the London Business School and Manchester University on the stress that dealers experience and on the personality of future traders.

No one suggests that economic forces do not matter, but I will argue that markets are also driven by the psychology of individuals, by how they respond to crowds, news, peer pressure and their own personal drives. For over a century economists have spoken of bears and bulls – bears who are pessimistic about the market and bulls who are optimistic. Recent research makes it possible to look in more detail at precisely how and why so many brokers tend to be bullish. It is a mixture of personality and situation. We are also well placed in 2001 to see how market professionals handle market falls.

I think, therefore, that now is an ideal time to look at the psychology of the markets and to try to be more specific about the many factors most financial analysis either ignores or pays lip service to without studying in any detail. These factors include greed, fear, the need for security, information overload, mathematical anxiety, peer pressure, over-optimism, denial, competitiveness, attitudes to technological change and confusion about personal goals.

Crisis 2001

In March 2001 I went to Moscow to make a film called *The Nuclear Game*. I was trying to find out how much nuclear material might be being smuggled out of the former Soviet Union. Moscow had changed totally from the end of 1988 when I had last been there. It had all the contemporary horrors, joys and toys of a modern city – bad traffic jams, muggers on the streets, endless ads on television, but food in the shops and money could buy you anything. Nevertheless, official paranoia still lurked. When we tried to film the outside of a pretty church close to Red Square, we were stopped by the police and told to move on. I was told that if I visited the Troyetsk Institute of Physics (where nuclear scientists had gone on strike because they hadn't been paid) I wouldn't just be arrested, but I'd have heroin planted on me. It was more fun being framed in the bad old Communist days when gorgeous sirens would try to lure you into bed to be blackmailed.

Still, 10 years after the fall of Gorbachev, Russia is moving towards becoming a market economy. President Putin, even though he had once been a KGB officer, is doing little to stop economic reforms. The Moscow stock market is still functioning and doing rather better than the NASDAQ.

I have no intention of being starry-eyed. Moscow is not a Western city. Some pensioners beg – and they don't have a drink problem. Old men and women whose only income is a state pension of around 1,400 roubles a month beg or sell flowers in the metro or in the street. In the countryside the poverty is far worse. But the old centre of Communism is now very much a capitalist city and one full of business opportunities.

Opposite the Kremlin, Christian Dior have a flagship shop which must make Lenin shudder as he lies in his mausoleum. The Dior shop is in a complex that used to be Moscow's leading department store Gum (or Glum as Westerners called it). In Gum the shelves were usually pretty empty in the late 1980s; today it's a fully neoned and styled shopping mall packed with goodies. Anyone can buy as long as they have the cash or credit cards. Hypermarkets are changing the way ordinary Muscovites shop for food – and, bizarrely, the leading chain is Turkish. I had dinner with an Irishman who had been in Moscow for 7 years and who had put together a consortium that had bought much of the Soviet glass industry for well under $1 million. The deal included all the patents developed by Soviet glass specialists since the Second World War and an office building in central Moscow. Gerry was ecstatic.

And so should the world economy be. Russia and the old Eastern block comprise a newly accessible market of over 500 million people. Some of these economies might be a little backwards, but the Czechs make excellent cars like the Skoda, the Poles and Hungarians have growing and skilled economies and even much maligned Russia is still the only country apart from the USA that can launch human beings into space.

Economic theory would suggest that the opening up of such huge new markets to capitalism would have a major impact; in fact, it has had almost no effect on the rather narrow world of the stock markets. What drove the bull market of the 1990s upwards was largely bio-technology, telecommunications and information technology.

When I started to write the first edition of this book in spring 1999, a share boom was in full swing. When the hardback version was published in February 2000 there were the first anxieties. Maybe share prices had gone too far. The intellectual debate was between analysts who claimed the laws of economics were changing and traditionalists who saw it all as bubble, froth and doom. The optimists claimed we had entered not just a new economy, but a new paradigm of perpetual growth. Technological wizards would devise ever more marvellous gadgets and gizmos that consumers had ever more need for. And labour problems were history, part of the bad old days we'd never see again.

As I finish the updated edition the optimists have been largely silenced. Economists now are arguing about whether the world is about to enter recession or depression, about how bad the landing will be and whether Britain and Europe will be hit as badly as the States.

Optimists in Britain claim the prudent policies of Gordon Brown mean that we are far less vulnerable to the boom–bust cycle than the Americans. Cynical left wingers point out that the recession is not just due to the cycle and the laws of economics, but also to the fact that yet again the American President is called George Bush. If you want the world's major economy screwed up, elect a Bush.

In the 4 months after George W. Bush won the election the slide on the world markets was real, as the following shows:

Dow Jones	11,009 to	9,975
NASDAQ	3,000 to	1,900
FT-SE 100	6,400 to	5,560
Nikkei	15,000 to	12,900
Dax Frankfurt	6,795 to	6,089
Tel Aviv	478 to	422

George Bush Senior mismanaged the American economy in the late 1980s and early 1990s. Perhaps it just runs in the genes.

The head of the Federal Reserve Bank, Alan Greenspan, has cut interest rates to try to boost the US economy and with interest rates down to 4% in the USA, shares climbed back by May 2001. But with such low interest rates how long will this last? Britain's last Tory Chancellor of the Exchequer, Kenneth Clarke, said Greenspan acted for better reasons than propping up the greedy guts of Wall Street. American growth is vital to the world economy.

In Britain, many shares that were aggressively hyped in early to mid-2000 have melted away. The number of companies going bust has risen through 2000 and early 2001.

The best known British case of a dramatic share flop is Lastminute.com which is now trading at 44p as against an offer price of 380p.

But the fall in Lastminute.com is far from the most spectacular. Baltimore Technologies have fallen from 1,479 to 61; the Money Channel which reached 578 fell to 7.5 and then stopped trading. Culturally, money itself is no longer quite so chic. Another cable channel which was launched on the back of our seemingly insatiable interest in money, Simply Money, has simply disappeared.

These were all new economy shares. It seems old proof of an old pudding. Optimism drives shares too high and then they have nowhere to go but down. As I shall argue in this book it is more psychologically complicated, but common sense is helpful – as in all things psychological.

When I first started to research this subject, Charles Clark, a broker with West LB Panmure, told me he had started to sell shares in mobile phone Nokia when he realized its business forecasts seemed to predict everyone in the world was scheduled to have a mobile phone by around 2002. Clarke had his doubts. Would Vietnamese villagers or Tuaregs in central and western Sahara really need mobile phones to keep in touch with their brokers or find out who the DJ was at the coolest nightclub? Might some sad-wits actually believe it was possible to live without a mobile phone?

When I was in Moscow certainly journalists had mobile phones, but ordinary people, like the English speaking receptionists at our hotel, did not, either because they didn't need them or couldn't afford them? I don't think I saw one person walking on the street making a call on a mobile phone. You could argue that means they can be sold phones; you could also argue the mobile business now is a more mature market and mature markets show slower growth.

Serious doubts have been expressed about whether the third generation of mobile phones will find millions of buyers. British Telecom left itself with £30 billion of debt and had to sell some interesting assets (denting its growth prospects) because it paid so much in the government auction for the mobile phone licences. The British government raised £22.5 billion for these licences. Everyone has assumed there will be an ever-growing market for add-on services to the phones. In the high-speed high-tech 21st century, status comes from your brands. Only the coolest get the newest. In the 1990s so-called first adopters always rushed to show off their latest new gizmos. But lifestyle analysts note a new scepticism, even puritanism. Anti brand is now stylish – see the success of Naomi Klein's No LoGo (Klein 2000). So now the confused chic ask themselves questions that worry some multinationals. Do I need the latest brand, the latest supersonic wizzo WAP phone? Will I get laid more easily if my date sees I can send and receive e-mails from my wristwatch? Will I feel less isolated if I can Internet connect while in the subway? First adopters may now be second best.

And then there are the health risks. Mobile phone operators have so far dismissed anxieties about the radiation hazards as exaggerated, but lawsuits have started in America where the plaintiffs claim that the radiation from mobiles has caused brain damage. I am not saying that mobile phone makers will not find a way of dealing with these anxieties, but the lifestyle problem is severe because the operators have assumed there will be a never-ending demand for new services.

Fears of recession in May 2001 are not just affecting these new-technology companies like Motorola. Steel makers like Corus are shedding a huge 6,000 jobs. The car industry continues to look vulnerable. What makes ecological sense – don't keep on buying new cars – does not make economic sense.

The best economic news, in fact, may be perverse. Real military tension has now returned to the Middle East since September 2000 with the continuing violence between Israel and the Palestinians, and, in South-East Asia, tension between China, Taiwan and America is as acute as ever before. Surprisingly, the Tel Aviv stock market has dipped much less than the NASDAQ where one of the top performing technological stocks has been the Israeli company BATM.

So we have moved in the space of 18 months from high optimism to deep pessimism. In the rest of the book I try to unravel some of the psychological factors involved.

In the book I also develop some ideas of an intellectual hero of mine, John B. Watson. Watson founded a school of psychology called behaviourism. He lost his professorship at Johns Hopkins University when he was 42 because he had an affair with a student. He was reduced to being a travelling salesman for 2 years and then went to work for the advertising agency J. Walter Thompson, where he made a fortune and perhaps most important he did not lose that much in the Wall Street Crash. In 1930 Watson was in England with enough cash to buy the most expensive shoes in St James. (For the rest of his life Watson had his shoes handmade in London and freighted across the Atlantic.)

Watson made all his students fill in a 'balance sheet of the self' in which they had to analyse their strengths and weaknesses. I offer two questionnaires – on attitudes to seek information and on attitudes to risk taking – which will allow investors to develop a profile of their financial skills. In a world where money matters and where many of us are not very sensible about money matters, understanding your psychological attitudes to investment and risk can only help.

By the end of the book I hope readers will see how these variables work both in theory and practice and will understand how to analyse their own strengths and weaknesses when they invest for themselves, invest for others or are just thinking about investing. I humbly tread in the wake of the *Talmud* because, when the rabbis wrote down what they took to be God's views on best investment practices, they were aiming to give the pious similar clues and insights.

I hope the book will be useful to professionals, large investors and those new to the market. I have tried to define key terms in the body of the text, but the book also includes a glossary.

one

A thousand ways of losing your pants

When I studied psychology, our tutors took us to visit one of Oxford's psychiatric hospitals, the Littlemore. An elegant psychiatrist, Dr Letemendia, 'demonstrated' two patients to us. One was a neatly dressed man in his forties. He spoke fast. He hated being in hospital. He'd never felt better in his life. He had friends, sex appeal and a feel for the stock market. He didn't like to boast but he was doing well. Spectacularly well. He was loud, a bit pushy and very restless, but these irritating traits surely did not justify locking him up in an asylum.

As students we were all fans of R.D. Laing, the anti-psychiatrist who argued that doctors labelled as insane anyone who did not conform to the straitjacket of society. The pushy man was an oddball, we argued. Shrinks, being the thought police, were making him pay the price.

Wrong, Dr Letemendia insisted. The pushy man had a well-established psychiatric illness. He was a manic-depressive building up to the full manic phase. When manic he might sound plausible, even charming, but he couldn't make rational judgements. He made passes at women who weren't interested; he spent money recklessly. After a few manic days he would crash into a terrible depression.

Most of us were not impressed by this explanation. Telling us that he was manic-depressive was labelling him, just as Laing had warned. It cut no ice that the American Psychiatric Association includes mania and manic-depressive psychosis among established psychiatric diseases and that poor financial judgement is a symptom of both conditions.

18

I thought of this hospital scene when I started to write this book because it is not just very disturbed people who get into manic states. On a number of occasions apparently normal and intelligent investors have behaved much like Letemendia's patient when he was in a manic state. Economists label these events speculative booms.

All the history you need about speculative manias

Some historians claim the first of these so-called speculative booms took place in classical Athens. In 333 BC, the price of Greek property and land rose sky high. But there are no documents for us to be able to understand any of the details, athough it is interesting that 'the' most rational and sophisticated of ancient civilizations succumbed ...

Since the mid-1600s there have been many well-documented 'speculative manias'. Prices for shares, land, gold, silver, railways or, most romantically, tulips, soared to incredible levels. In 1637 one rare tulip root fetched the price of 12 acres of city-centre land in the prosperous Dutch town of Haarlem.

In Britain a stock market of sorts started in coffee houses like Jonathan's and Garraway's around Exchange Alley in the late seventeenth century, but the public were suspicious of the new profession of 'stock jobbing', of selling shares. An Act of Parliament in 1697 imposed many controls because of fears of the 'pernicious' evil of stock jobbery. Despite these fears, the early eighteenth century saw the London South Sea Bubble of 1720 where people rushed to invest in trade in the Pacific.

A century later people dreamed of railways rather than of exotic gold and spices. The mid-nineteenth century saw the great railway mania. Some 50 years later, in 1907, America was brought to a financial standstill by crisis. But that did not stop investors getting excited by the Florida land boom of 1925, which was soon followed by the Wall Street boom of 1926–1929.

There is nothing new in hope and speculation. This is one of the many 'Bubble Cards' produced during the 1720 'mania'.

When I started to write this book the most recent of these bubbles was the Japanese stock-market boom of the 1980s. During that time the index of leading shares in Tokyo, the Nikkei 225 Index, reached about 35,000; in April 1999 it stood at less than 50 per cent of that. Between the spring of 2000 and the winter of that year, high-tech shares went into an even steeper decline. The NASDAQ lost 54 per cent of its value; shares in companies like Eidos which produces the Lara Croft games fell from 800p to under 250p and in Kingston Communications which runs the telephone system in Hull from £10 to around £1.40. High-tech frenzy in 2000 had many of the characteristics of a bubble.

The history of the latest bubble is too recent to have been written but there are a number of studies of more ancient 'speculative manias'. The Victorian journalist Charles Mackay (1852) in his *History of Extraordinary Popular Delusions* looked at three episodes that took place before 1850 – the tulipmania that swept Holland, the South Sea Bubble and the Mississippi land boom of 1718–1720 which led Parisians to buy land in America. The economist John Kenneth Galbraith (1933) wrote *A Short History of Financial Euphoria* and a study of the 1929 Wall Street Crash; the financial historian Kindelberger (1994) looked at speculative manias. Carswell (1993) has provided a detailed history of the South Sea Bubble. Recently Edward Chancellor in *The Devil Take the Hindmost* (1999) has given entertaining accounts of some of them. But none of these studies were really psychological.

Historians like to suggest that all these manias were similar. John Kenneth Galbraith claims investors are gripped both by mad greed and panic that they're going to miss out on fabulous profits. If others are getting rich, they think, I'd better get in fast or I'll lose out. In the end, all these booms ended in disaster.

With the exception of the Mississippi land boom, these 'speculative manias' gripped markets where investors had some experience. When they invested their money, well-to-do men and women were confident they were being sensible about the risks. However, I want to suggest that we won't understand these booms very well if we think that they're just a matter of simple greed and crude herd instinct. Also, in all speculative frenzies some win and some lose. Many investors did extremely well out of these manias because the rush of interest created profit. The losers were those who either bought too late or, more often, those who could not bear to sell in time when they had already made a profit.

Furthermore, the markets were stoked by the presence of many authority figures – the rich, the respectable, the famous. If they were playing, the less rich and less experienced felt it must be fairly safe. In all the bubbles too there were warning voices, Cassandras who warned that the price was too high, but they were not listened to by most people.

A third reason for distrusting the simple greed, fear and herd instinct explanation relates to the theory of cognitive dissonance. The theory offers some insights into why investors find it so hard to admit they are running potentially disastrous risks and to sell out in time. The theory also helps explain why many investors in two of the bubbles ignored recent evidence of the risks of speculation.

The short accounts that follow of five manias will show how complex they really were.

Money is the root of all evil – the tulip craze 1633–1637

Well before a tulip became a negotiable instrument around 1633 the Dutch loved the flowers. Every year ships brought tulip bulbs and roots from Constantinople to Amsterdam. Beautiful, exotic tulips were admired just for themselves at first; but they soon also became a status symbol.

In the 1630s Holland was the most financially sophisticated society in the world. Merchants could get credit from fledgling banks; and there was something of a stock market operating in Amsterdam. The Dutch were not by nature gamblers: many were Calvinists and the Protestant work ethic was strong. Dutch merchants were accustomed to calculating risks. They financed long sea voyages where there was a real chance of ships never returning but, also, a real prospect of great profits. It was a mercantile society, one unlikely, it would seem, to lose its grip over a bunch of flowers.

At the start of 1634 a tulip cost about 400 florins. Between 1634 and 1635, the price doubled, trebled and went 10 times higher than before. By the middle of 1635 prices for tulips were quoted on the exchanges at Rotterdam, Hoorn, Alkamaar and Leyden as well as in Amsterdam.

At first only rich merchants dabbled in tulips, but then middle-class people became excited. Some families sold their houses to raise the cash to buy tulips. People knew objectively that flowers could not be worth that much. Subjectively, however, they felt very different. Simon Schama (1994) argues that the Dutch ruling class were appalled by this money craze. People seemed unable to get any perspective on this phenomenon – and unable to behave with common sense.

The price of tulips went so high that roots started to be sold by weight, which was measured in perits. A perit weighed less than a gram. A tulip of the type 'Admiral Liefken', weighing 400 perits, was worth 4,400 florins. The most precious was 'Semper Augustus', which fetched 5,500 florins. One merchant wanted a single root of the rare 'Viceroy' tulip so badly that he exchanged for it (we owe the list to a contemporary commentator called Munting): 'two lasts of wheat, four fat oxen, eight fat swine, twelve fat sheep, two hogshead of wine, four tuns of beer, two tuns of butter, one thousand pounds of cheese, a complete bed, a fashionable suit of clothes and a silver drinking cup.' The value of all these items came to 2,500 florins. It has recently been calculated that this would be $244,000 in today's money (Hinshley 1996).

For about 18 months the craze flourished. Dealers in flowers kept the market bubbling, but their efforts would not have succeeded had thousands not been willing to suspend reality and believe a tulip could be worth far more than its weight in gold.

Newcomers to Holland could get into terrible scrapes. Munting describes a sailor who arrived in Amsterdam and went to see a silk merchant. The merchant paid him for some information and gave him a pickled herring. As he picked up his herring the sailor spotted an onion on the counter. He liked onions with his fish so he took it. He never thought the merchant would mind.

Ten minutes later, the silk merchant was frantic. He could not find a root of the highly valuable 'Semper Augustus' tulip. He searched the whole shop. Nothing.

Suddenly, he remembered. The sailor. He'd stolen the tulip. The merchant gathered some friends and searched the local taverns. When he finally found the sailor it was too late, the man was innocently finishing his herring and onion. The sailor did not know this was the most expensive onion in the world. It was the merchant's missing 'Semper Augustus', worth 5,500 florins or, given the calculations, over $600,000! The merchant had no sense of humour about the mistake and had the sailor thrown in jail.

The tulip market became so sophisticated that it even allowed futures trading. Munting described contracts where A agreed to purchase 10 'Semper Augustus' bulbs from B at 4,000 florins each, 6 weeks after the signing of the contract. One canny Dutch printer started to produce a Register of Flowers listing the price of tulips each week.

But in November 1636 faith in the value of tulips suddenly declined. Flowers that had been worth 4,000 florins suddenly dropped to 300 or 400 florins. Buyers refused to honour contracts.

Historians have not been able to show dented confidence or why, in the modern jargon, 'sentiment' had changed. Charles Mackay (1852) in his *History of Extraordinary Popular Delusions* only said, 'at last the more prudent began to see that this folly could not last forever.' As an explanation this does not go very far.

The aftermath was complicated. Buyers had sometimes borrowed money to pay for tulips; others had given tulip roots as security for loans. Those who had been tulip-rich now found that they owned mountains of almost worthless flowers. The Dutch government refused to interfere, saying it was up to the tulip traders to sort out the mess.

The eventual legal solution was interesting. All contracts made in November 1636 at the height of the mania were declared null and void. All contracts made later would be satisfied once the buyers paid 10 per cent of the agreed price. The sellers were unhappy, but when they tried to sue for payment they found the courts unsympathetic. Dutch judges refused to enforce the contracts, saying that 'debts contracted in gambling were no debts in law.' The buyers and sellers had not seen themselves as gamblers at all.

Dutch society was robust, and business soon recovered. Economists suggest that very similar mechanisms account for the South Sea Bubble craze, but there was an important difference. Whereas the Dutch were buying rare and exotic flowers at an absurd price, the Bubble buyers were buying a piece of paper and dreams of profit.

'Joynt stocks' and the South Sea Bubble

Both Jonathan Swift and Daniel Defoe, writing about the South Sea Bubble of 1720, painted a picture of innocent investors being conned by the rich. Swift's lines mocked the jobbers sitting in Garraway's coffee house who profited, writing:

Meantime, secure on Garraway cliffs,
A savage race by shipwrecks fed,
Lie waiting for the foundered skills,
And ship the bodies of the dead.

But the investors were not innocents. By the time of the Bubble, Britain had a 150-year history of stock-market trading. The first joint companies had been created in Elizabethan times to finance expeditions to trade with Russia and the East Indies. A company for bringing water to London was set up in 1607 as a joint-stock company.

In a recent article in the *Journal of Economic History* (1999), Castro and Lee point out that 'joynt stocks' were traded in London coffee houses from at least 1672. The expression stock exchange itself comes from 'joynt stocks'; stocks were shares. Castro and Lee analyse the buying and selling of shares in two seventeenth-century trading companies – the Royal Africa Company and the Hudson's Bay Company.

Perhaps more surprising is the fact that there was already a futures market operating by the 1690s. In the coffee houses round Exchange Alley you could buy shares and also what was known as a 'Refuse'. In a pamphlet published in 1694 John Houghton wrote that a 'monied man' could come into Garraway's coffee house and 'ask what he will have for Refuse of so many shares. That is how many guineas a share he shall give for the liberty to accept or refuse such shares at such a price at any time within the next 6 months or other times as agreed.' This is what we understand today as an option. Options give buyers the right to buy or sell a stock at a specific time ahead. Say you have bought the option to buy a stock at 50 and have paid 5 for the privilege. If the stock rises to 57, you are 'in the money'; you make 2 cents a share. The stock slumps to 49 and you have lost your whole stake.

Houghton also described the 'means of putting stock', when someone agrees to sell stock at a certain price. If the price rises you lose your money, if it falls you win. To continue the previous example, if you have bought an option to sell at 50 and paid 5 for the privilege, you would be 'in the money' if the stock went below 45 because you would then have covered your initial 5 stake. Houghton even outlined the dangerous practice by which groups could sell more stock in a company than existed.

It was against this background of both interest in joynt stocks and anxiety about speculation that the South Sea Company was started in 1710. The British government faced a financial crisis and the Earl of Oxford and other rich merchants agreed to take on the public debt which then stood at £10 million. To pay the interest the South Sea Company was given the income from certain duties such as that on tobacco. The Company was also given a monopoly of trade with the South Seas. The Company had a distinguished board of directors and did not start the enterprise meaning to cheat the public.

By 1710 Exchange Alley had some established procedures. Lee and Castro have dug through the records of the Royal Africa and Hudson's Bay companies and identified a number of goldsmiths such as William Shepherd who acted as brokers and market makers. Shepherd bought and sold shares in the companies; he charged commission and often held small parcels of shares so that investors could buy from him.

The social and historical context was also crucial for the South Sea Bubble. The British were fascinated by exploration and piracy. Pirates such as Henry Morgan, Captain Kidd, Bartholomew Roberts and Blackbeard were popular heroes. Roberts was famous for banning alcohol, as he claimed that drunken pirates fought less well than sober ones. His victories proved his point. His rum-less crews captured 400 ships and threatened shipping, forcing the navy to send a squadron to hunt them. Pirates were even believed to have set up a Utopian republic in Madagascar. There was continuing interest in where Captain Kidd had buried his treasure.

The South Sea Company offered investors a chance to share legally in the fabulous riches. People were convinced that Peru and Mexico had inexhaustible gold and silver mines and that heathen savages would hand over gold and silver in exchange for beads and cloth. Gold was a bauble to them.

Many historians claim that, even if the original intent behind the South Sea Company was honest, by 1720 that had changed and unscrupulous directors started to spread rumours designed to push up the price of the stock. They let it be known that Spain would concede four ports on the coast of Chile and Peru to the British. The truth was different. The only concessions Philip V of Spain had made were in the context of negotiating the *asiento*, the contract for supplying slaves from Africa to the West Indies. To show goodwill Philip agreed to let one British ship a year trade with Mexico, Peru and Chile but even in this he drove a hard bargain. Philip would get a quarter of the profits and a 5 per cent tax on the remainder.

On 22 January 1720, in the House of Commons, the Bank of England and the South Sea Company fought for the privilege of being responsible for Britain's national debt which had increased from the £10 million of 1710. The South Sea Company offered to pay off the debt in 25 years in return for the duties on tobacco and the privilege of trading with Spain and the South Seas.

On 2 February the South Sea Company won the vote, even though Sir Robert Walpole warned, if the South Sea Company won, 'that the dangerous practice of jobbing would divert the genius of the nation from trade and industry. It would hold out a dangerous lure to decoy the unwary to their ruin by making them part with the earnings of their labour for a prospect of imaginary wealth.' Walpole argued that 'the first principle of the project was an evil of the first magnitude; it was to raise artificially the value of the stock by exciting and keeping up a general infatuation and by promising dividends out of funds which would not be adequate to the purpose.'

Walpole's word 'infatuation' was apt. He asked the questions a good modern financial analyst would. How did the company propose to make the profits it needed to make? What was the company selling, in fact?

The day after the South Sea Company won control of the national debt, its stock rose from 130 to 300. The Bill then had to pass through the House of Lords. Historians who see the Company as a fraud claim that the directors spread more shameless rumours to talk up their stock: new treaties between Spain and Britain were being negotiated; Philip was about to make more concessions; the silver from Potosí was being sent to London to be worked.

One of the most interesting aspects of the South Sea drama was its ripple effect. Whereas in Holland the mania had focused on tulips and nothing but tulips, in Britain the South Sea Company inspired an interest in other joynt-stock companies and hundreds were started. Among the more amusing was one that specialized in 'trading in hair'. Others were more sensible, such as ones 'for importing walnut trees from Virginia' and 'for paving the streets of London'. Other companies were surreal, such as companies 'for a wheel for perpetual motion' and another 'for the carrying on an undertaking of Great Advantage but no one to know what it is'. Eager investors put in £2,000 in cash to get in on the Great Advantage but the main director then disappeared with the money and was never seen again. This ripple affected only the city of London but it was intense and all the more remarkable given the anxieties about stock jobbing which the 1697 Act had tried to allay.

Despite Walpole's warnings, the Bill passed the House of Lords by a vote of 83 for and only 17 against. The day after, the Bill got royal assent. Markets are peculiar, however. The South Sea Company had achieved its first – and very ambitious – aim and now controlled the national debt. The result: on 7 April the price of the stock went down from 310 to 290.

Again, there were positive rumours: the Earl of Stanhope had overtures from Spain, and Spain would exchange Gibraltar and Port Mahon for ports on the Peru coast. Were the company directors talking the stock up or was there so much group pressure to believe in the South Sea Company that good news just bubbled up?

By now Walpole was not the only influential sceptic. Jonathan Swift (cited in Mackay 1852) wrote:

> Subscribers here by thousands float
> And jostle one another down
> Each paddling in his leaky boat
> And here they fish for gold and drown.

Investors never learn

The Bubble was at its height from January to September 1720. The timing is significant. The year before, a scheme similar to the South

Sea one was floated in Paris by a Scotsman, John Law. Law's Mississippi scheme also offered investors shares in a company trading in the South Seas. This was the so-called Mississippi land boom. By May 1720 the Mississippi scheme had gone badly wrong. The shares – or *actions*, the French word for shares, which sounds much more dynamic – went into free fall. The Mississippi Company was bankrupt. Thousands of Parisians were ruined. On 27 May Law was being lampooned in prints as the 'Goddess of Shares'. One verse called him the first-born son of Satan who 'took all our money'.

People in London knew what was happening in Paris. After the Treaties of Utrecht there was constant trade and traffic between the two cities, and you could get from London to Paris in 4 days. Londoners should therefore have been alive to the dangers of trading in the South Seas which Law's scheme exposed. But most in London chose to ignore the lessons from across the Channel.

On 29 May in London the South Sea Company stock rose to 500 and many people swapped government-backed annuities for those of the company. Early in June the stock took a further leap, surging to 890. People believed the stock could go no higher and many now did sell out. On 3 June there were so many sellers and so few buyers the price fell to 640. Many people who had failed to get in at the start now scrambled to buy the stock, seeing 640 as a low price, a chance to get in relatively cheaply.

News of the Mississippi fiasco had no impact. The warnings of Walpole and Swift had no impact. South Sea stock kept on rising until in early August, the price reached 1,050. This was the peak. It then started to fall. By the start of September, it was selling at 700 – still a better price than in May, when news from Paris should have warned investors of the dangers.

The real problems for the South Sea Company started in mid-September. A fall in the price was triggered with the news that Sir John Blunt and other directors had sold some of their shares, making a huge profit. On 8 September a meeting of the Company was held, but it did not take place in a crisis atmosphere: the directors were praised and hopes were high. But, as so often, a meeting called to boost confidence had the opposite effect. By 12 September the stock had fallen to 540. It had now lost half its value in 5 weeks.

On 13 September a frightened MP Thomas Broderick wrote to the Lord Chancellor blaming the directors for the fall. Broderick said 'their most considerable men have drawn out, securing themselves, by the losses of the deluded, thoughtless numbers whose understandings have been overruled by avarice and the hope of making mountains out of mole hills. Thousands of families will be reduced to beggary. The consternation is inexpressible – the rage beyond description ...'

'The realist' and 'the dreamer' – a tale of Guy and Gay

The attitudes of investors differed enormously during what analysts today would call the boom/bust cycle and, here, I cannot resist including the tale of Guy and Gay. John Gay, who wrote *The Beggar's Opera*, and Thomas Guy, a merchant, are both interesting characters in London's history. Gay was given a present of 19 shares of stock, but he never managed to steel himself to sell. At the peak of the market his shares were worth £20,000. Gay's friends begged him to sell, 'but he dreamed of dignity and splendour' according to Samuel Johnson (1905) in his *Life of the Poets*. Gay would not even dispose of two or three shares, which would have guaranteed him an income of £100 a year for life, 'which will make you sure of a clean shirt and a shoulder of mutton every day'.

Once the stock started to fall Gay could not let go. He dreamed that his 19 shares would rise again in price. Once more he would be worth £20,000. When he lost everything, Johnson noted, 'the calamity sunk him so low his life was in danger.' Gay was a typical extrovert. He always wanted to please others and when his projects failed he often became bitterly depressed. His behaviour seems a typical case of denial and panic. Gay's behaviour recalls that of many investors who find it hard to take profits because they imagine that the value will keep on rising.

Thomas Guy was more astute. He was a Lombard Street bookseller who made his fortune selling Bibles. He sold at the height of the market and netted a fantastic profit of £234,000. He decided to use this altruistically and endowed a new hospital, Guy's Hospital,

The heart of the City of London with the Bank of England on the left.

by London Bridge. The greedy poet and the altruistic merchant – a nice pair.

Typical differences

Economic historians have not researched who did well and who did badly out of the Bubble but there are some interesting points. A number of Jewish bankers like the Da Costas seem not to have touched the stock very much and sold any they held in good time. Sir Theodore Janssen, a director of the Bank of England, lost a fortune but still had enough to be worth £300,000. A bluff Lincolnshire knight, Sir John Meres, was less well placed. He believed the Bubble would make him so rich he would become a national figure but he was bankrupted because he could not bear to sell. And Meres was not a provincial loon. King George I was foolish enough to go back into the market when the stock was around 900 and his wife feared the Hanoverians would be bankrupted. There is a rich seam of material here for a psychologically aware economic historian. The most balanced investor I have come across was Pulteney who wrote to a friend ' 'Tis ridiculous to tell what sum I might have been master of; but since I had not discretion enough to secure that (be selling in time) 'tis some comfort to me I have put my affairs in order so I will not be a loser.'

By the end of October the South Sea stock was down to 150. Apart from the fact that directors had sold some shares, nothing had gone wrong. The Company had not defaulted on debts; there was no bad news. Sea monsters had not suddenly made the oceans less safe and Philip of Spain did not issue a press statement saying that these rumours about trading with Britain were lies. So, again, what was it that dented confidence causing the swing from 'mania' to 'gloom'?

The aftermath was much more serious than in Holland. The British courts did not declare any deals null and void. If you had bought shares at 800 or 1,050, there was no going back. Thousands of people were ruined. The Postmaster General took poison. The House of Commons sent for the arch-critic of the scheme, Walpole, to sort out the mess. The House also established a committee to examine what had happened. South Sea stock was now worthless. Eventually the committee found that the South Sea Company had bribed many politicians to get their bills passed through Parliament. The directors were arrested and their estates confiscated.

Bribes may have allowed the South Sea Company to get bills passed and helped spread positive rumours. But no amount of bribery can explain why intelligent Londoners who knew that a similar scheme in France had just ended in ruin, continued to buy into the South Sea Company.

It could be argued that in these three seventeenth- and eighteenth-century dramas, investors were being sold the stuff of dreams – tulips and El Dorados in the southern seas. Yet those who risked money were not financially inexperienced by the standards of their time. From the start, it was only people with considerable funds – in 1720, £300 would buy you a fine house in London – who could play the Bubble. Still, economic understanding then was primitive. Banks were just beginning to function; paper money was an innovation.

By the middle of the 19th century, however, financial markets were much better understood. No one could have peddled a dream of tropical islands flowing with gold to Victorian investors.

Instead, they peddled railways but the railway mania was rather different. It was perhaps the first technology boom – and here we find the first evidence of the deviousness of ordinary investors.

The great railway boom of the 19th century

After railway engineer George Stephenson's historic engine run from Doncaster a number of railway lines were built, but by 1835 the first enthusiasm had petered out. Financial historians argue that so-called 'railway mania' started only in the mid-1840s. By then it was clear Britain needed a well-planned railway network.

Two devoted transport historians, H. G. Lewin (1936) and R. C. Michie (1981), have described how railway shares were promoted. Most railway shares were initially sold by direct subscription or by agents going into towns and holding meetings to persuade locals to subscribe. Stockbrokers had relatively little to do with the share offers. Most railway companies wanted local investors to help create traffic. Unlike the three earlier manias, railways were a real investment and the money individuals put up was needed to build track, stations and engines.

One of the earliest railways to be built, the Glasgow–Edinburgh line, was budgeted to cost £550,000. But all the money was not needed at the start. The companies knew that investors knew this and would refuse to pay the full price for shares at the outset. So the companies asked investors to put up only 10 per cent of the fully paid-up price. The investors had to pay the balance as and when funds were needed to pay for construction.

In some cases the railway companies asked for no money at all in the first instance. Investors were sent letters of allotment which confirmed they had been reserved so many shares.

There was so much interest that a market even developed in the letters of allotment. Lewin has calculated that in 1846 Britain could boast 1,190 separate railway companies. Some of these were tiny, having secured the right to lay less than 10 miles of track.

Many railway promoters just pocketed the initial subscriptions the public had sent in. But many individuals who bought the shares had no intention of ever paying the balance of the 90 per cent they had committed themselves to. Newspapers condemned them as 'sharp-shooters' who planned to sell on their shares at a profit before they had really paid for them. Michie (1981) has calculated that, at the end of 1845, 94 railways had been promoted in Scotland. The shares on offer had a total face value of £36.5 million but investors had coughed up only £180,764 – about 2 per cent of what they should have paid by that stage. In this situation most ordinary people were not that much at risk. What was at risk was the building of the railways themselves.

In the earlier manias ordinary investors do not seem to have had the chance to be dishonest. The railway mania was one of the first examples where greed led to dishonesty. It shouldn't shock us. When Prime Minister Margaret Thatcher launched the privatizations of the 1980s, people often illegally sent in multiple applications because they knew they were on to a good thing. Some were caught and prosecuted but to most 'gullible' ordinary investors it seemed a fast and easy way of making a buck.

As a result of the irresponsible speculation of the sharpshooters, railway companies had to raise money from banks and through debentures to finance the building of lines. Lewin argues that it was not until the end of the 1850s that the budding railway network recovered.

The Florida land boom – a warning to Wall Street

The most famous crash in history was the Wall Street crash of 1929. Between 23 October and 29 October the Dow Jones Index (which reflects values of shares on the New York Stock Exchange) lost over 25 per cent its value. It then continued falling until June 1932, when it reached 41.2 – the absolute bottom of that bear market – and down nearly 90 per cent from its peak.

The story of the Wall Street crash is economic, social and even cultural. The novelist F. Scott Fitzgerald was one of its great artists; many of his brittle bittersweet short stories have as their background fortunes suddenly wiped out. The photographs in the mind are also graphic. Black-and-white film, skyscrapers in the fog, desperate brokers throwing themselves out of windows ... better to die than not meet your margin call.

History is not supposed to repeat itself. Yet there had been anxieties about Wall Street since the start of the 20th century. Edith Wharton (1912) in her novel *The Custom of the Country* which is set before the First World War tells the story of Udine Spragg, an ambitious American girl in New York whose father, husband and friends are constantly in danger of having their fortunes wiped out by a bad day on Wall Street. And just as there had been a Paris boom–crash in 1720 preceding the London Bubble, there was a well-publicized crash in the United States before the Wall Street crash. Three years before Wall Street drifted into what Galbraith (1955) has called the 'wide blue yonder', investors in Florida saw their money disappear as fast as in the best European bubble.

At the start of the 1920s, Florida real estate started to rise steeply in price. A few local quirks helped. Investors could buy land and property without paying the price for it in full – just as in the railway mania. Deals were done on the basis of 'binders', binding contracts which required buyers to hand over only 10 per cent of the price. That 10 per cent payment gave them the right to pass on the full title to the land.

You could therefore buy a lot for $15,000, pay only $1,500 at first and borrow the rest on the property. If you sold it for $20,000 two months later, you could make a profit of $5,000, less the interest paid on the borrowed $13,500. The interest usually cost 7 per cent which in this example would be $525 for 6 months. If the market continued to rise it was easy to net $4,475 – literally without doing anything. In 1920 the average US salary was under $2,500 a year.

Property dealers started to market Florida land aggressively and willing buyers who believed they were on to a 'sure thing' invested from all over the USA. For a while the profits were, indeed, sure. In Miami strips of land were divided and divided over again. Once worthless lots miles away from the seashore were suddenly selling for thousands of dollars.

One broker called Ponzi offered parcels of land near Jacksonville; 'near' turned out to be 65 miles away. Another broker offered land in the fast-growing city of Nessie, a fabled city that did not exist at the time. Unlovely lots in Miami went for $15,000. Prime real estate on the Miami seashore fetched up to $250,000. Land prices spiralled higher and higher but buyers continued to snap up lots. However much they paid, someone else was always ready to pay more. Their profit, of course, was in the end someone else's loss.

Florida officials boasted that their state was the Riviera of America. Andrew Smithers, the economist, told me that at one point 55,000 people in Miami, out of a population of 110,000, were dealing in real estate. But before we mock the Florida folly too much, let us remember that in London in 1988 estate agents were marketing broom cupboards in Knightsbridge for £30,000.

Then in 1926 a hurricane hit Florida and over 400 people were killed. By the end of the year there were 17,000 homeless people. The tragedy hit confidence. For once it is possible to see that a definable event affected 'sentiment'. Slowly – and it was slowly – the boom came to an end.

By the end of 1926 land had fallen in price; and over the next 2 years the fall was dramatic, though never to the absolute zeros of the South Sea Bubble, as land had some value after all. The scale of the collapse is shown in the sums cleared through the Miami banks. In 1925 they cleared $1.06 billion; by 1929 their clearings had shrunk to $143 million.

The Florida collapse was big news in the States. To argue investors were innocent is to fly in the face of the facts. The collapse made headlines in the *Wall Street Journal*, in the *New York Times* and on the radio. It should have alerted investors to the reality that no market just goes up and up and up.

In his analysis of the Wall Street crash, Galbraith (1955) does not confront the key issue of why investors ignored what had happened in Florida. I do not claim to have the answers but some factors seem likely to have affected attitudes at the time.

In the 1920s, after the bleakness of the First World War, shares had glamour. It was cool to be in the market. If you did not have old money, investing made you part of a socially ambitious group. If you read Scott Fitzgerald you could be forgiven for thinking there was no one on the East Coast who did not play the stock market. (As we shall see, that was not true but it is the feeling that counts.) There were stories of valets who had made a $250,000 or more. Investors liked to feel part of this group and showed it in the most blatant of ways, crowding into brokers' offices to see how prices were rising.

Galbraith even argues this behaviour helped precipitate the crash. Many people who should have been working in their offices making money were instead in the brokers' offices watching share prices.

The market also was not adversarial. If Wall Street kept on rising everyone could get rich – and not at the expense of other people. No one had to get hurt. Psychologically that mattered.

The markets gloried in the latest technology. Radio shares were specially interesting, as Internet shares are in 1999. Smart new passenger ships had share shops on board so that you could radio or cable your orders to your broker. The composer Irving Berlin used one to sell 1,000 shares in the studio Paramount Famous Lasky when they were $72 – a wise, move as the shares later crashed to zero.

Part of the glamour was intellectual. Wall Street gurus were clever and they offered interesting new investment vehicles. The main ones were investment trusts. Investment trusts in themselves were not that new: there had been companies since the 1860s whose main business was to buy stocks and shares. But now respectable houses like Goldman Sachs – oh yes, they existed way back then – started investment trusts which bought not bonds or shares but the shares of other investment trusts.

The value of any trust was the value of its shares plus a premium for the goodwill, investment skill and so on of the house that developed it. If a trust invested in 10 different trusts, nearly half its value might be in the goodwill rather than in the value of the shares. Investment trusts investing in investment trusts were fragile pyramids. When the market was rising they looked ingenious, though the cutting edge of new finance.

Commentators have often written as if all 1929 America played on Wall Street. If that were so no wonder investors were gullible. Again, the truth was different. Of the population of 60 million, only about 1.5 million Americans had shares. Galbraith suggests that most of these lived on the East Coast and in California. What we now call middle America – Kansas City, Iowa and so on – was more conservative with its money. Geography mattered, as it had in Amsterdam during the tulip craze or London during the Bubble. The greater the physical distance from New York the less likely people were to be caught.

At the end of 1926, as Florida land collapsed, *The New York Times* industrial average, the equivalent of the Dow Jones, stood at 176. The next year the market started to rise steeply but it was only in March 1928 that it reached uncharted heights. It started at 245 and ended nearly 40 per cent up at 331. Galbraith claims that it was then that the 'mass escape into make believe' started. Investors started to poured into the market, staking large sums.

Some of the rises between 1926 and 1929 were astonishing. Dupont rose from 255 to 525. Wright Aeronautic rose from 69 to 289. The new glamour stock Radio rose from the mid-50s to 510. Between 12 March and 14 March 1928 Radio rose 40 points.

Galbraith identified a mixture of technical and psychological reasons for the steep rise in the market. He was very sharp on two technical points: the success of American industry and the relatively easy availability of credit. Many American companies were reporting large profits and there were a number of interesting new technology stocks such as Radio. The levels of prices in 1927 could be justified; Galbraith argued that even many of the prices for some of 1928 had some logic. The boom was based initially on a sane assessment of economic prospects.

Part of the mythology of the 1929 crash is that most investors traded on a 10 per cent margin and that this helped cause the crash. Trading on the margin means, when they bought shares, they only paid 10 per cent of the price. If the shares kept going up, their brokers never asked for more; you could, as in the Florida land boom, buy a $1 for 10 cents and then sell it at $1.15 collecting 15 cents profit a share. Galbraith showed that fewer people traded on the margin than myth suggests. Of the 1.5 million investors 900,000 were cash investors. The 600,000 who were buying on the margin, however, found it easy to get credit, but not because brokers were reckless. The margin was never 10 per cent. In fact, in 1927 brokers asked clients to deposit a margin of 45 per cent. Later that year, many brokers raised the margin to 50 per cent as they worried about the state of Wall Street. The brokers, however, found banks clamouring to lend them money. International banks could make good profits lending to the American banks that lent to the Wall Street brokers who, in turn, lent to clients. Banks could advance brokers money at 12 per cent; the brokers were lending it to their clients at 14 to 16 per cent. So it was always possible to finance the margin. At the start of 1929 clients owed brokers the staggering amount of $6 billion (around $60 billion at current value).

Galbraith argues, however, that these technical factors mattered less than the psychological ones. He suggests that there was a 'mood' which encouraged the idea of easy riches. Forget the Protestant ethic. No need to work hard. Invest, lie back, enjoy. Watch the Dow Jones rise. No effort needed. Galbraith speaks of 'financial euphoria' and argues that the Wall Street guru John Raskob (1929) caught the mood in his article 'Everyone ought to be rich' in the *Ladies Home Journal*, in which he advised everyone that if they put aside only $20 a month and put it into shares for the next 20 years, they would find, assuming they reinvested all the dividends, that by 1949 they would be sitting on a pot of gold, an $80,000 pot of gold. The art collector Bernard Baruch said in an interview that the world was entering a new economic age.

Moods of societies are never easy to define, quantify or explain. What follows is anecdotal, but I find it interesting because the subjects of my stories were all psychologists who had a good feel for many of the moods of America and in the late 1920s; none was in a get-rich-quick frame of mind.

Three reasons to think 1920s America wasn't totally get rich quick:

▓ the attitude of John B. Watson;
▓ the investment of Carl Rogers;
▓ the complaints of B.F. Skinner.

By 1928 the American psychologist John Watson had dropped out of academia and become the vice-president of the advertising agency, J. Walter Thompson. Watson often wrote for the popular press and he was in constant demand as a pundit. In the research I did for a biography of him I wrote in 1979, I found that Watson was not pushing easy riches at all. In an article for *NEA* magazine Watson (1928) stressed the need for hard work. He advocated the setting up of personality clinics where people could improve their career prospects. He offered some rules for business success. Hard work was key; everyone should be willing to work overtime. No one should expect to become president of a company overnight. It was sensible to learn about the whole area of the business you were in. Watson's advice was not astonishingly original but it hardly confirms the mood Galbraith sees as key – get rich quick, thanks to the magic of the market.

Carl Rogers, one of the founders of humanistic therapy, was doing his doctorate in the late 1920s. He came from a fairly wealthy family but had quarrelled with his father over money and needed extra income. He had all the contacts he needed to play the market. He did nothing of the sort, however. He made extra money by importing Chinese knick-knacks – he had visited China a few years earlier – and by teaching.

My third psychologist, B.F. Skinner, author of *Beyond Science and Dignity* and *Walden Two*, also does not remember the late 1920s in the way Galbraith suggests. In his *Particulars of My Life*, Skinner (1984) examines the state of his soul around 1927 when he was 23. It was a grumpy soul. 'The world considers me lazy because I do not earn bread,' he complained. The world expected him to get a job 'for eight hours of office work minus the time spent being friendly to other employees, in arranging for a party for the evening in arguing the merits of a baseball scandal.' Skinner reckoned that if he did all those things, 'I should be a man. It's not so much my "being a man" that people desire, it is my being one of them.'

I have culled these voices to suggest that the general get-rich-quick mood of the 1920s was not as general as Galbraith suggests and that to rely on the vagaries of mood to explain the scramble to invest just will not do.

In the late 1920s investors heard a good deal of conflicting advice. It is perfectly true that optimists such as Raskob, the oil magnate Rockefeller and the great financier Andrew Mellon were powerful. On 23 March 1929, when he sailed for Europe, Raskob spoke favourably of General Motors shares and insisted that, like many shares, they were too cheap. When the market had a brief blip downwards in June 1929 Mellon said there was no cause for alarm and that 'the high tide of prosperity will continue'. Later when the market again threatened to fall steeply Rockefeller bought shares, announcing there was no fundamental reason for anxiety.

With so much interest in the market, journalists sought the opinions of economists. Many of them were very optimistic and occasionally talked more like advertising men than academics. Professor Dice of Ohio University saw Wall Street 'led by these mighty knights of the automobile industry, the steel industry, the radio industry' going ever upward. In September 1929 Harvard economists announced that they saw no reason for serious anxiety. Professor Irving Fisher, one of America's most famous economists and a man whose reputation has lasted, claimed a month before the crash, that share prices were at reasonable levels. Fisher would, a year later, publish an interesting article on the psychology of investors, an article that has been neglected perhaps because of Fisher's own fate. He became a multi-millionaire but died in 1947 deeply in debt as a result of unwise investments. Rational economic man perhaps sees no reason to heed the work of an economist who ended up in the poorhouse.

But during the Wall Street boom there were pessimists too. Galbraith points to one analyst who suggested leaving money in cash or investing in gold. It is easy to understand why one lone critic should be ignored but there were also powerful voices which had absorbed the lessons of the Florida land boom. Paul Cabot, a writer on finance, accused the investment professionals of 'dishonesty, inattention, inability and greed'. The *Wall Street Journal* was a little hesitant about the rise in prices from 1928 on. The *New York Times*, traditionally the voice of the Eastern establishment, was definitely worried. It repeated time after time that the values of shares on Wall Street could not be justified. Galbraith counted at least 10 editorials in *The New York Times* which suggested investors sell out. The question is why so few investors were willing to listen. Wharton in *The Custom of the Country* offers an interesting if oblique idea. It dealt mainly with the men who played Wall Street and the fact that the men did not discuss money with their womenfolk. The women were infantilized, but greedy. The only way the men could placate them was by constantly buying them things, so many men gambled because it was the only way to keep their wives and mistresses constantly supplied with diamonds and haute couture! Wharton was an acute observer of high American society and there at the time.

When the market started to fall on 23 October there was a meeting of the richest men in New York. These sophisticated investors spent millions trying to prop up the prices of shares such as US Steel. It was no use. The final crash started on 29 October. *The Times* industrial average fell from 415 to 384 on the 23rd; on the 28th it was down a further 49 points and on the 29th down a further 43 points.

Police surrounded the stock market as the authorities feared riots. As in previous – and subsequent – market collapses, investors found it hard to believe this really was the end of a bull market and many kept looking for reasons to come back into the market.

Wall Street then declined until June 1932, when the Dow Jones Index hit 41. Again it is difficult to see just what triggered the initial loss of confidence.

In the turbulent markets of 1929 some lost terribly but there were investors like Watson who got out in time and preserved the fortune they had made from 1927. What makes the difference between the investor who knows when to sell and the one who cannot bear to? This question is perhaps specially pertinent as one of the curious features I have identified in this potted history of speculative manias is that on two occasions the bubbles followed one another and often investors clung on far too long before selling. A psychological theory may help explain why.

Festinger's theory of cognitive dissonance

In the 1950s an American social psychologist, Leon Festinger, was studying the sometimes contagious spread of rumours and came across an Indian study of earthquakes and their aftermath (Festinger 1957). A psychologist called Singh had collected 35,000 rumours from an area where a tremor was felt but there was no destruction. About 90 per cent of the rumours in that area predicted even worse disasters. Festinger could not understand why people would circulate rumours that would create even more anxiety.

In an interview Festinger explained to me how he came to understand the mechanics. 'The people had been very frightened by the shock. They come out from where they have been hiding. They have been through a great deal but they see that nothing has happened. They feel so frightened they become very interested in providing themselves with some context that will justify their fear.' In addition, they feel embarrassed by their behaviour.

Festinger argued, then, that the rumours of even worse disaster were not anxiety provoking but fear justifying. In a study with Stanley Schachter and H.W. Riecken called *When Prophesy Fails*, Festinger looked at a religious group who prophesied that the end of the world would come on a particular 21 December (Schachter *et al.* 1964). They sat around and waited for the great event. (Incidentally, they expected aliens, who would airlift them to safety in outer space.) By 22 December when the Earth was still in place, the religious group did not say they were wrong and give up their faith. No shrivelling away in shame. Rather, they went out and sought new converts, claiming that the world had been saved by their prayers.

Festinger set out his theory of dissonance formally. Two elements are dissonant if one statement is the logical opposite of another. For example, I know smoking is very bad for my health; I continue smoking. Festinger claimed that dissonance can be so psychologically uncomfortable that individuals reduce the discomfort by taking improbable attitudes as the religious group did. As a smoker, for example, I ignore all the research on the effects of smoking. I avoid reading such articles or I believe that the anti-smoking lobby are fanatics.

Many of Festinger's experiments involved money. He compared the attitudes of students who had been paid $1 or $20 to take part in a boring experiment. The ones who had been paid less rated the experiment as less boring. Less boring, Festinger argued, because that justified spending their time taking part for a mere dollar.

It will become clear now why Festinger's ideas may be useful in helping to explain investor behaviour in these speculative manias. Investors are not just out to make money but to give themselves – and others – a reasonable account of how they have behaved. They invest financially, of course, but also psychologically.

Bull markets are full of bull

In a bull market which is rising fast many investors will believe the following two dissonant propositions:

1. The price of shares is already very high and shares are overvalued;

2. I run the risk of missing out on profits if I do not keeping buying
   shares because so many others are in the market.

One way to reduce that dissonance is to ignore any information
which argues that equities are overvalued and seek out information
which supports the second proposition – 'I may miss profits if I
don't.' This will have the effect of persuading them to buy, and
the more people buy the higher the market will go.

Festinger likens the way we reduce dissonance to the way we
reduce hunger or thirst. His ideas, adapted to market conditions,
highlight the fact that when they reduce dissonance, many investors
also become emotionally attached to the shares they buy.

When the market turns down, these attitudes make it harder to
sell. To sell, investors have to jettison not only their financial investment but also their psychological investment and face an uncomfortable rise in dissonance again.

Rational economic man (described in the Introduction) would, of
course, notice that the losses have been growing and would act
promptly to change the situation. But investors who cannot face
cognitive dissonance become concerned to justify their past investment behaviour and cannot deal well with the present. So they cling
on until it is too late. They will seek out news that supports the idea
the market will improve or that their shares will suddenly turn up.
This is neither greed nor fear at work but a more subtle set of
psychological mechanisms, conscious and unconscious.

In 1929 many investors were forced to sell because they could not
meet their margins. Many were furious. They did not want to sell,
believing the market would recover quickly and that they would
make up their losses. That is precisely the reaction cognitive dissonance theory would predict.

All this matters today. Some optimists claimed in 1999 that, by the
year 2002, the Dow Jones Index would hit 36,000, more than trebling
in value. By the end of 2000, with the Dow having hit a high of
11,016 in the summer and then falling back to just over 10,000, the
optimists seemed truly cock-eyed.

As I interviewed financial analysts at work I found some good
examples of cognitive dissonance at work.

Roger Yates, of the major investment house Invesco, for example,
was at pains to rescue the reputation of John Raskob, arguing that he

had been more right than wrong. If you had put $20 in shares a month from early in 1929, 20 years later that modest sum would have grown to not quite the $80,000 he predicted but to a still lucrative $60,000; nothing else would have done as well. Wall Street crashed. Yet for Yates, Raskob was right, the markets deliver profits, all is going to be for the best in the best of all possible worlds.

I would not dream of suggesting that cognitive dissonance explains behaviour in speculative manias completely, but it offers useful insights.

The history of these manias suggests that a combination of personal and social factors drives investors. To really understand them requires a mix of economics, personal psychology, group psychology and communication theory. No one has yet looked at the differences between investors who get out in time and those who cling on hoping and hoping and, in the end, losing and losing. Chapter 2 offers some ideas on this point. It is a question of resistances and denial, dynamics many people remain unconscious of – unconscious because the roots are in their childhood.

two

The psychology of money and profit

Most market professionals argue that the only psychological factors to affect the markets are greed, fear and the herd instinct. I want to suggest that this is a far too limited view. These three variables matter but other factors are clearly at work.

In the aftermath of the Wall Street crash but well before he lost his fortune, the Yale economist Irving Fisher became interested in the psychology of investors. Fisher saw investment as rational; individuals faced a stark choice between spending money and investing it. Fisher painted a flattering picture of the investor. He was something of an idealist. He had strong will and great self-control. The investor had the patience to invest and to wait for his investment to become profitable. In his *Theory of Interest* Fisher (1928) devoted one chapter to six psychological factors which affected attitudes to investment. These were:

- Short-sightedness – a difference between investors and others was that investors were able to take a long-term view and, in particular, to limit their immediate spending so that they could invest.
- Weak will – in Fisher's terms it required strong will to save and invest and to stick with those investments.
- The habit of spending freely – which cuts down on the money available for investment. Fisher suggested a very direct link between self-control and successful investing. The self-controlled saved in order to be able to speculate.

- Emphasis on the shortness and uncertainty of life – selfish individuals were only too aware of the shortness of life and took the view that there was little point in investing if one were soon to be dead.
- Selfishness – investors, in Fisher's view, had to be able to control their selfishness and to delay immediate gratification.
- Slavish following of fashion – Fisher was acutely aware of how investors could be affected by trends.

Fisher did not see investors as either greedy or liable to panic but, in the best tradition of economists, he did not interview any investors. He theorized that individuals who had a steady income and could forecast their future would be less willing to take risks than others. Fisher's investor is a psychological ideal. He can cope with delayed gratification and he certainly is not obsessed with pleasing others. These traits are the direct opposite of those of extroverts. Extroverts are impatient and tend to want to please groups they belong to. Fisher did not develop his ideas after the 1930s, however. The rest of his book concentrated on traditional economic issues.

The only economist who showed the slightest signs of following in Fisher's footsteps was John Maynard Keynes. Keynes's father, an economist himself, had dismissed the idea that psychology had anything to offer economists. In 1936, however, Keynes proposed eight motives for saving. One of these was that it would allow people to speculate to gain more wealth. Keynes attacked Wall Street as a casino, talked of speculation as 'forecasting the psychology of the market' but did not study investors in depth. No body of research developed.

Both Fisher and Keynes were working on conscious psychological motives. One of the few recent studies of the motives of private investors (Nagy 1998) suggests these will not give an adequate account of the motives of investors. Nagy found that 40 per cent of private investors gave 'feelings about a company' as one of their main three reasons for investing in their shares. Nagy was surprised that most investors put most economic reasons below this. Nagy found that only 11 per cent of investors said they were influenced by recent price movements in shares. Coverage in the financial press and brokers' recommendations were an even less powerful reason for investment. There is some evidence to show that the kinds of feelings Nagy alludes to will not always be rational or feelings we are aware of.

There is a literature linking the desire to make money to extremely irrational aspects of human behaviour – fetishes, obsessive compulsive disorders, faeces, not getting enough at the nipple and squaring your account with God. We shall see that not everyone in the market is affected in similar ways.

A feature of my approach has been to interview analysts, brokers and traders. I talked to them about what led them into the City, their approach to investment decisions and how current pressures affect their decision making. From these interviews, similar to the ones I have done with psychologists (Cohen 1977), it's clear we should not generalize. Different individuals respond to situations that provoke fear and greed in different ways. Kahn and Cooper (1993) interviewed 26 dealers as part of their research on stress in the dealing room and found enormous differences in attitudes, though unfortunately they did not ask their subjects either why they had gone into the business or what continued to motivate them. It is even more true that not everyone responds to peer pressure or the herd instinct in the same way. Some people hate to conform and to be seen as part of of the crowd. Others like the security of being part of a group. These differences matter.

This book is not a scientific study but, as it happens, I interviewed, in all, 33 brokers, traders, analysts, slightly more than Kahn and Cooper did. Among them I found:

- conviction brokers;
- momentum traders;
- brokers by tradition;
- wealth preservers;
- true speculators – a group that often likes to stay a little anonymous. The City is about investment, it's not a casino.

Conviction brokers like Michael Barnard who runs his own company and Charles Clark of West LB Panmure have been fascinated with the business of finance from their teens. For them the actual game of playing with investments is deeply interesting in itself. They remember their first deals. Michael Barnard, a trim blond man, runs his own broking firm in Essex. 'My father was a hard-working photographer and he had a few shares,' he told me. 'I was 16 and I was growing out of collecting stamps. It seemed a more adult type of hobby.' Barnard still remembers his first share deal of £20 of unit trusts. 'When they went up £4, I was on cloud nine. I became addicted to it like someone who's addicted to the horses.' He soon preferred shares 'because the bookies stack the odds against you'. Barnard's story has a famous parallel. Warren Buffett, the only man to have made billions out of nothing but stock-market investments, was 11 years old when he first bought shares for his sister. This enthusiasm contrasts with the ideas of Jim Slater (1994), put forward in his *Zulu Principle*. Slater is one of the great investment gurus of the last 25 years. He has said that making money is easy, a little boring and really in the end not that satisfying. To Barnard, delving into shares is sheer joy.

Barnard and Buffett would never accept Slater's disdainful definition of moneymaking as boring. Others recognize that the lure of dealing has them hooked. A retired senior partner in a major stock-broking house said to me: 'I deal too much for my own good.' Ronnie who retired as a broker told me he still deals because he enjoys the excitement.

Brokers by family tradition – there is a second group of dealers and brokers who came into the business a little passively through family connexions. David Mayhew of Cazenove told me he had joined the Stock Exchange because his father, himself a broker in Liverpool, wanted him to do so. Mayhew had wanted to be a farmer. Hugh Priestley left Oxford and worked on *The Times Business News*. He found that boring and his father told him there was an opening in a company he knew. Ian Francis of West LB Panmure was also influenced by his father who was an engineer. He told his son that he had a good brain and should make money. The City was the place.

Entering the City through family connexions doesn't lead to a particular style of trading but I do find it interesting that Priestley who was influenced by his father should describe himself as a momentum trader.

Momentum traders are much more influenced by how the market moves than by seeking shares which have hidden value which only they can spot. Conviction brokers and momentum traders both stress the wish to make profits. They contrast profoundly with brokers like Paul O'Donnell and a Liverpool broker who insisted on staying anonymous.

Wealth preservers – these men emphasize wealth preservation and not taking risks. O'Donnell told me he had made more money for investors who were driven by fear than for those who were driven by greed.

No one admitted to being just a speculator. We don't necessarily, however, know everything we feel about money and investment. Money arouses complex feelings because it has a multiplicity of meanings – sacred, symbolic, personal. And we are not conscious of some of these meanings, as I shall show.

Some historians have argued that Protestantism, with its focus on the individual, helped create capitalism. If you were rich, you were one of God's elect and would go to heaven when you died. Good motive! Even for atheists, who have no wish to belong to God's elect, money represents power, status and security. If you can afford to fly first class, you are able to buy better treatment. In the recent film *A Civil Action* the character played by John Travolta and his colleagues come up to New York to negotiate with a rich firm. They book themselves into a suite at the Plaza because they do not dare let their opponents suspect that they are short of cash. Psychologically in this scenario there is not that much of a leap in thinking from 'I get better treatment' to 'I deserve better treatment' to 'I am a better person' to 'I am one of the elect'.

The psychological complications of money are many. In 1975, an article in *New York* magazine linked sexual potency among Wall Street workers with the state of the Dow Jones Index. When the Dow Jones went up, erections went down. Some 25 years on, the same pattern has been reported in London. In April 1999 a team of researchers announced that City executives earning over £80,000 often reported having more sexual problems than average; 90 per cent claimed to be bored with sex.

Neither of these findings would have surprised Freud. He suggested some people are driven by the most primitive instincts from childhood to make or to hoard money. Another crucial figure in trying to understand the psychology of profit is the American David McClelland, whose book *The Achieving Society* was a classic in the 1950s (McClelland, 1952). In their different ways, both Freud and McClelland point to the importance of unconscious motives and childhood experiences.

There has been much psychiatric research linking poverty with depression and even schizophrenia. Psychology and psychiatry have always been more interested in failure than in success, and in the abnormal rather than the normal. What concerns me here, though, are the attitudes of normal and successful people. Studies of how normal people handle money are surprisingly few. One centre in Exeter specializes in attitudes to taxation; the London Business School is studying the psychology of dealers. Nevertheless, in their comprehensive review Furnham and Argyle (1998) confess they are amazed by the lack of research. Some basic information, such as whether social class and level of education in Britain affect attitudes to money, is not available.

Yet though the research is sparse, much of the little available confirms our distance from rational economic man and the importance of the unconscious.

The Harvard historian John Forrester (1998) points out that it is no accident that the first types of money were gold and silver. Both were worshipped and seen as sacred long before they were used as coins or mediums of exchange. Forrester even likens the fetish for gold and silver to phallus worship. 'Gold, like the penis, has a long, distinguished and venerable history as a marker of value,' he writes. (Is that why we spend a penny?)

One economist saw the link between money and fetishes. John Maynard Keynes wrote that the love of money is 'one of those semi-criminal semi-pathological properties which one hands over with a shudder to the specialists in mental disease.' Keynes also pointed out that as a store of wealth money is 'barren'. All other stores of wealth – gold, jewellery, land, salt – 'yield some interest or profit. Why should anyone outside a lunatic asylum wish to use money as a store of wealth?'

In one of the largest-ever surveys related to money, the American magazine *Psychology Today* (Rubinstein 1981) analysed responses from 20,000 readers. The survey asked whether over the last year readers had experienced any intense feelings in connection with money and found that 67 per cent of men and 75 per cent of women had associated money with feelings of anxiety; 46 per cent of men and 54 per cent of women had linked it with depression. A quarter of men and a third of woman had experienced feelings of fear; roughly the same number had experienced guilt and panic. Very few reported feeling joy in the context of money.

The readers of *Psychology Today* were not poor. Only 23 per cent reported having problems making ends meet. The negative emotions were not therefore, in the main, the result of poverty. *Psychology Today*'s results, like those of Nagy, stress we need to recognize the importance of emotions in understanding attitudes towards money and investment.

Psychoanalysis and money

Sigmund Freud is a crucial figure in trying to understand the psychology of profit. This is not because he was fascinated by finance but because he kept finding a block, an issue, a problem in the lives of some patients. One of Freud's early patients, Baroness Von Lieben, had a 'hysterical psychosis for the payment of old debts', debts incurred over 33 years as the worthy Baroness always refused to pay. It is also interesting that in German the same word – *Schuld* – means both debt and guilt. She cannot have been incompetent, since she also managed to stay out of gaol. It took Freud 3 years to cure her. He developed his ideas about money in *The Interpretation of Dreams* (Freud 1900) and in *The Psychopathology of Everyday Life* (Freud 1905).

After the First World War Germany suffered the most appalling inflation of modern times. Many of the first-generation analysts were social critics and political reformers. Wilhelm Reich, for a time Freud's favourite pupil, joined the Communist Party and has the distinction of having his books burned by both Hitler and the American government. Reich argued capitalism was itself a form of mass neurosis. Alfred Adler, Sandor Ferenczi and Karl Abraham all wrote about the psychological distortions money could cause.

In the 1960s Erich Fromm wrote a cult book called *To Have or To Be*, in which he contrasted the immature, who measured their worth in terms of money and possessions, with better adjusted human beings who did not feel that their worth depended on how much they had in the bank. One of Reich's pupils, Ernest Bergler, developed personality profiles of what he called 'the great army of money neurotics' (Bergler 1958).

It is striking that I can find no reputable analyst who had much good to say about the money motive. In the 'Hidden faces of money'

Blanton (1957), an American therapist who hoped to make his readers learn to appreciate money, was critically mauled by his peers. His ideas were 'the nadir of psychoanalysis' (Bornemann 1976).

Freud's critique of money and his theory of psychosexual development

A clear idea of Freud's views comes from his writings about the tale of Midas. Midas was granted a wish and wished that everything he touched would turn to gold. Midas, Freud argued, suffered from a grotesque money complex. The greedy king's life took a tragic turn. He found that he could not touch his wives or his children because they too turned into gold. Obsession with money led to total isolation.

In his analysis Freud was not just critical of myths. He sniped at Carl Jung, the man who for a long time was seen as his natural successor, because Jung was too interested in money. Freud thought Jung a typical Swiss obsessed with money (and Jung thought Freud a typical Jew obsessed with sex). Freud teased and warned Jung, who had married a very rich wife and was financially secure, against his 'money complex' (McLynn 1996).

Around 1909 Jung complained to Freud that he could not afford to hire a promising young man as his assistant because it would cost too much. Instead the young man was sent to work as an assistant at a hospital near Montreux. He was bitterly disappointed because he wanted to study with Jung. Freud told Jung that he was letting his money complex get the better of him and, as he was financially secure, he really ought to employ the man if he wanted to.

Jung probably knew nothing about the fate of Freud's Uncle Josef and, for some years, Jung felt defensive. He explained to Freud that he was always conscious of money because it was a way of compensating for the fact that he felt so inferior when he compared himself to Freud – a wily reply, of course, because it seemed to flatter Freud enormously.

Acquiring money, Freud noted, was essentially an aggressive act because the rich have power over the poor. Freud was familiar with Marx, who complained that money changes fidelity into infidelity, love into hate and virtue into vice. But while Freud admired Marx, Freud said that communism made impossible psychological demands. In *The Future of an Illusion* Freud (1929) mocked the idea that money could be abolished or that a society could develop in which there was no private property. 'I am able to see that the psychological premises on which the system is based are an untenable illusion.'

The illusion was untenable, Freud believed, partly because responses to money and property stem from the most basic experiences of the human baby – sucking and shitting. (To financial analysts the following may seem bizarre and, even possibly, distasteful. If that's how you react, remember that Viennese doctors threatened to report Freud to the police because of his shocking ideas. Those doctors did not, however, become key influences on the culture of the 20th century.)

Freud developed a complicated and influential theory of psychosexual development. He argued that infants go through oral, anal and genital phases between birth and the start of the latency period when they are about 7 years old. The phases are each named after the orifice which then gives the child the most pleasure.

The baby's first pleasure is sucking. He or she grabs for the breast. The breast provides food, comfort and delight. Sucking is wonderful; the baby can never get enough of it. Some babies get fixated at this oral stage but, normally, 1-year-olds start to move on. They stop being quite so obsessed with their mouths, the breast and the bottle, and start being obsessed with excretion. Society reinforces the obsession by telling us that babies have to be toilet-trained – that's almost their first job. Freud argued that pee and shit are the first objects the baby produces.

Freud noted that certain infants find toilet-training harder than others and that this might be due to biological differences. Babies who find it difficult to learn to control their bowels invest anything anal with great importance. They linger on the pot. When they are 3 or 4 years old, they often still wet or soil their beds. Faeces have a real fascination for them. Some play with their faeces and smear them over toys and furniture. Their faeces are them. Such children, Freud claims, have a high degree of anal eroticism.

Parents and nannies are often irritated, and pester and threaten their charges. Good children are clean. Bad children are dirty.

Often children hold out against the wishes of parents for a long time. I remember once when my eldest son was 4 going to visit friends. Their $4\frac{1}{2}$-year-old was still put in nappies at night. They were embarrassed by what they saw as his failure but they had tried everything. My son Nicholas laughed at his friend when his parents put on the nightly nappy. Being made fun of apparently cured Nicholas's friend once and for all: he never needed a nappy again.

By the time they are 6, most anal children know they are somehow in the wrong. Some become disgusted with themselves. Freud argued that they feared the loss of control that not being toilet-trained represented. They now became ashamed and frightened of their dirtiness.

Sublimation and reaction formation are key concepts in psychoanalysis. These dirty children compensated for their dirty selves by becoming obsessed with cleanliness. The best way to be clean is not to produce dirt. If they do not shit, they cannot be dirty. Freud argued that these anal children now became anal retentives. They become constipated and cannot 'let go'. Some develop obsessive compulsive rituals like constant handwashing because they feel so unclean. They wash all the time because nothing can wash away the basic dirt.

This may all seem utterly remote from life in the City or on Wall Street? (I will not comment on the fact that a famous ad for Allied Dunbar was set in a company toilet.) In fact, Freud found evidence from a surprising source that linked money and shit. He was fascinated by anthropology and well versed in fables, the Bible and other myths. He noted there was an extraordinary tendency for money to be equated with faeces. In the Bible gold is called the devil's excrement; in some cultures shells which are used as items of value are called 'shit of the sea'.

But the most powerful evidence psychoanalysts have to offer comes from looking at slang and ordinary language. Freud observed that officials of the German Federal Bank went by the name of Ducatscheisser which means, literally, shitters of ducats. These ideas are supported by Bornemann (1976). In *Sex in Volksmund* he found hundreds of examples of German and English expressions that confirmed this link between money and defecation. In German, the anus is referred to as a gold mine and the toilet is called the gold mill, the bank or even the stock exchange. A chamber pot is called a piggy bank. In German slang toilet paper is referred to as securities, a treasury bill or an invoice. Going to the toilet is called doing big business. Newcomers to the London stock market in the 19th century were called 'shit breeches'. A more respectable term was to call them 'blue buttons'. It may be that the newcomer undid his blue buttons to get out of his breeches. In his *Dictionary of Slang* Eric Partridge (1984) pointed out that in Victorian times someone who cleaned out toilets was called a 'goldfinder'.

Bornemann argues that some almost normal respectable uses reflect this unconscious connection. In German, if you are in financial difficulties you are called constipated; your creditors are not satisfied. In modern English we call someone who is mean tight-arsed and, if your cash-flow crisis is suddenly and miraculously cured, you are suddenly liquid again. Bornemann argues that rich men wallow in gold just as children wallow in dirt.

Observations of children and clinical accounts of patients point the same way. The Hungarian analyst Sandor Ferenczi (1930) suggests there is a clear line of development which links faeces and money. He argues infants often play with their own faeces in the pot. Toddlers like to play with dirt or with mud. In kindergarten they learn that playing with mud or in the mud is not allowed so they start to play with that acceptable mud substitute, sand. Many child psychologists argue that when toddlers play with sand they are sublimating playing with shit. Ferenczi claimed that the next stage up from sand was playing with pebbles and stones. In primitive societies stones are often marks of value. So Ferenczi shows a nice ladder – from faeces to mud to sand to stones. And the child who plays with stones becomes the adult who plays with coins. There is an almost surreal, but poetic, logic to this.

In outline, then, this psychoanalytic theory is simple. Children with a high level of anal eroticism find it hard to be toilet-trained. They react against their childlish love of dirt and shit by becoming anally retentive. Later, they transfer the obsession and fixate not on hoarding faeces but on hoarding money. Just as they found it hard and painful to shit, they now find it hard and painful to spend money. Both involve letting go. (I look forward to the bank and building society advertising campaign which capitalizes on the saving–constipation connection.)

Freud's adult patients reported dreams and experiences which confirmed the link – at least to Freud's satisfaction. In *The Interpretation of Dreams* Freud (1900) cites a woman patient who dreamed she had found buried treasure inside a rustic little shed which was much like an outdoor toilet. The same woman reported a dream in which she wiped her little girl's bum.

In *The Psychopathology of Everyday Life* Freud (1905) tells a number of anecdotes in which patients who were ambivalent about therapy somehow managed never to pay their analysts' bills. Women patients were the worst. After an hour on the couch, they would rise and seem to have left their purses behind. But this was not just meanness, it was psychopathology. The women would have spent their session discussing intimate sexual details. That was bad enough but to have to pay for the privilege was too much. Some talked of prostituting themselves for the analyst. But prostitutes usually got laid and paid. Here they were being asked to pay for talking dirty.

In another link between money and sex, Freud describes an old man who had just married a young bride. When they reached the honeymoon hotel, the man had lost his wallet. If he had no money, they could not have a bedroom and if they did not have a bedroom, the man need not risk finding out whether he could satisfy his nubile young wife. The story had a sad end. The old man cabled Vienna for money. The hotel let them stay but the old man did not get an erection. But all the stress gave him an excuse. He would have been able to get it up if only he had had his wallet from the start.

Debt played an interesting part in one of Freud's most famous cases, that of the Wolf Man (Freud 1979). The Wolf Man suffered recurring fantasies that his anus was being gnawed by rats. Freud discovered that the Wolf Man's father had lost money at cards while a non-commissioned officer. A friend had lent him the money. Later the father became well off by marrying a rich woman and tried to find the friend to repay the debt. The Wolf Man did not know if his father ever found his benefactor. The Wolf Man became very concerned about this when he fell in debt to a lieutenant.

At a crucial moment, the Wolf Man told Freud about a dream in which he saw Freud's daughter with two patches of dung where her eyes should have been. The dream, Freud suggests, posed a key question. Should the Wolf Man remain faithful to the woman he loved despite her poverty or should he marry for money as his father had done?

Analysts often had slightly too direct proof of the money–faeces link. Bornemann describes a number of patients who farted loudly while they were on the couch, making the analyst pay through the nose for treating them.

Sandor Ferenczi discusses one patient who had an obsession with coins and from time to time swallowed them. He would then retrieve the coin from his stools, polish it and announce that there was no better way of getting a shine on a coin than to have them pass through your stomach and out again. Ferenczi also notes that he had learned from his patients that many rich people are extremely 'economical in changing their undergarments'.

Freud's pupil, Karl Abraham, discusses one case where a patient had a rich father (Abraham 1979). Papa trained his children not to go to the toilet for as long as they could so that they could squeeze the last ounce of nourishment out of their food. Food cost money. It was your duty to get the most out of your investment.

Furnham and Argyle complain that a number of psychoanalytic theories have not been put to any kind of experimental test and so it is hard to know whether they have any validity.

Oral personality and sucking

Psychoanalytic ideas on what drives people to make money have been less well explored but, again, Freud had a theory. The infant who gets enough milk when he sucks is set for a well-adjusted life. As Freud listened to his patients, however, he concluded that many of them did not get enough satisfaction at the breast and that dogged them for the rest of their lives. They always wanted to compensate for what they had never had as babies. And one way to compensate for their all-consuming hunger was to devour and possess everything they could get their hands and mouths on. Thus millionaires become rich in a desperate attempt to get over their oral frustration.

It was a losing battle, though. They might make millions but nothing could make up for having been left unsatisfied at the breast.

In the 1950s there was much popular development of these ideas. Bergler (1958) describes a number of psychological types in relation to money. From the point of view of the stock market, the most interesting are the gamblers who suffer from oral frustration and compensate by feeling nothing could go wrong for them.

The key question, of course, is whether these often exotic analytic ideas have a germ of truth. Furnham and Argyle complained that a number of psychoanalytic theories have not been subjected to any kind of experimental test and so it is hard to judge whether they have any validity. I think, however, there are two sorts of confirming evidence:

(1) empirical verifications of Freud, such as Kline's (1972, 1993);
(2) analyses of sell or buy recommendations

In an article for the *Financial Analysts Journal* Jerrod Wilcox (1998) wrote: 'it is often harder to decide to sell stocks than to buy them.' He noted out of his own experience that 'investment policies or decision rules are often harder to abandon than to create.' Löffler has come up with similar findings.

But the best proof is numbers. A number of recent studies have looked at brokers' recommendations to buy or sell shares. What is astonishing is the difference between buy, hold and sell recommendations. Carleton *et al.* (1998) researched just how influential recommendations were and, to do so, they logged 4,537 recommendations over a 5-year period. 51 per cent of these recommendations were buy recommendations; under 12 per cent were sell recommendations; 33 per cent were hold recommendations. The authors looked at the differences between recommendations put out by brokers and by firms that did not provide brokerage services. Among the brokers only 2.99 per cent were sell recommendations; the non-brokers were far more likely to recommend selling but, even with them, only 9 per cent of recommendations were to sell shares.

Wilcox concluded that the reasons for people finding it hard to sell were social and psychological. People felt committed to the shares they had bought. If a firm took a decision to sell, it could create conflict. Once you are familiar with Freud's ideas there is a different way to interpret these figures; they provide surprising confirmation of the power of the anal personality. To sell shares, to get rid of them, to expel them is something very difficult for the anal personality to do. Many unconscious resistances work against it.

Two other empirical studies suggest that Furnham and Argyle are being overcritical. The late Paul Kline was not a Freudian but one of Britain's great experts on psychometric tests. Interested in whether there was any link between obsessional behaviour and anal personality, he constructed a questionnaire which included questions such as 'When eating out, do you think of what the kitchens are like?' and 'Do you worry about keeping control of your finances?' (Kline 1972). These questions are all aimed at teasing out the extent to which a person is concerned about control, an issue we shall see is crucial in understanding attitudes to risk taking.

Kline also showed his subjects a cartoon of a dog called Blacky. Blacky was caught in a number of scrapes including defecating between the kennels of its parents. Kline asked his subjects how disturbed they were by this cartoon. He suggested that anal retentive subjects would be highly disturbed because it showed the dog doing its business – and around its parents. Kline found a strong correlation between obsessionality – including obsessionality about money – and being disturbed by the cartoon of Blacky defecating. Kline concluded that 'the study supports the Freudian hypotheses concerning the aetiology of obsessional traits and symptoms.' The anal personality does seem to exist.

Kline's study is an interesting addition to the faeces–gold–money link in myths and it suggests Freudian ideas have something to offer the psychology of the market.

The profit motive

Studies of the deep psychology of the very rich are rare. David McClelland's (1952) book *The Achieving Society* was a classic in the 1950s. He has done extensive studies in a number of cultures of people who are highly motivated to succeed. Like Freud he found that the roots of these drives began in childhood.

This picture shows a man playing golf. Do you think he's playing it:

a. because he loves golf;
b. his wife insists he practises;
c. he wants to enter The Amateur Championship.

In *The Achieving Society* McClelland argues that certain individuals have a high nAch or need to achieve. McClelland was focusing on economic achievement.

In this question these individuals would typically choose the answer *c*. They tend to be independent, hard-working, self-reliant and given to making plans for the future. They accept that it may take a while for them to achieve their goals and they are willing to put up with considerable frustration meanwhile. They will put up with short-term suffering in order to achieve long-term gain. Their need to achieve is the product of an upbringing where they learn that they do not immediately get what they want. McClelland's research has extremely interesting implications for recruitment into financial services as it suggests those who can cope with delayed gratification are most likely to do well in the long term.

McClelland came to this theory from history. He noticed that certain periods in history had seen an upsurge in economic success. In classical Greece there was a surge just before the 4th century BC. In Britain there was dynamic economic growth round the time of Elizabeth I and then in the middle of the 18th century. McClelland examined the literature of the time and found that just before an economic boom, literature tended to stress themes such as mastery.

The timing of the 18th century boom is very telling. The boom took place 30 years after the disaster of the South Sea Bubble. It seems very likely that people reacted against that key event, against the evil of stockjobbing and drilled into their children the need to do real work and be willing to wait for rewards.

In some of his later studies McClelland looked at children's stories. McClelland eventually set out to teach children to become achievement minded. He told me: 'we've found that certain sub-groups teach this naturally to their kids. All over the world, we kept on running into minorities who were very good at business. When we checked out, we found they were bringing up their kids that way, the way we were trying to bring them up artificially.'

The achievement theory has been tested extensively and proved robust. McClelland predicted Britain in the mid-1970s would suffer hard times because the level of achievement motivation in stories published in the 1950s was so low; he predicted post-war Japan would do well economically because Japanese children's stories published after 1945 highlighted effort. Both predictions turned out correct.

Fear and greed

McClelland, however, was not studying one of the main market motives – greed. Greed has been studied but not in a financial sense. Psychologists have long been interested in hunger and in what makes animals and humans over-eat but it is not sensible to assume that what makes people stuff themselves also drives them to orgies of money making.

There is also a long literature on fear but, again, it is not immediately relevant to fear on the markets. Gray (1993) in his masterly survey does not mention fear of losing money once. He points out that the first theories of fear assumed it was caused either by a loud noise or loss of physical support or novel stimuli. He reviews the extensive literature on anxiety and, later, we shall see dealers suffer excessively from certain kinds of anxiety. To get any sense of the role of fear on the market, we have to rely on studies not of investors but of savers. There is a large group of savers who are very risk averse but, as we shall see in the chapter on risk, the situation is complex.

Psychoanalysis does have a small say on greed though. The psychoanalyst Joan Rivière (1937) argued that greed was really a desperate search for love. The things we consume 'stand as proofs to us, if we get them, that we ourselves are good and so worthy of love.' When we lose something including money it feels as if we have been robbed of a part of ourselves that makes us deserve love. Alfred Adler, one of Freud's first pupils, developed a psychological theory based on the lust for power and claimed that those who suffered from avarice, the term he used, were trying to use money to prove their superiority (Adler 1929). Such generalizations don't help us much. In a later chapter I shall look at what analysts have learned about the motives of investors. Fortunately, it is a little more specific.

The psychology of conformity and 'noise' traders

There is more work available on the third often cited factors, conformity and the herd instinct. Most economists who rely on the herd instinct to explain behaviour seem to mean that everyone follows blindly; there is no opposition, no contrary forces pulling the herd the other way. Recent economic analyses have developed the idea of the noise trader who is tremendously influenced by noise in the market, by rumour and gossip and follows them blindly. Again, however, there have been no studies in which so-called noise traders have been interviewed. We are asked to infer their existence from statistical studies which model how the markets work. This is much like Benos's study that I criticized in the Introduction.

Many studies in social psychology do show that people tend to conform under social pressure. Solomon Asch was a Jewish psychologist who asked his parents why the door was kept open for Elijah on Passover. His father told him that if he looked hard he would see the door open a little as the invisible Elijah joined them. The young Asch stared and was sure he saw the door open.

Later, when Asch became a psychologist, he carried out a series of experiments inspired by his childhood experience (Asch 1952). Subjects sat in a dark room and looked at three rods of different sizes. Then they were shown a fourth rod and had to say if it was the same size as A, B or C. When all the participants were real subjects there was no dispute. The fourth rod was the same length as A. In a second experiment, however, Asch used stooges. He told all the stooges to say the fourth rod was the same size as C even though it wasn't. He discovered that if he then introduced a new 'real' subject into the group that subject was puzzled when the first stooge said C was the same length and as more people agreed, it got worse. The real subject became first confused and, then, agreed with the rest of the group. Never mind the evidence of their own eyes. Group pressure made them conform. Here is the herd at work. Asch was working in a very artificial situation, however, and it was never quite clear whether subjects 'agreed' with the group because that was what they perceived or because they did not like to contradict the others.

In the market the situation is not artificial. Social psychologists have also found there are considerable differences between individuals. Not everyone is as susceptible. In pioneering investigations of how suggestible people are under interrogation, Gudjudsson (1995) has shown that under stress over 60 per cent of individuals are very suggestible. The key factors that go with suggestibility are low self-esteem, a feeling that outside forces exert control (this is known as external locus of control) and a desire to please others.

Animal research over the last 30 years has also shown that herds are not quite as simple as we used to imagine.

The lack of studies of the motives and aims of investors makes it easier for people to assert market psychology is a matter of greed, fear and herd instinct. This absence of research is itself telling. One reason for the lack of follow-up may well be that it would have forced economists to consider the influence of subjects utterly unfamiliar to them, like childhood experiences and irrational and unconscious forces. Bornemann (1976) in his excellent *The Psychoanalysis of Money* highlights these irrational forces and concludes by saying 'the analysis of money must develop into a therapy that will cure us of our interest in it.'

In the next chapter, I look at more mundane psychological factors which affect how we deal with investment – anxieties about maths and analysing information.

three

The logical blues or how we learn to hate information

Richard Branson has recently confessed that, despite his success as a businessman, he used to have great difficulty in telling the difference between gross and net profits. The BBC has some delightful footage of him explaining this unusual problem for a millionaire. But is Branson's problem that unusual?

In his *Prelude to Mathematics* W.W. Sawyer (1951), Professor of Mathematics at University College London, argued that many people were frightened of mathematics. Sawyer, who loved numbers and saw rhythms in their patterns, felt this fear cut off many of us from a source of fun. For him numbers were a joy. Some market professionals love dealing with numbers and deducing trends from them. There's nothing they would rather do on a Sunday afternoon than dissect financial statistics. For many individuals, however, the idea that dealing with numbers can be fun seems weird, even perverse. For them, numbers provoke anxiety.

Sawyer was writing in the days before information overload. In this chapter, I want to look at how human beings handle information, and, especially, financial information, today. Rational economic man was supposed to be the perfect calculating machine. The evidence is, however, that many of us find it hard to handle statistics and to understand what inferences can be drawn from them. Some kinds of personality become very anxious about such issues and check for errors carefully; others assume they are always right and are in a hurry to move on to the next problem. Few books that offer investors advice deal with these issues. Perhaps they think it too rude to ask if someone who has the money to buy 500 BT shares has the skill to understand all the implications, let alone understand the company balance sheet or annual report.

Our attitudes and abilities to compare numbers, to dissect statistics are, however, crucial to investment skills – and to protecting our money. In this chapter, I want also to look at two closely related topics – the ability to analyse information logically and to draw correct inferences from a set of facts and numbers and how anxiety about lack of such skills affects people.

American research shows 89 per cent of investors feel they need a broker. One reason why we use brokers, of course, is we feel they have expertise we lack. Market professionals, as Jim Slater (1997) points out, may also not be that skilled since so many of them have no qualifications in investment at all. If your doctor had a degree in history or a diploma in car mechanics would you allow him to operate on you?

The ancient Greeks started the study of how to draw inferences. Some 50 years ago schoolboys in British public schools were drilled in how to solve syllogisms that had been first dreamed up by the likes of Plato and Aristotle.

Serious about syllogisms

Syllogisms state logically necessary relationships between propositions. A simple syllogism runs as follows:

If *A* is bigger than *B*
And *B* is bigger than *C*
A has to be bigger than *C*.

Whatever *A*, *B* and *C* are – cars, feathers, aeroplanes, Sumo wrestlers or psychology textbooks – the relationship between them is a logically necessary one. It is impossible to conceive a universe in which it would be different.

Another syllogism runs:

> All men are mortal
> Socrates is a man
> Therefore Socrates is mortal.

The inference from the first two statements is that being a man Socrates must share the characteristics of all men.

The Greeks argued that the study of syllogisms and logic allows us to spot faulty reasoning:

> All cats are mortal
> The Spice Girls are mortal
> Therefore The Spice Girls are cats.

This is an example of faulty reasoning. The conclusion 'Therefore The Spice Girls are cats' cannot logically be drawn from the first two statements that cats and Spice Girls are both mortal; indeed there's nothing else you can deduce about the Spice Girls or cats or mortals. We know they die. That's it.

In this example the faulty reasoning is obvious since we 'know' pop stars are not cats, but psychologists have found that when the premises are less obvious, mistakes occur often. Speed is also a factor. The quicker decisions have to be made the more likelihood of errors.

The following problem comes from a series of studies of how people work out the odds in various situations:

> Smith likes to work with precision. He draws and calculates with ease and did well at maths at school.

> Jones is a good communicator. He speaks well and knows how to get his audience to agree with him. At school he was good at classics and history.

Subjects are given a list of such short CVs and told that the files they come from contain a total of 70 per cent engineers and 30 per cent lawyers. If subjects are asked what jobs Smith and Jones do, nearly everyone identifies Smith as an engineer and Jones as a lawyer.

When subjects are told 70 per cent of the sample are lawyers and 30 per cent are engineers they give virtually the same answers. They ignore the probabilities in the given information – after all when 70 per cent of the sample are lawyers is it impossible for the meticulous Smith to be one too? Subjects still make inferences based on stereotypes – communicative lawyers and numerate engineers.

Such research shows how illogical we can be in interpreting information. Piatelli Palmarini (1995), in a book on cognitive illusions, claims that we have to guard against what he describes as 'deadly sins' in dealing with information: overconfidence, magical thinking, probability blindness, becoming too attached to certain authority figures and hindsight.

Anxieties about how we handle information are not new. The American sociologist Alvin Toffler (1974), in his classic *Future Shock*, warned that human beings would struggle to cope with increasing amounts of information. In 1974 there was no Internet, faxes, e-mail, mobile phones or pagers. Stock markets still had floors where brokers and jobbers traded by word of mouth and confirmed deals on little scraps of paper. Toffler predicted that well-educated women and men could adapt to new technologies but it would take effort and flexibility. The less skilled would lag behind and suffer. Toffler added that we would find it hard to handle the new information environment because it would make unprecedented and unnatural demands on our biology, which does not fit us for high-speed, high-accuracy data analysis.

The brain has been compared to an information processing machine. It is designed to handle information from birth. When a baby is born, two-thirds of his or her brain is already in place. Neural or brain cells do not sprout as the baby develops but connections between cells develop. Films show the process of connecting cells as being quite poetic. Little tentacles spread out from one cell and link up with tentacles (technically called dendrites) from other cells. The tentacles weave thousands of branches which link to mesh the almost infinite web we each have in our cortex.

As the baby sees, hears and feels, connections are created as cells connect for the first time as a result of the baby's new experiences. Think of it, as the fax machines say, as handshaking; but once two cells have shaken hands the line stays open. A typical adult's brain cell will connect to 10,000 other brain cells.

We humans could never have been such successful hunter-gatherers if our brains had not also made us good information gatherers; but, as we evolved from the apes, the pace at which we gathered and processed information was probably not too frantic. It is true, of course, that our ancestors had to deal with emergencies, matters of life and death, food and water. The Neanderthal brain could always snap into action. Leopard on the rampage – run like mad. Band from an enemy tribe with spears – gather friends, prepare to fight. In a crisis, the Neanderthal body went into overdrive, pumping adrenalin and increasing the flow of oxygen to make the brain more efficient. But emergencies were probably the exception.

Until the 19th century probably the only groups who worked in the kind of detail analysts and brokers now have to do were monks pouring over medieval manuscripts, Talmudic scholars and small groups of philosophers and mathematicians. Monks and Talmudic scholars had regular breaks for prayer and neither they nor mathematicians were expected to complete their contemplations in 3 minutes flat before the Osaka Exchange closed for the night. The human brain at the dealing desk is coping with unnatural tasks at an unnatural speed.

Recent research on genetics shows we share 98 per cent of our genes with chimpanzees. In a provocative essay on human cognitive evolution, Richard Byrne (1999) argues that the distance between us and apes is not perhaps as great as, in our vanity, we have imagined. And that prompts the funny question: Just how would a gorilla make out on Wall Street? And also many less droll ones. If we share so many genes with the apes, is it perhaps that surprising we often misinterpret information and get probabilities so wrong? Recent work on the numerical abilities of the most gifted, and tutored, chimps suggests a few manage to learn $2 + 2 = 4$. It confirms the pessimism of Desmond Morris's (1965) *The Naked Ape* where he argues that we are suffering because modern civilization had catapulted us into lifestyles evolution never designed us for.

The anatomy of attention

The area of the cortex that becomes most active when we make intellectual decisions is the prefrontal cortex. The prefrontal cortex sits in the front of the skull about $1\frac{1}{2}$ inches behind the eyes. New techniques of brain imaging now make it possible to see what happens in the prefrontal cortex.

There is considerable change in the blood flow to the prefrontal cortex when subjects are asked to do nothing more intellectually challenging than to count backwards from 50 to 0. This is not Einstein territory, but a task that requires a bit of concentration.

The blood flow to the prefrontal cortex increased by 27 per cent when subjects were counting backwards. This suggests that this relatively simple numerical task requires more than usual brain effort. Traders and investors have to do calculations which matter to them and much research like Kahn and Cooper's suggests they are under stress. Recent research shows that under stress one of the crucial areas of the brain, the hippocampus, starts to degenerate (Sapolsky 1996). Sapolsky studied the hippocampus as a structure that is involved in memory and that integrates information from other parts of the brain. Though none of these physiological studies were done in dealing rooms or brokers' offices, they still suggest that the kind of information financial professionals have to handle puts pressure on their natural brain biology.

The concept of information

The concept of information is itself the product of recent technology. We now understand the notion as it was first proposed by a telephone engineer, Claude Shannon. Shannon (1948) argued that telephone lines could be seen as channels of information. Each channel has a limited capacity, which Shannon measured in bits.

We tend to think that the brain is an unlimited channel and that there is nothing we cannot learn. Many experiments, however, contradict this optimistic view and suggest that human beings have definite mental limits. In a paper, 'The magical number 7 plus or minus two', the American psychologist George Miller (1956) shows that we can grasp only seven items in immediate perception. If you flash five dots on a screen people will know that there are five. If you flash eight they start to make mistakes and can as easily say there are seven or nine or ten. If the pace at which subjects have to judge the number of dots increases, the errors multiply. Often people get very irritated when they learn that they got such tasks wrong because they seem so simple.

Studies of memory show how over short periods of time, information decays. We forget much more than we remember. We forget most of what we perceive. Only freaks have perfect recall. Toffler predicted that, confronted with this information overload, people would adopt a number of strategies including ignoring new information, relying on stereotypes, narrowing the field and becoming emotional and attributing this to stress.

There is anecdotal evidence suggesting that traders behave in precisely this way. The editor of Reuters in-house magazine told me, as did representatives of other companies who sell financial information systems, that their clients do not use more than a tiny fraction of the information they buy access to. Particular clients tend to use the same small number of screens repeatedly. In other words, clients cut down on their information stream in order to cope. Some research fleshes out these points. Kahn and Cooper (1993) in their research surveyed 600 dealers. A total of 225 replied to their questionnaire. (The 26 dealers they interviewed were part of this sample and the subjects studied in most depth.) The most significant sources of stress included:

- 73.8 per cent suffered from fear of 'misreading the market';
- 70 per cent complained that having too much work to do caused them stress;
- 62 per cent complained about having to learn new techniques of handling information;
- 41 per cent complained directly of information overload.

These stresses are all related to acquiring and handling information.

Market professionals have the advantage of having sophisticated computers and computer programs to help deal with cascades of information. When I was talking to David Mayhew, senior partner at Cazenove, he took out a little pocket screen and said that it allowed him to know all the latest trades that he would normally keep tabs on. The instant access excited him. Mayhew added, 'These systems make everything more open and transparent,' which he saw as good. Mayhew has learned to be comfortable with the computer revolution but he may be an exception.

How private investors handle the information overload

Private investors are often at a disadvantage in the information universe. Many do not use computer models. Many often do not even realize how much they do not know. Many brokers and fund managers told me they were astonished by the way many private investors do no research and do not seek information. American mutual funds now recognize this and some send investors questionnaires to fill in before they take them on as clients.

In a survey of software packages in April 1999, the *Investors Chronicle* asked readers to think about a series of questions which might help them find the ideal information programme for them.The questions included:

- Do you find you are focused on the money rather than the strategic nature of the market?
- Do you feel rejection when you suffer losses?
- Do you feel able to assess information accurately or do you get too involved?
- Do you feel that you are an emotional trader?

Clearly the *Investors Chronicle*, which has 118,000 readers, worries that a large number of them cannot assess information about shares dispassionately. Many brokers 'blame' the bull market of 1995–2000 for this tendency. When it is relatively easy to make money, few realize how hard you need to work to invest well.

One of the issues the *Investors Chronicle* did not raise – I suspect because it would insult its readership – is the extent to which people worry about the essential skills needed to interpret financial information. I am talking here not about problems with calculating probabilities but about the most basic mathematics.

Early in 1999, when he was being interviewed on the radio, the Secretary of State for Education David Blunkett took an embarrassing 14 seconds to answer the question of what 9×12 was. The sum was the routine stuff of tables. I dread to think how long it would have taken him to work out 13×14.

The British education system does not fit people to deal with financial decisions. In 2001, significant numbers of teachers failed the very basic numeracy tests the Labour government insisted on. Confronted by complicated financial statistics – and often financial statistics massaged to sell products – many people feel inadequate and confused. Research on literacy shows that men and women who can't read go to extraordinary lengths to conceal the fact. There is less stigma in being poor at numbers, but people are still uncomfortably aware of their lack of skills.

Napoleon sniffed that the British were a nation of shopkeepers. Their soul was the profit and loss account. Napoleon today would be surprised how the shopkeepers – never mind the Richard Bransons – often cannot work out how much is in the till.

A non-mathematical nation

Take 1.22 away from 5.

What is 14×11?

According to a study by the Basic Skills Agency (1996) only 20 per cent of Britons could solve 12 such simple questions correctly. Standards of numeracy in Britain are poor, the Agency complains. If people cannot manage simple addition, subtraction and multiplication, what hope do they have with the following kinds of problem?

If a fund grows at 7 per cent and charges 1.5 per cent as an annual management charge, is it a better investment than a fund which grows at 12 per cent and charges a 5 per cent annual charge?

You bought British Telecom at 447 and now it's 890. You bought Ulster TV at 89 and now it's 196. Which share is the better buy?

Computer programs can solve such mathematical problems. They can also compute complex formulae, calculating the price of shares to the growth in earnings compared to their historical value. When it comes to private investors, no one knows how many of them use computer programs, however, or how well they handle the information they provide.

The amateur investor – and fear of logic

The research published by the Basic Skills Agency assumed that well-educated individuals would be able to pass simple numeracy tests. But in a study of British undergraduates Wason and Johnson Laird (1972) found that most undergraduates cannot think logically. In one study they presented students with four cards marked on one side as follows:

A   D   4   7 .

Students had to say which card needed to be turned over to confirm the proposition that if there is a vowel on one side there is an even number on the other. A total of 92 per cent of students contented themselves with turning over the card with the A on it and were amazed to discover that they had not solved the puzzle correctly. Only a truly logical 8 per cent realized that, to confirm the hypothesis, you also had to see what was on the other side of the 7. That could also be a vowel, after all. If there was a vowel it would falsify the general rule.

Psychologists have found similar results in America. Perhaps even more astonishingly, Golding (1980) found that patients with particular kinds of brain damage often did better than the students.

Most of us are not as familiar with manipulating logical equations as Golding imagined. Wason and Johnson Laird repeated the experiment using envelopes. They showed students a sealed envelope, one with a 5p stamp, an unsealed envelope and one with a 4p stamp. (The postage rates show how old the study is.) The hypothesis to be tested was that if an envelope is sealed it has a 5p stamp on it. To get that right, you need to look at the front of the sealed envelope and also at the back of the 4p envelope to make sure it is not sealed. With these more realistic materials 92 per cent of students got the right answer.

Computers can be programmed to solve logical problems like these. But investments often require choices which involve a mixture of mathematics, logic and personal preferences. Take the following situation. You have a windfall of £5,000. You have to choose between:

- Leaving the money safely in the building society, where it will grow by 4 per cent per annum but where you will have to pay tax. Whatever happens you will be able to take the money out to pay for that long planned cruise to the Caribbean.
- Putting the money into a blue-chip company such as BP Amoco, which has grown historically and where you will get a dividend of perhaps 3 per cent. Probably you could sell out and pay for the cruise but the shares could fall in which case you may also have to take some money from other savings.
- Putting £5,000 into a biotechnology stock, which could grow much faster than it would in a blue chip but where there is no history and a risk that it will fail completely. You might be able to afford to travel first class – that would be good – but you might also lose any chance you ever had of the cruise.

In this situation you have to choose between mathematically and psychologically complex options. The psychological options involve how much risk you are comfortable with and the relationship between possible level of profit and level of risk. I may be willing to punt £5,000 on Universal Biotech which could quadruple in value but also could collapse by 75 per cent. On the other hand I could invest in Baltimore Technologies, one of the stars of the high-tech market of 1999–2000 which reached 1,400p a share in June 2000 but has since fallen back to under 100p. Baltimore is unlikely to swing wildly upwards but it is unlikely to fall below 75p, a bottom line it has tested. If I buy at 100p, I could still lose 20 to 30 per cent but probably not more and it's quite feasible to imagine Baltimore would hit 200p. One is a very high-reward/high-risk option, the other is still quite high risk but also a far less high-reward option. Which option a person chooses is as much a matter of personality as of mathematics. To calculate the options perfectly right you would also have to throw in an estimate of:

- the commission you pay the broker;
- the differences between the price you buy and the price you sell;
- capital gains tax you will have to pay if there is a profit.

We are all individuals with different plans, different attitudes to risk, different obligations. You can calculate the possible risk of uncertain investments; you can, using certain scales, arrive at some measure of how much the cruise would mean to you (you could ask people, for example, how many weeks they would work to earn the cruise). But the sums would attempt to add up different things. Two bananas and three oranges make five fruit. But what do three bananas and three dreams make?

This example of a typical decision assumes that the individual is well informed – and trained to analyse it. In its software survey, however, there was another key question the *Investors Chronicle* did not ask: Just how motivated are private investors to be well informed?

Information overload and the private investor

The broker I found most passionate about what he saw as the shameful ignorance of the small investor was Michael Barnard whom I saw at the small broking firm he runs in Essex. Barnard's passion stems partly from his background. His father was a professional photographer who had dabbled in shares. Some 30 years after Barnard bought his first £20 of unit trusts and became addicted, it almost offends him that amateurs should be so dilettante. He taught himself. They should put in the same effort if they want to deserve to make a profit.

Barnard moved his firm to Essex to cut down on travelling time and that has given him more time for researching shares which is what he says he loves. He laments the fact that he also has a business to run with 19 staff and many clients who want to chat for ages. He does not mind that usually. What he does mind, it seems, is the stupidity of many small investors.

Barnard told me, 'I often get people ringing up and saying to me "can I buy them shares for a penny" because they think if the share only costs a penny, it has to be cheap. Or they ask for BT and I tell them that each share is £6 and they say "No, that's too expensive." '

Depending on the company, of course, a share at £6 can be very cheap, decent value or insanely expensive. Barnard worries that many small investors do not understand that penny shares are more likely to be a risk than a bargain. Tell an investor he is getting a share for 2p and he (or she) usually thinks he's getting a big bargain, Barnard argues, but often these shares are expensive. Until recently there were so-called bucket shops which specialized in penny shares. Many bucket shops had bought penny shares in companies for far less than a penny. They then made a profit selling these shares to mug investors for a penny. The bucket-shop operators knew that most of these shares were probably worthless. Nice con, especially as it was perfectly legal.

'The companies doing that have been largely forced to close down here but there are still companies registered abroad doing it here,' Barnard told me. Newsletters recommending penny shares sell well. Some penny shares, Barnard admits, may do well but most are exceptionally high risk. Research suggests that out of 100 penny shares, 85 are likely either not to improve or to become literally worthless. Many clients seem to prefer to dream that their penny share will soon be worth 10p. Proof that they'll soon rival financier millionaire George Soros.

Many amateur investors 'buy shares in companies they don't even know and certainly haven't studied,' Barnard complained. They are not even intelligent in their greed. 'The first question they always ask is what's your commission. Well, that sounds sensible, but very few ask how hard I'll try to get them a good price.' Someone who went into the Skipton Building Society would almost certainly pay less commission than if they went to him, he admitted. 'But the deal would be done screen to screen. I often save the commission because I'll get on the phone and I do try to get clients the best price.' But people either do not realize that or do not want to think about it.

The press and financial understanding

The private investor also gets less help than you might expect from the burgeoning financial press. All the broadsheet newspapers have weekly sections devoted to 'Your Money' or 'Personal Money'. Even tabloids like the *Sun* now carry regular financial features. The *Daily Mirror*'s City Slickers column has been the subject of controversy. But it is very possible that ordinary intelligent readers (who may be or become private investors) find financial reporting not easy to understand because that reporting assumes far too much knowledge.

As a simple test, I looked through the *Evening Standard* and *The Times* business pages on 13 April and 16 April 1999. The following sentences and terms seemed to me to require explanation:

- 'Chemical companies would always be poorly rated because investors and analysts did not understand commodity cycles' (reported in a piece about ICI selling a company called Huntsman).
- 'The theoric value of the 3i offer is also some way behind the 915p asset value that the Electra board said was the underlying true value of the trust shares.'
- 'Windfall hunters who made a rare excursion into the fixed income markets by buying bond style issues from the Birmingham Midshires Society are likely to sell from next Monday causing downward pressure on the price of so-called Permanent Interest Bearing Shares.'

The papers included phrases such as **'net debt'**, 'leveraging growth', *'complex leveraged recapitalization'*, 'golden share', **'goodwill write-downs'**, 'adjusted earnings per share', 'covenant terms on loans to accommodate write-offs', 'convertible *Eurobond* issue', 'perpetual subordinated debt' and **'short positions'**.

It is not easy to write about complex financial matters and I am only too aware that I may be vulnerable myself to accusations of obscurity, but it is telling that neither paper tried to define these often technical and complex terms.

The Times and the *Evening Standard* are not selling particular products and they present information critically. Much financial information, however, is presented very differently. Adwatch, the advertising pressure group, complained recently that a number of reputable companies used misleading comparisons in their publicity materials. Companies compared their performance, for example, with the average or the worst in a sector rather than with the best. If Fund *A* has delivered a 20 per cent profit and the average fund in that sector delivers a 15 per cent profit, that sounds like a good argument for investing in Fund *A* until you discover Funds *C*, *D* and *F* scored a 35 per cent profit.

We have, therefore, a consumer and market environment in which there is information overload, deficiencies in numeracy, anxieties about logical skills and less awareness than we might imagine of the problems these cause. One help in coping with information overload is education and training, developing what human resource professionals call competencies.

The qualifications of market professionals

Jim Slater (1997), the investment guru, is cynical in *Beyond the Zulu Principle* about the qualifications of market professionals. He argues that investment advisers and brokers have puny professional qualifications compared to those of lawyers and accountants, let alone doctors. Any skills they have are skills they will have learned on the job. Brokers' qualifications are recent. As both the City and Wall Street have long and snobbish traditions, it was assumed that new recruits simply fitted into the job. Kahn and Cooper (1993) found only 20 per cent of their dealers had any kind of specific financial qualification.

As I interviewed brokers and analysts I became aware of the truth of Slater's point about lack of qualifications. Charles Clark of West LB Panmure is one of the most outspoken brokers I met. He told me, 'I'm rather proud of having passed the exams well first time round. Not that many people do that. In the past, families would send the really stupid son into the Church or the Army, the clever one to be a lawyer and the middling one to be a broker. It's changed – in theory,' he said.

Charles Clark wanted to go into the City from the age of 16. He is what I call a conviction broker, a person who was fascinated from his teens by the mechanics of shares. 'I left school and went to the States. I had my first taste of the market then in New York.' His father thought he should get his hands dirty and insisted he go into the Army first. 'It did me good because it showed me my weaknesses.' He finished his short-service commission and went into Panmure having obtained his qualifications including an MBA (Master of Business Administration).

Bryce Cottrell who became senior partner at Phillips & Drew went to the City from Oxford because he could not get finance to do the research he wanted to do. He had a degree in PPE (philosophy, politics and economics) and, as a result, had some relevant professional training.

But many brokers were educated in very different disciplines. Hugh Priestley went to Oxford and specialized in French. 'I read Anthony Sampson's *Anatomy of Britain* and clearly one of the places to be if you wanted power and influence was the civil service. Luckily for me – and them – I failed the Foreign Office entry at the interview. A friend told me there was a job on the City pages of *The Times*. Any specific financial training he got there. But after two years it felt a bit repetitive.' Connections now helped a little at least. 'My father told me there was an opening at Hendersons, where he knew someone.' Hendersons interviewed him and took him on.

Roger Yates of Invesco read history at Oxford, had two marvellously eccentric tutors and went into teaching. Then someone told him he should be in the City. I said that reminded me of a friend who had gone into the City but kept the teaching certificates in the drawer in case the market collapsed. Yates laughed 'I do the same.'

Other dealers like Simon Rubins at E. D. & F. Man studied law. Mike Lenhoff of Capel Cure had studied economics.

David Mayhew went into stockbroking 'really I suppose because my father was a broker in Liverpool and I did what I was told to do. You did in those days. I was completely untrained and my first job was scribbling up prices on the board.' He did that in chalk. 'I also knew it was an over-rewarded profession; though, of course, people then weren't paid anything like they are now.'

Many brokers in Britain have an accountancy qualification like Michael Barnard who used that to go into the City. But though accountants have to be numerate, the skills they need are very different from those of brokers. Paul O'Donnell of Brewin Dolphin too obtained an accountancy qualification. However, he did not like the job much and his reasons offer an interesting insight into the differences between accountants and stock-market professionals. 'I was looking at history all the time. I was bored. I did a few investigations and they were more interesting but I realized it wasn't for me. It wasn't quite a road to Damascus experience but nearly.' He got a job as an analyst 'because I could read a balance sheet' and eventually started to manage private clients. This task requires numeracy, of course, but also many different skills.

A number of brokers and dealers had no qualifications at all. Ronnie left school at 15 and worked in a post room earning just under £2 a week in the 1950s. He saw an ad for a job in the post room of a City firm which offered the princely wage of £2. 10s. 'and luncheon vouchers'. The luncheon vouchers were an incentive. Ronnie jumped ship and started to show a talent for trading. Roger Laughlin who has spent 20 years as an oil trader first started to work for his father who was in commodities. Laughlin actively distrusts academic training and, fundamentally, the numeracy skills he looks for are basic.

The situation is changing for analysts as high-level mathematical skills are needed to understand the sophisticated computer models of the market that big companies use. Nat West Global receives something like 3,000 applications for the 30-odd graduate jobs it has each year. Most have maths and physics qualifications. But brokers and advisers who talk to investors are very unlikely to have those skills. Both Paul O'Donnell and Matthew Orr of Killiks stressed they looked for ambition in their recruits. Orr, however, recruits many who have been in the services and insists on people skills more than mathematics. Roger Yates of Invesco still has more history graduates working for him than any others, 'probably because I did history', but that is changing. 'We hire more and more people with mathematics degrees who are developing sophisticated models of how share prices behave. I don't pretend to understand the algebra myself but I'm very confident in their ability to understand the algebra.'

Some 30 years after computer systems started to be used as cutting-edge tools in investment the City and Wall Street are still full of brokers, investment-fund managers and dealers who have, as Slater argues, no professional training at all. This doesn't just affect how they perform, it also affects their levels of anxiety, I suggest. Two of the three main causes of stress Kahn and Cooper (1993) found in *Stress in the Dealing Room* – misreading the market, having to cope with new techniques of information – stem from intellectual failures. One of the benefits of good training is that it makes workers less anxious about their ability to perform.

Re-analysing the past

I want to analyse in a little detail one of the great anecdotes in stock-market history in the light of these arguments. I gave a brief account of Nathan Rothschild's coup after Waterloo at the start of this book. Without taking the awesome name of Rothschild lightly, I want to imagine how Nathan Rothschild might have coped with information overload.

The Rothschild dynasty was started by Meyer Rothschild. His ancestors had been small merchants. In spring 1764 Meyer returned to the Jewish ghetto in Frankfurt, having turned down a job as an apprentice in the Jewish banking house of Oppenheimer. Meyer then developed a business in old coins. He travelled to remote castles and bought thalers, dinars and other obscure coins. Some he sold, some he kept. They were interesting trinkets to show to important people. One of the collectors who used Meyer was General Von Estorff, a courtier of Prince William at Hanau. Prince William was a grandson of George II of England and nephew to the King of Denmark. Blood did not come bluer.

Prince William was rich and wanted to be richer. He rented troops to the British to keep peace in the Colonies and any time one of his men died, William got compensation. William was impressed by one of his son's tutors, Carl Buderus, who also did some accountancy. He won William's heart by working out that if the Prince refused to accept payments from his tenants and debtors which involved fractions of a penny, his annual income would rise by about 120 thalers. Two thalers were worth a pound; William's annual revenues were about £60,000. Buderus improved the cash flow by only 0.1 per cent, but it was enough to make his career.

Buderus became interested in Meyer's coins and, as Buderus became an important person, he gave Meyer some business, cashing the Prince's drafts from London banks. For 19 years after 1785 Meyer built up his connections with Buderus and did many useful small financial services for the Prince. The House of Rothschild was launched. Meyer also trained his five sons.

Meyer and his sons established an international network of a kind the world had never seen before. They had agents, means of transport and fleets of homing pigeons. As Napoleon conquered Europe, these were all valuable. The Rothschilds could provide safe transport for money; they could collect debts from Manchester to Vienna.

In 1804 Denmark was broke. Her king desperately needed money and he happened to be Prince William's uncle. William had not told his relatives quite how rich he was. He was willing to lend millions to his uncle – Denmark was decent security – but William wanted the source of the money to remain a mystery. Meyer got the chance to arrange the loan and the Rothschilds had fixed their first large deal.

The Rothschilds developed many ways of flitting through Europe. Meyer had a coach built which had a false bottom. He and his sons communicated in codes and a language which was a mix of Hebrew, Yiddish and German. English invesments were called stockfish; old Rothschild was called Arnoldi and Prince William was given a nice Jewish name – Herr Goldstein.

In 1804 Meyer sent his son Nathan Rothschild to live in London. Nathan soon became a well-known figure on the Exchange. He started to provide services no one else could – there was no system of international banking or credit then.

In 1811, as Napoleon limped towards Moscow, the British, led by the Duke of Wellington, were fighting him in Spain. The British army needed money but it was not safe to send £800,000 (value now perhaps £80 million) by sea. At the request of the British government, Nathan developed a plan. He sent his 19-year-old brother James to Paris. James's mission was to smuggle the £800,000 of gold through France and into Spain to pay Wellington's army.

Politics came naturally to the family. James let it be known that he had come to Paris to invest money that was being smuggled out of

England. The British government wanted these exports stopped because they were depressing the value of sterling. Napoleon's finance minister believed James's story. Spies were sent to observe the young Rothschild. His behaviour fitted with his story.

At Calais and Dunkirk, James met ships carrying British guineas, Portuguese gold ounces, even French gold napoleons. James saw these monies to Paris. Then the Rothschild networks took over. Coaches with false bottoms, couriers racing through the night, secret hideouts were all used. South of Paris the money disappeared. The French could not keep track of the routes they used. Most of the money reached its destination – the British army across the Pyrenees.

By 1811 the Rothschilds were famous in London – and their reputation as international dealers was vital for the coup Nathan Rothschild pulled off in the hours after the Battle of Waterloo.

For 30 hours in June 1815 the fate of Europe hung in the balance. Late in the afternoon of 19 June a Rothschild agent called Rothworth jumped into a boat at Ostend. He was met at Folkestone by Nathan Rothschild who hurried back to London, went to the Exchange, sold Consols till the price was rock bottom and then placed one gigantic buy order. This famous coup depended on just two things. First, Nathan got the information about Waterloo before anyone else. Second, he dealt solely with one stock – Consols.

The Times's listing of stock-market prices in 1815 consisted of 140 shares. Also Nathan was not having to scan 28 screens to check if another dealer in Singapore or Sydney had spotted his strategy. He was not having to calculate whether he might make even more money if he were dealing in oil futures as opposed to Consols.

Memories of the 1720 South Sea Bubble discouraged people from speculation, but after the Battle of Waterloo interest in stocks revived. By 1826 there were nearly 200 companies being traded. Even in 1842 there were less than 300 shares quoted on the Exchange – 66 of which were railways but R.C. Michie estimates that 89 per cent of the business done was in government securities. The late 19th century saw a rise in the number of shares quoted but, even so, by the mid-1950s there were just over 1,400 shares quoted on the London Stock Exchange.

In the last 15 years the situation has changed enormously. The number of UK shares listed on the London Stock Exchange has risen

Table 1 Stocks quoted on the New York Stock Exchange.

Year	No.	Year	No.
1864	136	1950	1,472
1870	147	1955	1,508
1880	250	1960	1,570
1890	342	1970	1,802
1900	376	1980	1,895
1910	454	1990	2,215
1920	756	1999	2,854
1930	1,308		
1940	1,230		

from 2,070 in 1994 to 2,722 in 1998 – a 25 per cent rise in 4 years. The Alternative Investment Market now adds to the opportunities in London.

The New York Stock Exchange was incorporated in 1817. In its first decades it was usual for no more than 6,000 shares to be traded a day. Again there was an increase in shares quoted in the late 19th century, but it is since the end of the Second World War that the number of stocks traded on the New York Stock Exchange has increased dramatically.

Table 1 charts the rise and rise of stocks quoted. The figures for 1990 and 1998 omit one of the most significant of the new exchanges – the now all too volatile NASDAQ – which had over 5000 shares listed by the end of 1998 including giants like Microsoft. The total number of shares traded in 1900 – 157 million – equalled the amount traded in the first hour of 17 June 1988.

London has seen a similar huge rise. In what financial analysts call the dull period 1956–1958, the average number of bargains done each day on the London Stock Market was in the region of 7,000 to 8,000. By 1970 that had risen to 16,070 bargains a day on average. Since then the rise has been constant (Table 2).

There are not just more stocks but more stock markets. Africa had some stock exchanges in the 19th century. The Cairo exchange started in 1898, the South African exchange in 1887. In the 1990s the number of African exchanges doubled to 16. Footsie is about to launch an index based on Global Stock Market Indices, which will

Table 2 London Stock Exchange bargains.

Year	Bargains per day
1975	18,774
1985	22,007
1990	27,315
1994	38,247
1997	52,752

The average size of a bargain was just over £75,000

include trades from London, Paris, Oslo, Stockholm, Frankfurt, South-East Asia, Japan, South America and Africa.

The collapse of communism has seen the development of stock markets on the other side of what used to be called the Iron Curtain, with flourishing stock markets in Warsaw and Prague especially. Some investment funds now specialize in these.

If Nathan Rothschild were again in the position of being the ultimately well-informed dealer who knew the result of say a Middle East war in 2000, he would have far more investment choices. He would have to decide not just whether to buy or sell Consols. In his infinite sharpness, he would have to juggle the following alternatives:

- buy oil shares, because the price of oil would soar;
- sell UK equities because the war would affect trade badly apart from defence industries;
- sell US equities for the same reasons;
- sell US government bonds because the US government deficit would soar as it has to finance the Israeli war effort;
- buy options to sell Israeli stocks because these might collapse totally if there were a new Middle East war;
- buy shares in oil-exploration companies, because there would be a desperate need for alternative sources of supply;
- buy shares in suppliers of alternative energies, because these would become more profitable as oil became dearer;
- buy shares in companies such as British Aerospace and Lockheed which provide military equipment.

Nathan Rothschild would have to predict far more variables accurately or someone might moan that clever Nathan was not so clever because his fund could have performed better if he had bought a mix of Hungarian, Korean and Turkish equities instead of UK stocks.

Most brokers, despite the problems, have a love–hate relationship with the increased flow of information. But if everyone knows more, it is also harder to bring off the great coup – and that increases the pressure to invest in much the same way as others invest. It makes it more difficult to be a 'contrarian' and take a position that differs from that of most of those in the market.

As markets change it is not just a question of understanding traditional stock-market concepts but of keeping pace with new ones.

The creation of complex financial instruments

Increasingly the markets deluge investors not merely with more information but with frighteningly complicated new kinds of investment opportunies. When historians write of the economics of the end of the 20th century, they will be intrigued by the change in the class, personality and ambitions of those who were recruited into financial markets from 1975 onwards.

The 1970s made the financial markets glamorous in a way they had never been before. Michael Lewis (1990) describes how the best graduates of his generation fought to get jobs with Merrill Lynch, Salomon Brothers and Goldman Sachs. Finance became high profile, high income. Today good graduates going into the City know that they can command £30,000 in their first year. If they are competent, they will be earning £50,000 or more in 3 years. Goldman Sachs in going public announced that the average annual income for members of staff would be $126,000. When, in early 1999, there was much negative publicity about a group of young dealers who called themselves the Flaming Ferraris (the name came from a cocktail they all liked which cost £13 a glass) recruiters reported that the publicity led to even more than usual interest from graduates.

Such changes meant that Wall Street and London were much

more open to risk and innovation. Pension funds had refused to invest in shares at all till the early 1950s. By the 1980s, however, finance became half in love with risk, creativity and innovation. The evidence for this is largely anecdotal, however, and comes from 'memoirs' and journalistic accounts like those of Lewis's (1990) and Chapman's (1988) of personalities in the market.

In Chapter 2, we saw that 17th century London understood the concept of options.

With the creation of the Chicago Futures market in 1851, options trading became more common. At first, though, futures were not that speculative; rather they offered a way of coping with the vagaries of harvests. Food producers wanted to be sure of being able to buy supplies of corn, barley or other crops at a known price. Future contracts were protection against farming risk. If Kelloggs knew it was going to buy wheat 3 months ahead at $100, it could make sensible plans for the price of cornflakes.

However, one of the features of the post-1980 market environment has been the creativity of financiers in dreaming up versions of futures the world never needed before – and of markets to trade them in. Since 1980 exchanges like the London International Futures Exchange and the International Petroleum Exchange have been created specifically to deal in new forms of risk.

Another form of creativity has been in what was once considered the safest of all trades – bonds. A bond can be issued by a government or a company. Typically the British government issues £100 bonds which pay interest of say 7 per cent for 10 years. At the end of the 10 years, the investor gets his £100 back. If the company that issues the bond gets into trouble, the bonds are worth less because there is a risk that, eventually, the investor will not get his £100 back. The American Michael Miliken invented high-yield so-called junk bonds to finance takeovers in the early 1980s (a high-yield bond offers a better rate of interest). In the past, governments, local authorities and some large companies had issued bonds. The 'issuer' was nearly always large and safe; the interest rate was modest. Miliken saw that he could issue bonds on far less safe companies and offer investors a far higher rate of interest. You could use the money raised by these bond issues to finance takeovers.

A company raised money by issuing junk bonds with high rates of interest. The security was the assets of the company the bonds were being created to buy. It was said in the 1980s on Wall Street that you could set out to take over large companies without having any money. You used the money the company would make in the future to finance buying the company now.

Miliken's junk bonds at least had some connection to the value of the company. If a new management bought a firm, sold some of its assets, slashed the workforce and brought in new energy to make the business fizz profits, there would be enough to meet the junk-bond payments. Risky, sure. Creative, of course. Criminal, occasionally. But it had some reality. But in retrospect Miliken was quite conservative.

In his book *Liar's Poker* Michael Lewis (1990) explains how one of his first successes at Salomon Brothers was to help invent a new trading vehicle. In 1986, a Salomon customer was buying hundreds of millions of Deutschmarks of German government bonds. Lewis wondered if there was not 'a more daring play' to be made. The client liked risk. If they could find a way of packaging risk he would buy it.

With this insight Lewis and a colleague invented a new security. It was a warrant or call option for German government bonds, which investors could buy or sell. Lewis notes that it was a way of transferring risk from one party to another. Investors who bought these warrants would, in fact, be buying risk from Salomon Brothers, who were making the market in the warrants. Salomon Brothers created the warrants; they themselves took no risk. The company would get commission whatever happened to the market.

Many investors would not realize they wanted to buy or sell risk on the German bond market until Salomons' sales force suggested the idea to them as part of the campaign for their new warrant. Lewis describes the joy he felt on making the invention. Like other inventors he and his colleague got carried away. They had done nothing about gaining German government approval. But Lewis shows how easy it was then for the house of Salomon to persuade the German government that the new warrant was respectable, a force for stability in the market. The German government was a little worried that it might encourage speculation. But Salomon did not promote gambling. Heavens no. Frankfurt fell for it, Lewis records. It was not quite like inventing roulette but Lewis and his colleague had created a new game for the casino. Just like the investment trusts that invested in nothing but investment trusts, which Goldman Sachs were so proud of in 1929.

These new warrants like futures are hardly that complex in theory. But Lewis was amazed by the response at Salomon. 'As incredible as it may sound to those unfamiliar with the business, none of the bosses in either London or New York fully understood what we had done,' Lewis writes (1990, p. 168).

Just as Salomon's bosses did not fully understand their German warrants, the collapse of Barings suggests that none of its senior management grasped what their rogue trader Nick Leeson was doing (see Fay 1996). Barings did not question his activities for two reasons. First, on paper, Leeson was delivering a third of all Barings profits – and those profits meant more bonuses for all staff. Second, the senior management did not really understand derivatives and did not dare admit that they did not understand derivatives. Because no one asked a series of questions, because they were frightened of framing them in a way that betrayed their ignorance, Leeson bankrupted a bank that was 200 years old. Yet the concept of a derivative is hardly one that requires a PhD to master. Leeson himself just had O-levels and failed A-level maths.

Leeson initially made money for Barings by seizing on tiny differences in prices for the same bonds and stocks quoted on the Singapore, Tokyo and Osaka exchanges. If you have an index that is worth 100 today and that may be worth 115 in 3 days' time, you can bet that the index will stand at 108 or more in 3 days' time. If then the index stands at 111, you are in profit. If it stands at 107, you lose money. You can hedge the bet by doing hundreds of trades for different values.

Leeson started to trade in Nikkei 225 contracts. The Nikkei 225 is the main Tokyo stock-market index based on the value of 225 leading shares. The index is not a stock. When Leeson was buying Nikkei 225 contracts, he was buying a stake only in what its score would be next week or next year. It was much like betting that the England cricket team would make 250 or more the next time they batted. If they score 255 he won, if they score 240 he lost. This is why these are called deals in derivatives. Leeson was trading in the future value of a score derived from the value of stocks in the Nikkei 225.

Eventually Leeson took the greatest possible risks. Normally if you buy an option for 3 cents and the stock does not move your way, the most you can lose is 3 cents. But Leeson usually sold straddles – in effect, bets other people could buy that the Nikkei would either go above 21,000 or below 19,000. If the Nikkei stayed between 19,000 and 21,000 Leeson would make a profit because it would not be worth the buyers' while to exercise the options. If it went below 19,000 or above 21,000 he would have to buy Nikkei 225 contracts at whatever the price was in order to honour his positions. If the Nikkei dipped to 18,650 he would make large losses on each contract because the Nikkei was 350 points below his bottom price.

I do not mean to repeat the story of the failure of Barings to control Leeson. But I am struck that this management failure took place in a period when there was some publicity about derivative disasters. Channel 4 News ran a 15-minute item about derivatives in August 1994, for example. The news was responding to a series of crises. In March 1991, Allied Lyons had lost £150 million on currency trading in the Gulf War. In 1993 the German giant Metallgesellschaft AG announced 1.8 billion Deutschmarks of losses from oil futures trading and further losses that might run to 1.5 billion marks more. In April 1994, Procter & Gamble announced it would have to take a $102 million, after tax, charge because of losses on derivatives.

Just as suspicions about Leeson were surfacing in December 1994, there were two more derivative disasters. Bankers Trust New York had to pay $10 million to settle federal charges stemming from its sale of derivatives to Gibson Greetings Inc. Then Orange County, one of the richest areas in the States, discovered $1.5 billion losses on its portfolio. The County had been playing the derivatives market and had to file for protection from creditors. As in the South Sea Bubble and the 1929 Crash, evidence of problems elsewhere was blithely – and ruinously – ignored.

Leeson was already concealing some losses in his secret account numbered 8888. After the Kobe earthquake in January 1995 his position was hopeless. The Nikkei dropped to below 18,000. Barings incurred £380 million of losses. Leeson then tried to recover his losses and lost a further £400 million.

Now out of jail, Leeson is in much demand as a speaker because he is actually able to explain in detail what he did – speculations that investors still don't find easy to grasp.

It is against this background that we have to look at a story

Michael Barnard told me. He explained that when a private client asks him to buy futures, regulations now require him to send the investor information that sets out the risks and warns that he may lose everything. The investor has to sign a declaration and swear in effect that he or she grasps the extent of the risk. Only then does Barnard as a prudent broker agree to deal.

Since so many professionals do not seem to understand the complexity of these new financial instruments, how many individuals are competent to make the declaration the regulators require Barnard to ask for?

I have tried to show how information overload affects the market today. Just as it is naive to suggest the markets just run on greed, fear and the herd instinct for everyone, it is naive to assume individuals respond the same way to information – and information overload. Investors and professionals both need to be aware of their ways of dealing with it.

Personality and coping with information

We often hear people describe their friends as extroverts or introverts. The systematic study of personality goes back to the ancient Greeks. Around 400 BC Hippocrates suggested that personality was determined by the nature of a person's bodily humours. He identified four different personality types: the choleric or angry individual who had too much yellow bile; the melancholic who had too much black bile; the phlegmatic who had too much phlegm, which slowed him down; and the sanguine or well-adjusted sort who had strong blood. These ideas influenced Carl Jung and, in turn, the late Hans Eysenck.

Jung argued that people were either extroverts or introverts. He did not propose any very scientific measure of these personality traits. Hans Eysenck (1967), however, devised a series of now well-established psychological tests – the Eysenck Personality Inventory which allows us to quantify how extrovert or introvert anyone is. The EPI is a paper and pencil test in which subjects are asked questions such as:

▓ Do you enjoy going to parties?

■ Do you often feel depressed for no apparent reason?
■ Do you get easily bored with ... ?

Subjects have to answer yes, no or tick a question mark. The typical traits of extroverts and introverts have been verified through fairly large-scale studies.

People are not total extroverts or total introverts. They score somewhere along the continuum. At one end of the scale, extroverts get bored easily and they need constant stimulation. They are social, like going to parties and are more willing to take risks than introverts precisely because risk keeps them stimulated. They also tend to be more optimistic. Introverts, at the other end of the scale, are meticulous, anxious, interested in detail and eager to get things right. Eysenck argues that the differences between these two extremes are biological. Extroverts have low levels of cortical arousal; introverts have high levels of arousal. At first this seems the wrong way round: you would expect an active extrovert to have high levels of arousal. But Eysenck explains that one function of the cortex is to inhibit and control more emotional centres of behaviour in the brain and cortical arousal produces high control over more spontaneous behaviour.

Introverts are nervous about making mistakes and more prone to feeling ashamed. When they get things wrong, they tend to blame themselves and they generally want to make sure it will not happen again. This attention to detail is obviously useful in analysing research data. Ironically, however, introverts have a personality style that finds it hard to trade. Introverts are also more averse to risk. Jeffrey Gray (1993) found that introverts responded better when they were punished for their mistakes and extroverts when they were praised for their successes.

Ideally, a well-run investment house will therefore recruit a number of extreme extroverts, who will be able to see the big picture and spot new investment opportunities, as well as introverts, who will not lose patience with the sheer detail of the information and who will be likely to analyse risk more methodically. In a big company this balance may be achievable but few private investors will have that perfect balance of personality – an extrovert's taste for risk allied to a introvert's relish for detail. And I have yet to see recruitment ads for City jobs demanding such psychological niceties.

___

The consequences of not examining information

The consequences of not paying attention to details can be very real.

When I was in my teens I lived through a now-forgotten financial scandal. My late father, Benjamin Cohen, worked as a company doctor after he came to live in Britain. He had been a lawyer in Palestine and a banker in Switzerland. When he did not have his work permit renewed, we came to London.

My father went into the unlikely business of renting television sets to hotels but he also did some financial consultancy. In the early 1960s he helped put together a rescue for a company called British and Overseas.

One day, after an argument with his bank manager, he decided to seek new sources of finance because he had an order to put hundreds of television sets in the Savoy group of hotels. He went to borrow money from a company called Pinnock Finance. Pinnock took deposits from the public. When high-street banks were offering interest rates of about 4 per cent, Pinnock was offering 8 per cent. It was assumed that they had a magic formula.

Within a few days of his first meeting with Pinnock, my father found himself asked to take charge of rescuing the company. The subsequent events made headlines. Pinnock's founder, a Mr Wright, disappeared. One day Wright was extremely sick in the London Clinic, one of the most expensive hospitals in town; the next day he could not be found. Also not to be found were most of the millions people had banked with Pinnock. No one ever saw Mr Wright again.

My father took over a 'bank' which had about £100,000 in cash and two sewing-machine factories. Pinnock owed depositors over £2 million. It soon became all too clear what had been happening. Wright used the new deposits coming into Pinnock to meet high-interest payments as well as the few withdrawals. The rest of the money just went.

In 1974 the Inquiry Report chaired by Basil Wigoder QC concluded that the investors in Pinnock had been blinded by the good returns they were getting (Pinnock Report 1975). No one had asked Wright sensible questions.

In the history of financial scams, bubbles and rip-offs, Pinnock was small beer. To those who lost money it was a big tragedy. I took phone calls from people in tears because they had lost all their savings. My father never got enough votes to take the company over so Pinnock was liquidated. In the mid-1980s, 12 years after he had been forced to give up running the rescue, my father still got phone calls from Pinnock depositors asking after their money. Sometimes they pleaded that they really needed it now.

Yet none of the investors I talked to ever owned up to the fact that they had been unwilling to ask questions because the profits seemed to be so good. Few thought of themselves as greedy or wondered if one of the reasons Pinnock attracted them was because it gave them permission to be greedy. None had asked themselves about their own attitude to risk.

My personal experiences were backed up by a study in the *British Journal of Psychiatry* which looked at people who had invested in a company that went bankrupt. Many of the investors were depressed and angry. Salesmen had come to their homes, been nice, cracked jokes and persuaded them the investment was safe. If they had asked a number of questions, they might have thought twice about the company. The 'victims' found that they lost more than just money. A number were elderly people who had been looking forward to a comfortable retirement. Now, they could not do many of the things they had set their hearts on. That cruise to the fjords of Norway would remain a dream. Some had to look for work again. Many developed symptoms similar to post-traumatic stress.

In many of the financial scandals to hit the press in the last 20 years, small investors were tempted by high interest rates only to find the company go bankrupt. Investors did not have either the motivation or the confidence to ask important questions.

Information overload is a fact of life now. No one can hope to master all the information available in and about financial markets. A psychological truth follows. Whatever specific investment strategy we might follow, we should accept the kind of discipline Charles Clark and Michael Barnard accept and only focus on a manageable number of stocks in a few sectors. Having set that limit, we should try to understand them in as much detail as possible.

It is important for investors to understand not just their own attitudes to risk (which we shall see may be hard to change) but also their own attitudes to gathering and paying attention to information. The questions that follow should give you some idea of where you stand. We shall see that we can alter our attitudes to information gathering and get to see information gathering not as a chore which somehow cramps your intuitions but as a vital preliminary to good decision making.

Information questionnaire

1   You have invested £2,500 in a unit trust. Do you check the price of the fund

    a   once a week?

    b   once a month?

    c   once a day?

2   Which of statements a to d is most true for you? I try to read the financial pages of the newspapers every day but

    a   I often don't manage it because I'm too busy at work

    b   I find them too technical

    c   I am only concerned with checking the investments I have

    d   I try to look at what is going on in the markets generally.

3   I try hard to do my income tax return

    a   on time

    b   at least 3 months in advance

    c   I get my accountant to do it because I'm scared of making mistakes.

4   At school my attitude to maths was

    a   I hated it

    b   I loved it

    c   It didn't seem very relevant to my future plans.

5   A friend tells you there's no point in reading the small print because insurance companies, banks and investment funds never tell the truth about their charges and commissions. Do you think your friend is

    a   a fool

    b   realistic

    c   lazy. If you make the effort to understand the details you are less likely to be fooled.

6   A friend of yours takes a job as a proofreader

    a   you feel sorry for him

    b   you see what might give him or her satisifaction but it's not for you

    c   you think it must give a lot of pleasure to know you've proofed something correctly.

7   When you make mistakes which of the following best expresses your feelings

    a   I was just in a hurry, it doesn't really matter

    b   I'm sorry but everyone makes mistakes

    c   the next time I'll be more careful to check my figures

    d   it's very unlike me to make mistakes and I get very nervous when they happen.

8   Which of the following is your response to the daunting amount of financial information available

    a   I try to read at least one of the following papers a week – *The Economist, Investors Chronicle, Shares*

    b   I find the financial pages boring

    c   I watch the financial channels on TV.

9 Which of the following is closest to the truth for you? I'm attracted to tracker funds

a because they seem to be doing well

b Virgin have a tracker fund and they know what they're doing

c it's easy to understand what they mean.

10 If I'm faced with too much information I respond by

a making a careful selection of what I need

b ignoring it all

c choosing those items which I suspect will bore me.

11 The yo-yoing of high-tech shares up and down between 2000 and 2001 is

a just too complicated to follow

b really fascinating to watch

c not as interesting as the football results.

Answers

1   a 1   b 2   c 3

2   a 1   b 1   c 2   d 3

3   a 2   b 3   c 1

4   a 1   b 3   c 2

5   a 1   b 3   c 1

6   a 1   b 2   c 3

7   a 1   b 1   c 3   d 2

8   a 3   b 1   c 2

9   a 3   b 1   c 1

10   a 3   b 1   c 2

11   a 1   b 3   c 1

The total possible score is 33.

If you score between 25 and 33 you are open to seek the information you need and not scared of being overwhelmed by information.

If you score between 18 and 25 you are reasonably open to information but you could improve.

Any score under 18 suggests you need to take serious stock of your strategy for getting information and that you may run two risks. You may invest impulsively or you are just the kind of personality who can become too dependent on expert advice.

To improve your attitude to information, you need to create a routine for yourself. Read the financial pages of your newspaper every day and give yourself an hour a week to study an investment paper like the *Investors Chronicle*. Keep a diary in which you note what you have done because you will be likely to fool yourself into believing you have done more work than you have.

In Chapter 10, I give hints on how to alter, if you want to, your attitudes to information.

In these first three chapters I've introduced a number of psychological ideas which affect how people behave in financial situations. The theory of cognitive dissonance suggests that people tend to avoid information that will increase contradictions in their positions. Information theory suggests that most of us are not that good at analysing information. Much evidence suggests that market professionals are not well trained and this may cause them anxiety. Personality theory suggests that extroverts who like risk often fool themselves and ignore the details. At the end of the book I will attempt to explain what we can learn from these all too human defects. To do so let us first explore what we can learn from analysing the analysts.

four

Inside the markets – the analysts

My late ex-father-in-law, William Isaac La Tourette, prided himself on being able to pick good stocks in a bear market. Any fool, he said, could make money in a bull market. He had studied economics at Columbia University, done a doctorate and ended up as a vice-president of a big Wall Street firm, E.F. Hutton. His trick was to look for unglamorous stocks which produced goods and services people and businesses needed even in hard times. He was a fan of the Xerox Corporation, for instance, when photocopying was still novel.

Until the middle of 2000, few contemporary stock-market professionals had much experience of bear markets other than the long Japanese crisis of the late 1980s and 1990s which saw the Nikkei 225 fall to 13,000 and the collapse in South-East Asia in 1998 which shredded the stock markets and currencies in Thailand, Indonesia, Taiwan and Malaysia.

On 8 January 2001 *US Today* reported that American companies were in the grip of 'the worst credit crunch in a decade'. The paper noted gloomily that Montgomery Ward, a large department-store chain had filed for Chapter 11 bankruptcy and laid off 28,000 workers. Californian electricity companies had warned they could go bankrupt and household names like that same Xerox found they had to pay huge rates of interest in order to sell bonds. The Californian situation affected Wall Street with the Dow Jones down by 2.3 per cent and the NASDAQ down a staggering 6.2 per cent. Banks like Bank of America plunged 7 per cent. For many young, even middle-aged analysts, this situation was novel and frightening.

Roger Yates is a tall, enthusiastic man in his early forties who is one of the directors of Invesco. 'In our entrance,' Yates told me, 'you'll see a plaque which was awarded to our Japan fund.' If I had invested money in it in 1998, I would have lost money, which would not seem to merit any kind of award. When Japanese stock markets were tumbling in 1998, Invesco's Japan fund, however, lost only 1 per cent of its value; the average loss for Japan funds was 7 per cent. 'So if your research is really good, you can win awards for losing money,' Yates smiled. Through the irony, he is proud, as he likes to see 'what we do as a little academic' and his story underlines his belief in the value of good analysts.

Research into equities has changed radically over the last 50 years in Britain. In 1950 no one would have described their profession as a stock analyst. Even enlightened brokers did not do systematic research into equities. One reason for the lack of research was that shares were seen as more like a gamble than an investment until George Goobey, who controlled the pension fund for Imperial Tobacco, decided this was an ancient prejudice that made no economic sense. Goobey switched his fund from investing mainly in bonds to equities – and helped change the nature of investment. As a result of his policy change, pension funds entered the stock market. Shares became respectable as never before. Today, pension funds hold some of Britain's largest portfolios.

Financial markets today devote enormous resources to research. Balance sheets are analysed; forecasts are mulled over; computer models crunch different visions of the future. Theorists look at the values of Fibonacci curves, Elliott wings and papers in *Nature* which try to model stock-market behaviour on the principles of particle physics. In Santa Fe, there's a Prediction Company run by researchers with a link to Los Alamos physicists. In London and New York researchers boast about their latest computer-modelling techniques. Being vain, analysts pride themselves on how often journalists pick up their tips.

Analysts perform a key role in the market. As these issues affect both analysts and brokers it seems useful to look at the whole set of these studies at this point. There are more American analysts than in any other country. A 1998 study compared the work of 4,275 American brokers with 476 British ones, 495 Japanese, 798 French and 479 Germans. The 4,275 American analysts had studied 6,018 firms.

Most analysts specialize in one sector of the economy. Analysts use computer modelling, add a dash of intuition, read trends and recommend stocks. Analysts are essentially in the business of prediction. What will go up? What will go down? Prediction is as much an art as it is a science, but analysts have a vested interested in claiming that what they do has a rigorous base.

In the summer of 1999 the differences between analysts showed up all the problems of prediction. Controversies abounded. In the gloom corner there were the pessimists, who thought shares were priced too high. In the happy corner there were the optimists, who believed that the world had changed and that all the old rules about how to value stocks no longer applied. Bull markets for ever. They sniped at the Cassandras who were not sharp enough to buy when shares were cheap. Many agreed that markets were overvalued but also suggest paradoxically that shares may get even more expensive.

At the end of 2000, after a year which had seen the Dow Jones lose 14 per cent of its value and the NASDAQ lose 57 per cent of its value from their peaks, analysts remained divided between those who argue that this is a blip in the ever upwards path of equities and those who claim like Smithers and Shiller that markets are dangerously overvalued. One reason for the division is that predicting the behaviour of markets remains elusive. We can say that many variables affect share movements but we can't wholly explain what these economic, psychological and political variables are.

All analysts work against the bulge of chaos, the pressure of events. In what follows I try to describe the sane, sensible methods many large companies use to study how shares and bonds move, but it is a little like predicting the behaviour of volcanoes. Markets keep their mysteries. Few experts in 1998 predicted what would happen in South East Asia. The tiger economies were supposed to be teaching the rest of the world how to make money rather than collapse.

A more local example of a trend most analysts did not predict concerns the high-street retailer, Dixons. In May 1999 they announced they would float its Internet Server Freeserve. In the 6 months between December 1998 and May 1999 the share price of Dixons doubled because of the Internet potential of the share. Good management, yes. But certainly a move that does not seem to have been spotted by many analysts writing in the autumn of 1998 even though Internet shares were so popular. Then, once Freeserve had been floated independently, the price yo-yoed partly because e-shares were no longer such dreams. In 2000 Freeserve's share price went as high as 1,000p and then fell right back to 300p before finally being taken over by Wanadoo, the French company.

Today analysts claim to be better informed and better tooled up than ever before. In theory, they should therefore be more accurate.

The Cow & Gate coup – a brief history of stock-market research

To understand how the science of financial analysis developed, I went to Tonbridge, Kent, to see Bryce Cottrell. He was the senior partner at Phillips & Drew until 1985, when the broker was bought by the Union de Banque Suisse, and was one of the first equity analysts in this country. Today Bryce Cottrell is in his mid-sixties. It would be easy to dismiss him as a slightly vague country gentleman. He lives in an olde worlde cottage in Tonbridge – leaded windows, dark, heavy furniture, nice antiques. Round about 11.30 a.m., he confessed, 'I still keep to old stockbroking habits,' and offered me a drink.

But the country-gent manner is deceptive. Cottrell remains a sharp observer of the City scene – and he has a long memory. He studied PPE (philosophy, politics and economics) at Oxford. He found the philosophy boring and so he concentrated on economics. After getting his BA in the early 1950s, he wanted to do research. His family did not have the money to fund a further degree, however, so he had to look for work. He went to see Phillips & Drew. Phillips & Drew was not a old City firm like Barings or Cazenove. It had specialized initially in government stocks like the Consols that Rothschild had traded in. The firm had grown under a legendary bond dealer called Perry who worked out how to squeeze a little extra profit from bonds in the 1930s. Bryce Cottrell's first job was to build up the Phillips & Drew library.

In the early 1950s stockbrokers did not suffer from information overload. Deals were done on tips, nudges and winks on the old-boy

---

network, the traditional British way of doing business. According to David Mayhew at Cazenove, 'There was a lot of business done just on pure gossip. If you knew something about a company that someone else didn't, you used it to your own advantage.'

'The equity market operated on tips and no one thought that was immoral,' Cottrell told me. The idea of insider trading did not exist. (Insider trading is using privileged information to buy or sell shares when you know something the rest of the world does not. If I were married to a director of the supermarket chain, ASDA, for example, and I knew they were talking to Wal Mart about a takeover and I bought 80,000 shares 3 hours before the merger was announced, I would be guilty of insider trading. Now it is illegal; in the 1950s it was accepted.) 'Someone told you that there was going to be a plan or move at a company and you bought them and the shares went up – that was the mechanism,' Cottrell told me. Insider trading was the tradition. 'I don't think people are more moral now. I think that we operated by different standards,' Mayhew said.

Research had little place in this world. 'A lot of members of the Stock Exchange lived off their private clientele,' Cottrell told me. These clients were charged fixed percentage commissions. 'Remarkably few brokers did front-running – i.e. buying stock and then recommending clients to buy them,' he added. Front-running encourages brokers to analyse the prospects of shares. 'One of the few reliable sources of information was the Lex column in the *Financial Times*,' Mayhew said. Lex looked at the prospects for different shares each day – and still does. Every company felt they had to talk to Lex 'and the column had an enormous amount of influence on the price of stock,' Mayhew added.

All this was to change in the 1950s. 'The 1948 Companies Act was the really big change because until then it hadn't been necessary for company accounts to be reliable. So there was no hope of doing any systematic research,' Cottrell told me. Phillips & Drew did not have a vision of the science of security analysis but he had gone to work for a firm which, at least, was not opposed to the idea of research. When a big client offered them a brilliant deal if they were willing to invest in research, they grabbed the chance. Phillips & Drew were brokers to the Mars Pension Fund. Mr Mars who owned – and, indeed, was Mars – believed in the American way. Study the company's history, grill the management, toothcomb the accounts, visit the factories, draw up scientific forecasts and then, if numbers look good, buy the shares.

Mr Mars also insisted Phillips & Drew hire an American expert, Professor Sidney Cottle of Georgetown University, who was supposed to have perfected a technique of researching companies. When Cottle came over to talk to them, Phillips & Drew were impressed with his slick presentation – a nice way of suggesting that actually he did not have much to teach them about the art and science of picking shares.

Good research pinpoints opportunities other people do not see. Cottrell worked with Dennis Weaver, who eventually became one of the founders of the Society of Investment Analysts. Early in their collaboration, Cottrell and Weaver spotted an opportunity. 'We saw that there had been a huge rise in the statistics of milk for manufacture so we thought that Cow & Gate (who make milk products) must be having a good year.' So they bought into Cow & Gate and recommended it to a few privileged clients.

'No one else either troubled to do the research or spotted the likely link between milk manufacture and the company that turned out products that required that milk. No one else tumbled to it for something like 4 months,' Cottrell told me. They did not plan the operation in great secrecy as they would have to do now. 'Today, you'd have the idea ahead of the opposition for 4 minutes.' The hunch was good. Cow & Gate shares rose. Clients were pleased. Phillips & Drew became more convinced of the value of research.

Before the 1950s there was a tradition of men from the City going to visit companies. As David Kynaston and Bill Reader (1992) point out in their history of Phillips & Drew, these visits were mainly sales expeditions. The salesmen built up knowledge of potential customers and wrote up notes on these visits. The notes included details on the hobbies of the executives they were trying to sell to. A Mr Lunan of Scottish Widows liked gliding but he was not interested in any risky shares. A Mr Kelly of the National Commercial Bank of Scotland complained that the salesmen who rang him were too junior, agreed that shipbuilders John Brown were a bad bet, and quarrelled over the rating Phillips & Drew gave Butlins.

In the mid-1950s, the purpose of many of these visits changed. The men from the City often became much more interested in finding out what the management of particular companies was doing. Should they buy or recommend their shares? They wanted insider knowledge. 'Companies began to feel a little nervous about telling you things that were confidential,' Cottrell told me. And the finance directors often gave away nothing.

'We slowly discovered that a good way of getting inside knowledge was to ask them not about their own company but about the competition. If you visited a company like Tesco, they might not tell you anything much about themselves but they might well spill the beans about Sainsbury's and say that they're finding it particularly tough at the moment.' They also played games of bluff and counter-bluff. Cottrell often took a more junior analyst with him and left it to him to ask the questions. The finance director often thought that he was so important he should only be talking to a partner. 'The analyst would say that we were thinking your profits might be £180 million and the finance director would reply, I think you're being a bit optimistic, and give the analyst a steer.' Cottrell would wonder whether the finance director was feeding them a line to boost the price or to damp down expectations to make poor results look less bad.

The visits also gave the analysts the chance to meet the management which, as we shall see, remains psychologically important to many who seek to predict shares. Unfortunately the Phillips & Drew records have no notes at all about how they judged managers.

'We'd look at a company's past performance and particularly we looked to see if a company was in a growth industry. The Economist Intelligence Unit would often identify growth areas,' Cottrell said. 'Our thinking was that it was easier to expand if there was growth. There was less pressure on profit margins. In a declining market it's hard for dog not to eat dog.'

By the end of the 1960s, the place of research had been established and computers were installed in stockbrokers' offices. But attitudes died hard. Jos Drew, who ran the private clients' department of Phillips & Drew, offered youngsters timeless and slightly cynical advice: 'If you've got breeding it may help. If you've got brains it may help. If you've got both you're unstoppable.' Jos Drew offered other pearls: 'Bullshit always baffles brains' and 'Trees do not grow to the sky.' And one gem that would invite a visit from the City of London Fraud Squad today. Drew said: 'One tip is worth a million analyst's hours.'

Today no one would dare voice Drew's opinion but analysts often exhibit an ambivalent approach to their skills. They often shift between assuring you that their work is scientific and hinting that really art and intuition are also involved. Several firms, however, insisted their analysis and the decisions that flowed from it was systematic, if not scientific.

One feature of 1998–1999 was that analysts became extremely nervous because of the success of tracker funds. Computers can track the Footsie 100, they argue; traders can then do the deals. Analysts counter by talking of 'active fund management'. An active fund manager will not limit himself or herself to these 100 big shares but will actively seek the very best buys throughout the market. As there is increasing evidence that tracker funds perform better than most analysts, analysts are increasingly under pressure to justify both their methods and the results they achieve.

Systematic selection of stocks

Roger Yates told me that, at Invesco, he had 400 people whose job it was to research stocks 'and we do so in a very organized way'. This huge intellectual effort has two basic aims: spotting stocks which are worth more than the market currently thinks they are worth and identifying the right moment to buy or sell.

Mike Lenhoff, a slightly sombre man who heads the research effort at Capel Cure Sharp, a firm that specializes in private clients, approaches share analysis with the same high seriousness as Smithers. Lenhoff told me: 'If people don't have £150,000 to £200,000 they don't really have enough to make it possible to have a diversified portfolio.' Capel Cure Sharp has a very clear investment message and gives the impression that if you want your money used differently, you are probably not the client for them. 'We have quite a structured organization. We believe in a very regimented approach to investment decisions.'

Capel Cure Sharp was generous enough to give me a detailed account of how it made its investment decisions. I think it is worth reporting in detail because it reveals the decision-making process in one firm that is committed to an orderly process.

'We are a top-down firm,' Lenhoff told me. Account managers have a lot of discretion about when to buy and sell for clients, but they have to work within the policy limits. They cannot decide to buy Amalgamated Onions for Mr Jones if the share has not been approved by the various committees.

Two key meetings every month – one, asset-allocation, and two, sector strategy – decide the policy. These meetings feed a weekly stock-selection meeting.

At the asset-allocation meeting Lenhoff, two other analysts and five key practitioners meet to decide on asset allocation, the general policy for allocating the money managed by Capel Cure Sharp. Should they have more in cash, more in equities, more in bonds, more in commodities? For this they have their own jargon – whether you should be overweight or underweight.

'We believe that major macroeconomic forces drive the market,' Lenhoff told me. So his department brings to the asset-allocation meeting 'a briefing paper which gives our overview of the global market situation'.

The April 1999 paper ran to 12 closely argued pages (Lenhoff and Rubinsohn 1999). It started with the punchy assessment that 'restructuring will hurt the Japanese economy in the short term so the risk is that last month's rally in the equity market will prove to be a damp squib like many others before it.' In the paper Lenhoff and his co-author Simon Rubinsohn contrasted the situation in Japan with that in the rest of South-East Asia. They argued that Malaysia, Korea, Indonesia and the Philippines were likely to recover profits in the next 12 months but the markets would be sceptical so the shares would still tend to be cheap. They recommended 'overweight South-East Asia'. Looking ahead to April 2000, they forecast that the Nikkei Index would be at 12,410 down from 16,328 on 31 March 1999 while the Pacific Rim Index would be up from 192 to 217.

The paper then offered an analysis of the key markets – the USA, the UK, Europe, Japan and the Pacific Basin sector – and gave a few sharply phrased recommendations and warnings. Trying to predict risks is central to the briefing. In April 1999 in America the key risk was that the Federal Reserve Bank would tighten interest-rate policy. 'Both bonds and equities could collapse,' the briefing warned. In Europe the key risk was that the euro would rise, profits fall and

City towers.

'equities would lose out'. In Britain the key risk was rising interest rates, which would make shares fall.

In Japan the risk was less that shares would fall and more that they would miss an opportunity. The paper recommended being 'underweight' on Japan. If the Nikkei rallied to 20,000 from 16,000 and then raced ahead, an analyst who suggested 'underweight Japan' would have missed a big profit opportunity.

Lenhoff presents his briefing paper to the asset-allocation meeting 'and I make recommendations. There's then a discussion, but the actual decisions are made by the practitioners. It's the account managers who are responsible. All the research people do is recommend and advise.' Nevertheless, Lenhoff has a vote on this committee. This kind of group decision making has an interesting social psychology. The shifts are usually not that dramatic. 'I might recommend we switch from being 30 per cent in UK equities to being 33 per cent. We then discuss it and the consensus might be that we end up with 32 per cent.'

The monthly sector strategy meeting, Lenhoff told me, 'was to identify those sectors in which we should be overweight and underweight. It's a question of looking at the impact of new regulations, of understanding where new technologies may have something we ought to be following.' Again the researchers recommend and the practitioners decide. Lenhoff added – and here the science ends and the intuition begins – that there were many experienced heads in the firm who had seen the markets in many moods.

The weekly stock-selection meeting has to translate all this analysis into action. Capel Cure Sharp, like most large firms, has a buy and sell list of shares which the meeting reviews. They also look for new shares to recommend.

Any methodology has to try and prove its worth. Lenhoff showed me the quality scorecard he and his colleagues have designed to highlight key facts about a company and assess its potential quickly. The scorecard trumpets that it provides 'an easily readable snapshot of that company's business and current prospects'. There are six key items on his scorecard, 'the sensible measures you need to look at', Lenhoff said. Each of the six items has a maximum that an excellent company can score:

financial strength	2 points
business diversification	2 points
historic record	1 point
earnings/divided growth potential	2 points
management strength	1 point
marketability	2 points

It is worth going through the scorecard in detail.

There are four elements to score for financial strength. On each element a company can get a maximum of 0.5 points.

The first element is the gearing of the company. Gearing is the ratio of borrowing to the assets of the company. A company with net cash in the balance sheet, which means its gearing is 0 per cent, would receive the highest score, 0.5. If the gearing was 75 per cent the score would be 0.

The second element is cash flow. Positive cash flow is always a good sign. A company that does not have to borrow to be able to function with good cash flow will score 0.5. A negative cash flow scores zero.

The third element is return on capital employed. If a company with a capital of £10,000 makes £200 profit the return is 2 per cent and, even in these low-interest days, you would be better off putting your money in the building society than in the company. Lenhoff uses a traditional formula to calculate this. You divide the operating profit by the capital employed – that is, the shareholders' funds, borrowings plus any provisions for bad debts and other disasters.

If a company makes a profit of £1.2 million and if its shareholder funds amount to £10 million and it has borrowed £1.5 million and made £500,000 of provisions, its return on capital would be:

£1.2 million divided by £12 million (made up of £10 million shareholder funds plus £1.5 million borrowing plus £500,000 for provisions) = 10 per cent.

This is a respectable to low return. Interesting companies worth buying show a return on capital of over 20 per cent. That would score top marks – another 0.5.

The fourth element is how well the dividend is covered. If the dividend is covered twice over the company gets full marks – again 0.5.

With business diversification, again worth 2 points, the judgements are much more subjective. The idea is to analyse a company's position in the relevant market. To get 2 points the company needs to be a leading company in a nicely growing market. It does not rely on one or two big clients who can scupper it and it has a nice geographical spread, so that if there is a recession in Wales, for instance, it should not hurt it too much. For example, many textile firms whose main client is Marks & Spencer are poorly diversified and so in a bad position to negotiate on price and if Marks & Spencer cut their orders the result is a crisis.

Historic record is worth only 1 point because history is at best a guide and the past is no guarantee of the future. Lenhoff recommends looking at 5 years of earnings and dividends. A company will score the highest marks only if it manages 5 years of uninterrupted growth. A dividend cut loses 0.25 points; so does any loss-making year.

Earnings/dividend-growth potential, the fourth criterion, is assessed on the forecast for the next 2 years compared with the market average. All analysts look for momentum shares where the earnings keep on growing better and better.

Management strength, the fifth criterion, requires much more subjective judgements. Does the company comply with Cadbury proposals for corporate governance? Is there a separate chairman and chief executive? Are there a reasonable number of external non-executive directors? Lenhoff argues that management strength is worth only 1 point for two reasons. First, it is a subjective judgment; second, poor management should show up in the mathematics because a badly run company should produce worse results.

Marketability simply means how large the company is. A company that is in the FT-SE 100 gets 2 points; a company with a market capitalization of over £2 billion dips down 0.25 points to 1.75 points and then even lower. The less the total value of the company, the less it gets for marketability. A company that has a capitalization of under £750 million but over £500 million will only get 0.50 points. A small company that doesn't make the index of 250 leading shares, the FT-SE 250, gets no points at all. Big is beautiful.

On the quality scorecard the maximum score a company can get is 10. Companies get an *A* rating for above 8 points; a *B* rating if they score between 5 and 8 points and a *C* rating if they score under 5 points. If a company makes an *A* grade it is a 'buy'; *B* grade is a 'hold'. Below that it is not worth bothering with or should be sold. *D* and *E* ratings suggest the shares should be sold.

'Apart from the numbers, we also look at charts of how shares move and the underlying momentum of shares,' Lenhoff told me, 'but there's a lot of judgement and skill. In our meetings there are people who have been there and seen similar market conditions often before.' Cottrell had warned me that all investment houses 'would give you the guff.' Praise ancient experiences, old intuition. After all, the real business of analysts is to sell their analysis either to their colleagues in their firms or to private investors.

Here Lenhoff smiled a little self-deprecatingly. But, apart from the quantifiable features, there is that old and odd entity, sentiment. An analyst with good intuition understands the mood of the market, the sentiment. 'It is a nebulous concept,' says Lenhoff. 'It could be the result of a good feeling because he's been with the shares before or good newsflow.' It is nebulous, vague and psychological but it does matter. It is one of the oddities of the stock market that in a place where people quantify everything the one thing they do not know how to quantify is sentiment. I came across three studies which attempted to examine how we measure sentiment. One involves the Bullish Sentiment Index, an index based on how newsletters recommend shares and the other a small study by the American Association of Individual Investors. Merrill Lynch have also developed a sentiment index based just on newsflow. None of these measures seems to present a rounded approach to measuring sentiment.

Lenhoff has been at Capel Cure Sharp for over 14 years and his colleagues have never broken the discipline of having only their scheduled meetings. 'Nothing is really that disastrous. You'd dilute the value of meetings if you called them because the market fell by 300 points. I don't think we even had a meeting in 1987 when the market fell. The markets always overreact and the best thing to do when they fall is to stay away, stay calm and take a leaf out of history. Historically these collapses are good buying opportunities.'

Psychologists might see this differently – a splendid example of denial of reality reinforced by strong group pressures. If your procedures are traditional enough nothing will make you change them. For some analysts the methods described by Lenhoff miss a crucial element – the ability to learn from history. One of the most interesting divisions to emerge from my interviews was how some brokers and analysts currently take a totally different view of history.

The cock-eyed optimist and the catastrophic pessimist

I want in particular to contrast the views of Hugh Priestley of Rathbone and Andrew Smithers of Smithers & Co. Both are highly educated men. Yet one suspects optimistically the market is entering a new period of history while the other sees nothing but frightening omens because we ignore history.

Hugh Priestley is a subtle man who read French at Oxford. After our talk I was quite clear where he stood on issues such as whether active management is better than passive management, whether we should be momentum investors or look for value and whether we are seeing a market whose values cannot be justified or whether the world really has changed and made its prices sane ... for the time being at least.

Hugh Priestley suggests history teaches us that the recent past is an aberration. 'I've talked to historians who say that most of the time since 1611 there has been low inflation and less power in the hands of workers.' Until the 19th century trade unions did not exist. Victorian capitalists were able to exploit the workers. The 1930 Depression made people desperate for jobs. The situation only changed after the Second World War. 'The period from 1945 to 1979 was an aberration because workers had so much power and shareholders relatively little,' Priestley said. That recent period of history is, however, the one most current commentators and senior financial professionals grew up in. Its memories are strong. Our idea of sane prices for shares may date from an abnormal period, Priestley argues. 'If that has happened historically, we are reverting to normality,' he added. And then we should not be scared the market is too high. Priestley has had only two experiences of bear markets – in 1973 and briefly in the autumn of 1998. He sees 1987 as having been hardly a crisis.

Andrew Smithers is an intellectual analyst who takes a radically different view. He is in his fifties and very relaxed. He lived in Japan for some time in the 1980s and takes a long, wide view. 'I'm not a trader,' he smiles. He's a back-room boy with a taste for pithy epigrams and a gift for mathematical equations. He read economics at Cambridge and decided then 'to help the world'. The World Bank, however, told him they did not take anyone who was under 28. So he went to work for a Commonwealth charity. He did not like charity work 'because I discovered that charity begins at home. It was very much like the world of Dickens's *Bleak House*.' An interesting allusion as Smithers' views are desperately bleak.

Aged 23 and a little disillusioned Smithers ran into John Nott, whom he had known at Cambridge. Nott suggested Smithers go to Warburgs for an interview. 'And they hired me.' Today Smithers's company provides in-depth analysis to fund managers.

'The City was a much less intellectual place than it is now,' Smithers said. Clever graduates went into the civil service, academia and the media. Economists thought money was a little grubby. But even if the City is more intellectual today, 'I'm not sure that's necessarily a good thing,' Smithers grinned.

The City may have acquired more brainpower but 'virtually no one admits how complex the behaviour of markets are,' Smithers told me. Until 20 years ago economists 'tended to assume that markets were simple and could be manipulated. It took a long and painful process of learning to realize that interventionist economics was a monstrous ego trip: if markets could be manipulated, economists become ever more important.

You can understand things you cannot manipulate but the evidence is that all models of markets do not work that well. Smithers has scanned the computer models, the economic models, the models that compare market movements to the behaviour of subatomic particles. None is perfect. 'But markets have one great virtue: they are the source of some of the best data in economics.'

In his best academic manner Smithers challenged the rationale of this book. Was I claiming that markets were affected by irrational forces? Very doubtful. For Smithers the one reason individual psychology may help explain market movements is because of the time horizon. Most investment decisions are made on a short time horizon and so from generation to generation people do not learn and mistakes get repeated. Smithers believes that this is particularly true because brokers and traders do not stay in their jobs for very long.

In *Stress in the Dealing Room* Kahn and Cooper (1993) argue that the majority of traders only last a few years. My contact at Nat West Global Markets made the same point, saying that the majority of their traders had either made enough money by the age of 35 to retire or had become managers rather than traders. Simon Rubins at E. D. & F. Man said that on the LIFFE, the London International Futures Exchange, traders did not often last for more than 10 years.

Smithers believes that the truths of the last great crash in the mid-1970s, when the price of oil soared and, in London, foolish lending to property companies nearly crippled the banks, have now been lost. 'Provided crashes don't happen more often than once in every 20 years, people will not learn the lessons,' he said.

'You're a pessimist,' I said.

'No, no, I'm a catastrophic pessimist,' Smithers insisted.

'People in the City today will not have jobs in 2 years' time. They'll be apple farming or something else. The banks will go on to something else and the people who trade often don't understand what they're doing but they do understand that they don't want their bosses to understand what they're doing.'

Smithers argues that 5 years is too short a time horizon to really measure performance. 'Over 5 years, if the investment fund managers OK the game of assuming the market will go up and there is volatility, that's a good bet.' It's a good bet, he argues, because volatility requires investment managers to trade and trade makes commissions. He pointed out, however, that, ' so much trading may not be in the best interests of clients.' There is, as we shall see in Chapter 6, growing evidence of conflicts of interest in some broking houses between what is best for clients and what is best for the house.

As a catastrophic pessimist Smithers is well aware of past bubbles. 'You can measure extremes of overvaluation. The only profoundly bad economies you get are after an asset bubble. Japan saw it in stock and land in the 1980s. South-East Asia saw it.' His favourite bubble is the great Florida land boom because in 1925, at its peak, 55,000 people in Miami (population 110,000) were real-estate dealers. 'We now have the same with mutual funds in the States,' he smiled; indeed, it sometimes seems that there are more mutual-fund managers than the whole of the population put together. But it is hard not to feel that it is not just analysis but personal experience that has influenced Smithers. He lived in Japan when the market bubble of the late 1980s bloomed – and then burst. He has kept in close touch with Japan since then visiting a number of times each year and seeing in effect not much of a recovery in that market.

Many contemporaries think that Smithers's focus on the long view is quite unrealistic. Roger Yates, who likes him, said that if he had followed Smithers's advice he wouldn't have a job because he wouldn't have invested in equities. Yates told me, 'I've listened to Andrew and if I'd been cautious as he suggested I probably wouldn't be here'. Smithers' time horizon is too long. For most analysts research has to lead to short-term action – buy, sell or hold.

Move the time horizon, Spock

Roger Yates loves the long term, because in the long term shares do well. Virtually the first story he told me was of the ill-fated market genius John Raskob whose article in *Ladies Home Journal* predicted riches for the investor who squirrelled away $20 a month in shares (Raskob 1929). Where Galbraith saw Raskob as a foolish optimist, Yates sees him as something of a hero. Raskob did not foresee the 1929 Crash and yet when someone did the calculations after 20 years, it turned out the abused analyst might have had a point. 'It's true that you wouldn't have made $80,000 but you'd have made $60,000. The rate of return was about 15 per cent annual growth.' On the long time horizon, shares do well.

'The problem is that the time horizon of our clients is very different.' Invesco handle both huge funds such as the BBC pension fund and the money of thousands of small clients, men and women who save £100 a month. In 1997 the company merged with Amvescap and looked after $132 billion worth of different funds. 'We made more profits than ICI,' Yates smiles. 'It's an international group. We have the guy in Taiwan who is saving a hundred Taiwanese dollars a month. Investors can switch money quickly and cheaply from one fund to another and they do it.' Yates has seen that investors react fast if one of the Invesco funds is named as one of the poor performers – and they take their money elsewhere.

Yates's job now is to manage analysts and traders. And while he is critical of too short term a perspective, he cannot afford to let one of his funds drift down because investors will take their money away. If that starts to happen, he said, 'we then have to take very robust action.' There is a hint of steel beneath the gentleman. It reminded me of my contact at Nat West Global markets, who regretted having been a nice guy and allowing a poor trader to go on trading for a month. The human touch, giving the man the chance to redeem himself, had cost the bank close to £1 million pounds.

One consequence of the shrinking time horizon is that analysts are judged on their decisions in the short term. In Chapter 9, when I look at the movements of 13 shares, we will see how their recommendations often change within weeks.

The limits of computer models

Some professionals I talked to are rather proud of their computer skills like Michael Barnard. He said: 'My first big break came in 1973 when I studied how to use Datastream Software. I don't know if you remember Extel cards, but you used to have to shuffle through them to find which shares met your criteria.' The criteria might be shares which had a high rate of growth and where there was a 5-year pattern of growth in profits. 'In those days brokers were just beginning to come to grips with computers. I was supposed to do a valuation on a portfolio using it.' When he started to do that, Barnard became interested. 'I read the manual and I realized you could use the software to find the shares that met the criteria for private clients.' It allowed him to sift through far more shares than before to see if they met his criteria.

Roger Yates made much of the fact that his analysts have better computer models at their disposal than ever before. He pointed out that in the late 1980s the chess computer Big Blue had no hope of beating world champions. Yet in 1997 Big Blue managed to beat Kasparov, even though he is reckoned to be one of the greatest ever chess players.

Even with the new computer models available today and skilled graduates to write and interpret them, Invesco recognizes that it is impossible to focus on all the 2,500 stocks traded on the London Stock Exchange. Yates told me that the company concentrates on about 300 and studies these intensively. As I walked through the offices, people were hunched over their computers. I said the offices did not have a frenetic feel at all. 'Good,' Yates smiled. He is at his happiest when the company only trade a quarter of the stocks in a year.

Yates gave me two examples where the models worked on something which made intuitive sense but which he claimed no one had either spotted before or acted on systematically. 'If a company makes a profit warning, telling you it will not do as well as expected, the traditional response has been to adjust the price of the stock downwards,' Yates told me. Once the profit warning has been absorbed, that information is out in the open, the price goes down and 'Everything's OK.' The models suggest, however, that when a company issues a profit warning, in 75 per cent of cases there will be a second profit warning within the next year. It made sense intuitively to him but markets, being locked into short-term news, had not adjusted to that fact.

'When you think about it, it's not that surprising,' Yates told me. 'For a publicly quoted company – and we're a publicly quoted company – if you think that you might have to put out a profit warning, you'll have looked at all the possibilities. You'll have cut all the fat, looked for anything that the company might have squirrelled away and then some, so if anything else goes wrong, you're going to be in trouble.' In the great tech stock meltdown of 2001, many companies have had to issue just such repeated profit warnings and have seen their shares plummet down.

The reverse also seems to be true. Yates also has evidence of earnings growth or momentum. The models again show that when a company is doing well and reports significantly better than expected growth it is likely to better that performance in the immediate future. Invesco looks for above average growth and growth in the dividends that the company is able to pay.

Many analysts deliberately reduce the information they have to consider. Charles Clark at West LB Panmure, for example, excludes whole areas of the economy as not being really viable. The car industry seems to him totally out of the question at present. 'I will change on that but I need persuading.' Michael Barnard, who works solo, will deal only in UK equities for the fund he manages because he cannot hope to handle other things. These, like Invesco's focus on 300 leading shares, are classic strategies for coping with information overload by reducing the spread of what you consider.

Professionals like Clark and Barnard use computers to check their ideas but the computers don't have the last word. The most acute problem analysts face is that computer programs may do their job better than they themselves do. There is evidence of this in other fields. It has been found, for example, that computer programs are more accurate in diagnosing illnesses than most GPs are. In a field like financial markets, where half the workers are not trained it is hardly surprising shares picked by the financial equivalent of Big Blue should do well.

What has made this issue so central to debates is the recent success of so-called tracker funds.

Tracker funds

Tracker funds automatically invest in the 100 leading FT-SE shares. They adjust how many shares they have in each of these 100 companies depending on how well these shares do. The composition of the FT-SE 100 also changes every month.

Most researchers I talked to fretted that these tracker funds distorted the market – and have introduced a new variable into the market. 'They're one reason why large companies have done so much better than small companies. If you have a tracker fund and ICI is in the index, you have to buy ICI,' Yates explained. Everyone needs ICI shares and so their price rises whether or not that price represents good value. Small shares are not tracked or needed. A fund may buy Associated Lentils if the managers think lentils are going to boom, but there are not hundreds of buyers who have to have Associated Lentils in their portfolio too.

I put it to Yates that the logical conclusion is that everyone will have exactly the same portfolio. He laughed and said that that was indeed the logic. More and more money will be driven into the top 100 companies in the FT-SE 100 Index. On 3 May 2001 for example, the market capitalization of BP Amoco was £13.2 billion, which represented over 9 per cent of the Footsie Index. The shares were traded both in London and in New York. In 2001 Vodafone had overtaken it with a market capitalization of £15.2 billion but then dropped to £12.3 billion, the number 2 spot. Great Universal Stores, also in the FT-SE 100, had a market capitalization of a mere £4,798 million.

On 3 May 2001 tracker funds have, therefore, to have 9.5 per cent of their funds invested in BP Amoco and 9 per cent in Vodafone and far far fewer in Great Universal Stores. The result is that Vodafone and BP Amoco shares become scarcer and their price goes higher.

Tracker shares became popular because, in a bull market, they offer investors an easy way to make profits. Yates believes this success is affecting the psychology of those who work in the markets because analysts and brokers are being asked to perform against various benchmarks – and the main benchmark is the FT-SE 100. It is not a question of absolutes, of how much money you make for clients, any more but whether you are doing better or worse than the index. 'You go to see a client and you say the bad news is that the market is down 20 per cent and the good news is that we've only lost 19 per cent of your money and they're pleased.'

Lenhoff does not worry about tracker funds as much as Yates does. He thinks they are quite efficient 'for the chap who doesn't want to be bothered to check his shares every day. It's simple but it doesn't mean that there isn't a real value to active management where you choose shares on the basis of the kind of processes I've described.'

At Capel Cure Sharp fund managers have created a portfolio called Mr Benchmark to measure themselves against. Lenhoff said they wanted to see how much value they were adding to a portfolio by active fund management. It was 150 points up. The problem for analysts and brokers, however, is that we are seeing increasing evidence that their skills do not outperform the market. Since nearly all the studies have been done on brokers who forward their analysts recommendations I look at that evidence in detail in Chapter 6.

In this chapter I've suggested that the systems used by analysts to pick shares tend to ignore the role of intuition and that, at the same time, the intense controversies between optimistic and pessimistic analysts suggest analysts' decisions and assessments do not just depend on cool intellectual reading of the evidence. Many companies dislike analysts too. While I was writing this book the ex-chairman of ICI, Sir Ron Hempel, attacked analysts. My Liverpool broker told me that he had a great deal of sympathy with Sir Ron Hempel, 'though he's probably been misquoted'. Hempel has complained that analysts are so driven by short-termism. In 1999, Merseyside stockbrokers had had a dinner with Peter Davis, the chief executive of the Pru, 'who's a Merseysider'. Davis said that now he was at the Pru, he operated on a 20-year plan, but that was different from the way he had worked before. The Pru was not in the business, it seems, of anything as crude as short-term gains. Davis has since left the Pru for Sainsbury's. But analysts see themselves being judged on much shorter timescales.

In the next chapter, I look at what is a central factor in understanding how different people react to the market – to their attitudes to risk. Here again we shall find more than reason at work.

five

The psychology of risk and risk takers

Before you read this chapter, you might like to fill in the Risk Attitude Questionnaire on pages 151–161. If you answer after you have read this chapter, there's a risk that you will have picked up clues that will influence the answers you give.

In 1968 psychiatrists at Broadmoor Special Hospital released Graham Young. The hospital believed that Young, an intelligent young poisoner, had been 'cured'. The psychiatrists turned out to be tragically wrong. After 4 months Graham Young murdered again. Again, he did it with poison.

The press pilloried Broadmoor. In their defence the psychiatrists argued that assessing risk was as much an art as a science and that their record was good. That was not an idle boast. A 15-year follow-up (Bowden 1981) found that only 4 per cent of the patients released from Broadmoor in the early 1960s had committed any subsequent act of violence.

Tony Black (1980) studied 128 patients released into the community a few years after Bowden's sample. The results of this second study were more worrying: over 10 per cent had been reconvicted for offences involving personal violence. But as these patients were amongst the most dangerous 'criminal lunatics' in Britain, a 10 per cent failure rate did not suggest Broadmoor had assessed the risks that poorly. Yet the mistake with Graham Young did cost lives as did other mistakes. So was Broadmoor's record good or appalling? Assessing how others assess risk is as difficult as assessing risk in the first place.

There is a large body of literature on risk, risk takers and predicting risks, most of which, like the examples I have given, deals with psychiatric patients, criminals, vulnerable children or dangerous sports. Financial risk taking has been studied much less.

To some extent the City has only itself to blame for this lack of research into real-life financial risk taking. Financial institutions are wary of allowing outsiders to study them. Scandals like the collapse of Barings have started to change attitudes but the process is slow. A comprehensive London Business School study of how dealers handle risk, for example, found institutions nervous about giving all the information needed.

Perceptions of risk

Researchers speak of the safety risks, health risks, environmental risks, financial risks, relationship risks or insurance risks people run. Logically there does not have to be a connection between how fast you drive your car, how likely you are to risk your health by smoking too much and how likely you are to risk your money. But, intuitively, we feel there should be a connection. Timid souls who never break the speed limit, we think, are unlikely to gamble recklessly in casinos or on the markets. Some large American companies like Fidelity Fund send their would-be investors questionnaires to assess their attitudes to risk but, as we shall see, these are very flawed.

In this chapter I want to examine what we know about the psychology of risk takers. Some personality characteristics are associated with high risk taking; others with fear of taking risks. The conditions under which some people work in financial markets may encourage some personalities to take greater risks than they might do otherwise.

We know the extremes, the almost caricatured types – ultra-cautious Mr Triplicate Jobsworth who will not lift a finger unless the task has been approved by everyone and cannot possibly go wrong, and Ms Punter Gung Ho who loves mischief, will do almost anything not to be bored and adores the buzz, the adrenalin, the edge. There should be some pattern, 'caused' by personality traits, childhood or work experiences or even our genes.

One problem is that many studies of financial risk are based in the laboratory where subjects play simulated betting games. They are asked whether they would stake $1 on a 2 to 1 bet rather than $1 on a 10 to 1 bet. A typical finding is that subjects will rather risk winning a small sum when the odds are good than winning a large one where the odds are much less favourable. The sums involved are small; the atmosphere artificial. These studies are also hard to interpret because while investment can be a gamble, a gamble is never an investment. If you place a bet on Lucky Loser in the 2 o'clock you can lose the whole stake. When you invest in equities it does not feel the same – and for good reason. However lousy your judgement, history says you are unlikely to lose all the £1,000 you invested. Total wipe outs are rare; only in option trading or derivatives do investors stand to lose all their stake. Even Lastminute.com is still worth something.

Investors don't always find it easy to judge the risks they are taking. Derivative markets do, of course, offer greater risks than gambling because investors expose themselves to a so-called 'open' position and can incur losses they did not know they had – unlimited losses. Names at Lloyd's were in that situation but most did not always see it like that. Tradition told them that Lloyd's was an old club for the rich. It had made money for names since the 18th century. When they signed up, new names were told they were risking everything they owned. 'You could really lose your shirt, even the cufflinks,' was a phrase sometimes used at the interview. But few believed the formula meant anything. The committee had to say 'unlimited liability' for the record.

When some Lloyd's syndicates started to post enormous losses in the 1980s, many names were furious. No one had ever made it clear that unlimited really meant unlimited, they claimed. Their behaviour was typical of 'victims' in financial catastrophes – a mixture of bitterness, anger and denial.

I do not find that surprising, because even very sophisticated investors can be blind to the true nature of the risks they run. This is not just blind greed. Today risk is packaged in ever more exotic vehicles. To protect investors the Financial Services Authority now insists that anyone who trades in options signs a certificate that says they realize they can lose all their stake.

Building on the work of Piatelli Palmarini (1994), Hilton (1998) argues that seven deadly sins affect financial decision making.

He stresses in particular overconfidence (which may be increased when traders work in groups) and irrational risk aversion. He cites work which shows that when investors have to choose either a sure loss of £30,000 or a 20 per cent chance of losing nothing and an 80 per cent chance of losing £40,000, the majority choose the second option.

Equations never go wrong – the masters of risk in financial markets

The blindness of the most sophisticated is best illustrated by the story of August 1998 and the Long Term Credit (LTC) fund. I want to contrast two accounts of this – those of Andrew Smithers and of Michael Lewis (1999).

In August 1998 the world's banking system was threatened by the possible failure of the major hedge fund, LTC. A hedge fund gets its name from 'hedging bets.' LTC specialized in interest-rate swaps, long-term stock options and other derivatives. (An interest-rate swap is where Bank A has mortgages in Denmark which produce 7 per cent interest but the interest is variable. Bank B owns debt in Poland which produces 10 per cent interest but there is more risk of defaults and also the risk of a fall in value of the zloty. Bank A and Bank B swap the interest. Bank A may do this because it thinks Poland will do well, the zloty will rise and so the bank will earn more than it would in Denmark.)

The LTC fund was run by John Meriwether. Meriwether had made his name at Salomon Brothers in the 1980s – and especially when the market crashed in October 1987. Meriwether had gathered a team of young academics. On the day of the crash he saw the total confusion in the bond market and saw an opportunity. To under-stand what he did it's necessary to understand what selling short means. To sell short is to sell something you do not currently have. You agree to sell me on 30th July 1,000 bonds or shares. Today you do not have these but I, being the buyer, pay you today's price to take delivery on 30 July. If at 9 a.m. on 30 July, you can buy those shares or bonds more cheaply than you could today, you make a profit. If on July 30 the shares or bonds cost more than they did today, you are 'out of the money'.

Meriwether persuaded his young team to sell short the 30-year US Treasury bond (let us call it Bond A) which had just been issued and to buy identical amounts of the 30-year US Treasury bond issued 3 months before (Bond B). Bond B was in effect a $29\frac{3}{4}$-year bond by October 1987.

Meriwether had studied patterns of bond trading and seen that newly issued bonds like Bond A carried a so-called 'liquidity premium'. They were easier to resell – just like nearly new cars – so bond traders were willing to pay fractionally more for them. In the chaos of October 1987 the price of newly issued US government bonds rose steeply; they seemed safer than equities and could easily be sold. Bond A climbed high.

By selling millions of Bond A short, Meriwether and his young academics were betting that the crash would hit the bond market less than expected. The fall in the equity market would not be so steep and, as a result, bond prices would not keep on rising. Give it a few weeks or months and the chaos would simmer down. Bond A would become significantly cheaper and so, by selling it short, Meriwether would cash in. Buying Bond B was doing what hedge funds exist to do – hedging that bet. If the price of bonds rose the losses Meriwether would take on Bond A would be offset to some extent by profits on Bond B because it would have risen.

Meriwether was proved right. A few weeks later, when the markets had calmed down, bonds were cheaper. Selling Bond A short gave Meriwether's small team a profit of $150 million. It cost him $150 million less to buy the bonds he had agreed to sell than he paid for them in the middle of the panic. Mighty Merrill Lynch by comparison posted a total profit of just $391 million for the whole of that year. Meriwether had understood the market at a moment of total confusion and pulled off an even smarter trade than Nathan Rothschild's Waterloo coup. (Unlike Rothschild, Meriwether did not have privileged information; he just saw the financial universe falling apart and predicted its future correctly.)

This coup made Meriwether famous. He left Salomons and set up a fund of his own. Long Term Credit had to borrow money to set up.

Its backers included major Wall Street players such as Goldman Sachs and Morgan Guaranty. Meriwether gathered a number of very able traders. One man turned down an offer of $28 million a year to work for him. The team devised complex mathematical formulae that predicted future price differences between different bonds and formulae for interest swap deals. Two Nobel Prize winners in economics were part of the team.

Meriwether abolished the distinction between researchers, analysts and traders. All his group called themselves strategists. From 1987 to 1998 Meriwether and his men made enormous sums of money. In 1995 the fund reported profits of 43 per cent return on capital, in 1996 they were 41 per cent, in 1997 the profits declined to a mere 17 per cent. The 16 partners even put much of their personal fortunes – a total of $1.9 billion – into their fund. Then in the summer of 1998 it started to go wrong.

On 17 July Salomon Brothers sold a large portfolio in interest swaps; these were very similar to the interest swaps Meriwether had. As these were big sales in the market the price of these interest swaps fell. As the interest swaps were being used as security by LTC, the security they were offering banks fell sharply. The value of the LTC fund dropped by 10 per cent in July. Just as brokers in 1929 called on their investors to supply more money to maintain their margins, LTC found itself being called on to provide cash. Then on 17 August Russia defaulted on its debt. Panic gripped the market.

On 21 August 1998, LTC lost $550 million in one day – two-thirds of the amount Barings had gone bust for after months of Leeson's rogue trading.

There is an interesting difference of view about what happened to LTC. The conventional position is that LTC took too great risks and got out of control. Andrew Smithers argued that it was worrying that banks invested in the fund. 'The banks were getting a 40 per cent return,' he told me. 'That kind of return presumes you are running big risks – yet the banks thought it quite normal.' Banks normally lend money at a base rate plus up to 5 per cent.' If banks never asked why they should get such a phenomenal return, Smithers hinted, they almost deserved their losses. They were getting extravagant returns and should have wondered whether they were not running extravagant risks.

Michael Lewis is much more sympathetic and suggests that LTC did not deserve to lose (Lewis 1999). He sees the pigmy minds of Wall Street as the main cause of the débâcle. No-brainers did not understand the true nature of the risks Meriwether was betting on.

Also, after Russia defaulted on its debts, Meriwether's no-brain backers lacked True Character – the 1980s' version of the 'right stuff' Tom Wolfe's *Apollo* astronauts had (Wolfe 1979). The backers of LTC panicked. Their panic made their worst fears come true.

Some of the backers were major firms. In August 1998 they started to trade to protect their own positions, even if this went against the fund they had invested in, Lewis alleged. If, for example, they knew LTC had a position in Danish mortgages, they sold Danish mortgages as fast as they could, thus bringing the price down. LTC needed the price of Danish mortgages to stay high because they were security for other trades. As the value of Danish mortgages, for example, fell, LTC's banks demanded more collateral. By the end of August LTC needed $1.5 billion to keep afloat.

Alan Greenspan, head of the US Federal Reserve Bank, organized a rescue. He said that August was the most terrifying period in international finance he had known during his long career. International banks had to pump in $3.5 billion at a few hours' notice into LTC to stop it defaulting. If LTC had gone bankrupt there would have been domino effects in the world's banking system, especially as Russia had just defaulted on its debt. The total losses of LTC were $4.4. billion. The Union Bank of Switzerland lost $700 million; other banks lost $1.8 billion but the 16 partners of LTC took the biggest hit. Between them they lost $1.9 billion.

Lewis argues that the banks panicked because they still did not understand the complexities of derivatives properly. He even hinted in the *New York Times* that there might have been a plot. Major Wall Street interests saw a chance to crush LTC so that its brains would be working again for them rather than for themselves.

The story illustrates how complex risk has become. Is Smithers right? Did LTC take too great risks? Or is Lewis right? Would LTC have survived if its backers had been more brained and given the fund time to recover its losses? The plea that it would is typical of gamblers. Eventually they say the wheel will spin their way.

For investors the lesson is that risk is hard to understand these days.

Bernoulli – the father of risk theory

Risk research has its roots in mathematical theory. Much thinking about risk goes back to the 18-century mathematician Daniel Bernoulli. Bernoulli who came from a family of distinguished mathematicians made many contributions to mathematics and, especially, to probability theory. He linked many of his ideas to so-called utility theory, which the 18th-century philosopher Jeremy Bentham also developed into the moral and political philsophy of utilitarianism. It is from that we get the maxim of the greatest good for the greatest number.

Bernoulli argued that individuals are motivated not to maximize financial returns but to maximize the expected utility of their actions. This is a convoluted way of saying that a poor man who has a chance to gamble £10 to win £100 sees a huge possible gain but the stake of £10 is also huge. For a rich man, on the other hand, it is barely worth betting £10 to win £100: he will not notice either the loss or the gain. 'The utility resulting from any small increase in wealth will be inversely proportional to the quantity of goods previously possessed,' Bernoulli wrote. The rich bastard may bet £100 to win £1,000, however.

Bernoulli also argued that people will find it 'more inconvenient' to lose £5 than convenient to gain £5. This idea eventually led to the notion of the so-called equity risk premium – investors will want a reward for taking a risk in equities as opposed to leaving their money 'safe as houses' in the bank or in government bonds.

Bernoulli did not study the perception of risk, the contrast between mathematically accurate calculation of risk and how people see or feel the risks they are running. Risk researchers Tversky and Kahneman have built on Bernoulli's ideas (Kahneman and Tversky 1974; Tversky and Kahneman 1992). They also claim that as people own more they become more risk averse. Their main aim is not to make money but rather not to lose their wealth. The extent to which a person is risk averse will, according to this theory, depend on their wealth. Unfortunately, as nearly all the experiments into risk involve bets of between 50 cents and £50, these studies do not reveal much about what motivates people to make real-life investments. Excuse me if I'm sceptical, but in my view if this reply were true, no one with over £20,000 would invest any of their money in equity markets.

Stockbrokers like Paul O'Donnell of Brewin Dolphin often told me that their clients, and they themselves, are more concerned to preserve their money than to make profits. But stockbrokers preaching the gospel of 'wealth preservation' are doing something they love – giving the guff – and the particularly English guff of not boasting about money.

Outside the lab the behaviour of investors and markets suggests that Bernoulli's utility theory does not work perfectly, however. Wahlund (1991) studied 1,700 Swedish savers. A total of 48 per cent of them had sizeable liquid assets of an average of 82,000 Swedish kronor and saw themselves as wanting to increase their wealth and being willing to take some risks to do so. Wahlund defined risk-free investment as putting money in the bank or with the Swedish equivalent of a building society. A later study of 503 investors showed that 14 per cent were security savers who saved in order to have money on hand for troubled times. A total of 9 per cent were what he called risk hedgers who were willing to take some risks and 6 per cent had portfolios which were very diverse and included significantly risky investments. Unfortunately no attempt was made to look at the different personalities and thinking styles of these different investors.

Rever (1999) argues that economists see themselves as scientists, on a par with chemists and physicists. Chemists and physicists do not carry out interviews. They produce beautiful equations and explain reactions. Therefore economists do not need to carry out interviews. Never mind that chemists and physicists are studying objects and processes while economics study subjects and processes.

In fact, the relatively little research has produced a number of interesting answers. First, there seems to be a link between age, wealth, education and the willingness to take risks. Studies in Holland by Wärneryd reported in *The Psychology of Saving* (1999) suggest that as investors get older they are willing to take more risks. Wärneryd argues that this is because they have less need of income for family emergencies, for example. More educated investors are also readier to take risks. Less surprising perhaps, richer investors are more willing to take risks. They can afford to lose and small increases in wealth will mean less to them.

Some personality traits go with a propensity to take risks. It is still not totally clear how those 'risk propensities' affect behaviour or what the differences are when you are handling other people's money or your own money. But the research has useful clues nevertheless. One intriguing theme to emerge is a connection between feeling you are in control and willingness to 'go for broke'.

E.J. Langer (1975) in *The Illusion of Control*, argued that people often behave as if chance events are subject to control and that this may be due to the fact that they pick up some cues in the situation that suggest skill is involved. Langer (1975) and John Burger (1986) also found that some individuals are more liable to feel they are in control of events whether this is reasonable or not. To make sense of this we need to understand two different concepts – desire for control and locus of control.

Desire for control is a personality variable. Individuals range from control freaks who want to control their own and other people's behaviour totally to happy-go-lucky souls who do not mind leaving their fate in the hands of others.

Locus of control refers to whether you tend to ascribe responsibility for success or failure to yourself (internal locus) or to forces outside yourself – luck, those bastards at head office, your ex-husband, the usual suspects – which means you have an external locus of control. Suggestible individuals will have an external locus of control.

Think of each of these as a spectrum. You can be high in desire for control, low or somewhere in the middle.

How you rate depends on reasonably well-verified personality tests such as the Desirability of Control test which asks subject to rate, on a scale of 1 (the statement does not apply to me at all) to 7 (the statement always applies to me), their response to questions like:

1. I would rather run my own business and make my own mistakes than listen to someone else's instructions.
2. Others usually know what is best for me.
3. I like to wait to see if someone else will solve the problem so that I don't have to cope with it.

There has been considerable research on how attitudes to control affect financial behaviour. High-desire-for-control subjects gamble more on games where there is an element of skill. They prefer poker to roulette. No one has asked whether they are more likely to play the stock market than the horses but it seems very likely, because few people see investment as just a matter of luck.

Burger looked at how these high-control individuals react to probabilities. He first made them sit through 100 tosses of a coin and say how often they had been right in choosing heads or tails. The high-control subjects believed they had guessed 60 per cent of throws correctly when their real scores were much nearer 50 per cent.

In a second study subjects were asked to bet whether or not two dice had landed on a target number. The odds were peculiar. If the target was 9 and if the dice fell right, subjects would get paid at 9 to 1. If the target was 2 they would get paid only at 2 to 1. There were two conditions. In condition 1 subjects knew the target number before they placed the bet, so they also knew the odds; in condition 2 the target number was written down but the subjects did not see it before they placed the bet and so they did not know what reward they might win. Without that information, high-control subjects bet far less – a perfectly reasonable strategy given their personality characteristics.

Burger discovered, however, that high-control subjects became less rational when they got a string of answers right at the start of the experiment. A little success distorted their perceptions. They then rated their level of control as far higher than it really was.

This tendency to overestimate how much control they had also emerged in another study. Subjects sat in front of an array of coloured lights that flashed on and off in different sequences. By pressing keys the subjects could affect the sequence of how lights went on and off. Some of the sequence was always random. In one condition 25 per cent of the sequence was random but pressing the keys controlled the other 75 per cent; in another condition 75 per cent of the sequence was random and the keys controlled just 25 per cent.

Subjects did the task and were then asked to say how much control they had. In the 75 per cent control condition the high-control subjects said they had 64 per cent and the low-control subjects said they had 50 per cent control – (i.e. both groups underestimated the amount of control they had). When the keys were only controlling 25 per cent of the sequence, however, the high-control subjects were wildly out. They thought they exercised twice the amount of control that they did, saying they had 48 per cent, while the other group said 30 per cent.

Burger's studies did not touch questions of vanity, and the buzz and the social approval dealers get when they pull off a good deal. You could become a master of the universe, Michael Lewis claimed, with a big coup. Kahn and Cooper (1993) found in their interviews that dealers were very aware that their performance was being watched. A good result made them a bit of a hero. Lewis's phrase is telling, of course. Masters of the universe have total control. Once you are seduced into that self-image, it is all too easy to believe you can shape the markets to your will.

A person who has brought off some very successful trades may attribute this to good luck or to their own brilliance A high-control subject will tend to think he has succeeded because he is more in control. To use one of the buzz phrases, he knows how to take advantage of 'market asymmetries'. A market asymmetry is a situation where the price of a share does not reflect its true value. But will that make him take more risks?

The next factor to consider is locus of control. If you think external forces rule, you will be less likely to take risks unless you feel particularly lucky. But if you have a high desire for control and an internal locus of control, you tend to think success or failure are the result of your own actions. Luck is for the birds. You will be more likely to take risks if you feel you have assessed the situation correctly. But you have a weakness; you will be prone to think your assessments are correct.You will be a poor judge of how much information you need. You will see yourself not as gambling but as judging well. The-high-desire-for-control, internal-locus-of-control person is most likely to take big risks on limited information – and feel they are being rational. In an interesting comment on his Dutch studies, Wärneryd (1999) found that some investors who took big risks did not see those investments as being that risky.

Nearly all the experiments on perception of risk, however, assume all subjects are alike. They exclude factors of personality. This, it seems, ignores useful psychological evidence.

Excitement, anxiety and the personality of risk takers

Freud said that human beings seek to reduce arousal. If you are sexually aroused, you feel tense and need to make love. Once you have made love, you feel satisfied, your arousal level reduces back to nil and so you can relax. The same model applied to hunger and thirst. Reducing arousal or tension has been a key concept in psychology.

However, by the 1960s it was clear that the tension-reduction model could not completely explain either human or animal behaviour. Experiments showed, for example, that rats would perform the same tasks (pressing a lever) hundreds of times to get food rewards in order to be allowed to explore a rich, interesting environment. When the rats explored they showed all the physiological signs – quicker heart rate, for example – that normally accompany a rise in arousal and tension. According to Freud and other tension-reduction theorists, the rats should have experienced this rise in tension as stressful and a punishment; the rats obviously did not, however.

Human beings are not so different. During foreplay, people do not usually dislike the rise in sexual tension and physiological arousal. Sex has a clear biological purpose, which may be an explanation as to why we tolerate the tension – but what is the biological purpose of dangerous sports?

In 1977 a survey in the American magazine *Human Behaviour* was sparked off by an increase in deaths in hang-gliding accidents. *Human Behaviour* noted there had been a boom in so-called 'escape centres' where people could take part in scuba-diving, bungee-jumping, fun aviation and other dangerous sports.

Since the 1970s we have become more interested in dangerous sports. In the States now 1,000 people a week leap off tall buildings or bridges doing bungee jumps. France considers the sport so dangerous it has banned it but in America it is legal and enjoyed by thousands. Dangerous sports are so popular that a whole television cable channel, ESPN 2, is devoted to them.

Peter Greenberg (1977) found that most customers of escape centres were tied to their office desks for most of their working lives.

Dangerous sports gave them a chance to test themselves. Even when things went wrong people often did not have regrets, as David Klein, professor at Michigan University, found when he studied 500 snowmobile accidents.

Ira Matathia and Marian Salzman (1999), who spot trends for marketing, suggest those who climb mountains or bungee jump or race motorbikes feel they have accomplished 'a grand experience'. The American therapist Abraham Maslow talks of people having peak experiences. He is not so literal as to mean mountain climbing but among other things is referring to a buzz of achievement you get from surviving a major challenge, physical or psychological.

The 1977 survey of dangerous sports unfortunately did not give people a personality questionnaire. In the 1960s Hans Eysenck suggested that extroverts like risk taking better more than introverts, arguing that there was a biological reason for this (Eysenck 1967). Extroverts have lower cortical arousal and, therefore, need far more stimulation than introverts to keep their brains working at a comfortable level.

Some 30 years of research have made the situation more complicated but there is some evidence which supports Eysenck's ideas. He saw extroversion as one end of a continuum. Introversion was at the other end. As psychologists examined his research, picked over his original questionnaires and developed some of their own (Zuckerman 1991) it seems clear a number of factors contribute to extroversion.

One factor is sociability which, it seems, has little connection at all with risk taking, but there are other aspects of the extrovert's make up which do. The most important are:

- Broad impulsivity – the willingness to act on impulse without calculating the consequences.
- Narrow impulsivity – by which psychologists mean 'not having detailed plans for the future'. The narrow impulsive does not have to know what she is going to be doing on Saturday night and is quite happy with that situation. She will not obsess about what to wear at the last moment.
- Sensation seeking – the sensation seeker gets bored easily and wants new experiences, even if they are not predictable. Extroverts are much more sensation seekers than introverts.

The impulsive extrovert is clearly the person who is most likely to take risks – and to take risks without having bothered to spend the time to assess the situation properly. He suffers from one of the cardinal sins Fisher outlined in his 1928 study of investors' psychology – impatience.

Many of us, when we take unusual risks, feel anxious. As we have seen, subjects with an internal locus of control are likely to feel more anxious than average. Kogan and Wallach (1964) looked at how men and women played gambling games in the laboratory and found a link between impulsivity and willingness to take risks but only if subjects were not too anxious. When they were highly anxious they settled for the more cautious options in the games. There was an exception, though. If, at the end of a sequence of games, subjects had to choose between a cautious strategy or betting all their winnings on one gamble – and had to do that face to face with a male experimenter – then even very anxious men tended to plump for the one gamble.

The men, Kogan and Wallach suggested, found themselves in what I would like to christen the macho crunch – a situation where you have to show you are a real man, to put up or shut up. The majority chose to put up and risk losing money in order to gain face. They preferred feeling the stress and the anxiety to chickening out. This has interesting echoes of Wharton's observation about American men on Wall Street before 1929. They felt they had to invest to impress their women.

Kahn and Cooper found that dealers suffered to an unusual degree from free-floating anxiety. They talked with one man who had reported feeling his pulse race after he had sold $10 million, bought $6 million and was waiting to see how the dollar exchange rate would go. Roger Laughlin, a dealer in oil futures, explained to me that he supervised dealers who had to be able to cope with the anxiety of knowing what the price of oil would be a few hours ahead. If the price shifted by 2 cents a barrel it could mean losses or profits of millions. Kahn and Cooper found that their male dealers were 30 per cent more anxious than the average.

In the light of Kogan and Wallach's research it's possible to see how some market professionals deal with such situations. They feel the anxiety but they are in a very public situation. So they cope by suppressing that anxiety. It comes out later. While Edith Wharton's losers rarely admitted their losses to their wives and families because that would be considered so improper, today Kahn and Cooper reported that many dealers worried they took their stresses out on their families when they got back home. Showing anxiety in private, after the deals were done, was acceptable.

Today's extrovert risk taker pays a price, therefore. He becomes anxious but cannot show his anxiety. Some dealers, of course, will not feel the anxiety as much.

Reversal theory

Michael Apter, an English psychologist, has tried to bring these various strands together into a model he calls reversal theory (Apter 1992). He argues theories like Freud's and Eysenck's do not reflect the complexity of either life or personality. There are times and situations when some of us want calm and other times when we want excitement. Only freaks do dangerous sports 24 hours a day.

Apter suggests we move between two states all our lives:

- telic state – where low arousal will be felt as calm and is pleasurable, while high arousal is felt as anxiety and unpleasant;
- paratelic state – where low arousal will be felt as boring and high arousal will be felt as fun.

People switch or 'reverse' between these states. Personality dictates how often people do this and which is the more normal state for a particular person. Apter divides individuals into those who are telic dominant and those who are paratelic dominant. The telic dominant is serious-minded, ambitious and finds it hard to relax; the paratelic likes fun, play and buzz. But the point, Apter argues, is that even telic people spend considerable time in paratelic states – and vice versa. To understand behaviour – and this applies to risk taking – you have to know if you are basically a telic or paratelic person and whether at any particular moment you are in a telic or paratelic frame of mind.

Apter has developed a scale – the Telic Dominance Scale – which helps pinpoint how playful people are. Typical questions ask how people prefer to spend their time, what activities make them relax, whether they like to feel excited, what their attitude to meditation is.

The more telic dominant a person is, the more he or she will avoid arousal; the more paratelic he is, the more he will seek arousal. Apter asks us to visualize the following model in terms of how we feel in relation to experiences:

■ trauma zone;
■ danger zone;
■ boredom.

The paratelic individual will find a situation boring when a telic individual will not. Their boredom zones will be quite different. The telic individual may feel a situation is dangerous while the paratelic will find that same situation an amusing challenge. Every individual has an optimal level of arousal. This level is the product of both subjective experiences and objective basic biology.

Even your pulse rate is a clue to what your personality style is and how much risk you like. A Norwegian psychologist, Stan Svebak, argues that greater muscle tension, faster heart rate and breathing rates all indicate whether you are more arousal seeking or arousal avoiding.

One of Apter's most interesting insights is that our optimal level of arousal is related to our sense of playfulness. Apter (1992) quotes a *Playboy* interview with Donald Trump, where Trump says that life for him is a psychological game 'and a series of challenges' – the challenge of developing real estate, or deciding whether or not to buy the Eastern seaboard shuttle – but he had a college friend, a man with an IQ he estimated of 190, repeatedly on the phone worrying about his mortgage. Trump contrasted his own success with his friend's relative failure and attributed it to the fact that he did not freak out with anxiety when taking risks. From Apter's point of view, Trump, being essentially paratelic dominant, is the kind of personality who seeks out and copes with risks. Such a person might say that it is better to live through crises and failures with their accompanying dramas because that is less boring than a steady routine. Trump is a master dealer and survivor. We can't know whether he has much less free-floating anxiety than the dealers in Kahn and Cooper's survey, but he seems to cope with it better.

George Soros when he famously sold sterling short seems again to have coped magnificently with his anxieties. His aides suggested selling £1 billion short. Soros insisted on selling £10 billion short. He went to bed and slept soundly. A few hours later he had made a profit of $968 million.

The large American investment house Fidelity Fund send their investors a questionnaire and it includes some questions on attitudes to risk. It asks investors to say which of the following fits them best:

 i. You are willing to take a lot more risk with all your money;
 ii. You are willing to take a lot more risk with some of your money;
 iii. You are willing to take some risk with some of your money.

Investors are also asked if they have invested on the stock market before and to say if they would be comfortable with the risk.

The questionnaire is scored oddly. If you answer i. you get 16 points. If you answer ii. you get 6 points. Fidelity do not explain the logic. Their scoring manual also assumes that anyone who has ever invested in equities is more prone to risk taking, ignoring totally the possibility that if you invested and lost badly you might never want to invest in shares again. With a nice parochial touch, Fidelity class as supremely risky any non-US equities so a flix and fluxing American Internet stock would be seen as less risky than Great Universal Stores.

Illusion of control

We have seen that illusion of control affects people in experimental situations. Is this also a factor that affects how dealers trade in real markets?

This kind of dynamic is being studied by Fenton O'Creevy et al. (1998) others at the London Business School. They have developed the Risk Assessment Tool (called RAT) as one technique for measuring how cognitive bias affects decisions.

The London Business School team argue that a key factor in assessing risk is this question of control. They point out that City traders and dealers are under pressure to produce good results; at some level they know that markets cannot be controlled but some delude themselves.

Again let us squat in the mind of a lucky trader. Two good months. Hefty bonuses earned. Is this luck? Hell, no, it is skill. It is art. I am a master of the universe. In an environment where you have to compete against other dealers you need confidence. Confidence turns into overconfidence fairly easily. Dealers can become unrealistic; they think they have control, and think risks are not so great because they are the ones taking them.

Fenton O'Creevy and his London Business School colleagues suggest there are three elements in understanding how traders see and take risks:

- A dispositional or personality element – some people will be more likely to have unrealistic perceptions of control.
- A learned element – good trades can become a snare. An overconfident trader can refuse to change tactics because, even if they are losing now, they believe their approach will come right in the long term.
- The context – traders operate in a very competitive and noisy context. Hockey (1970) found that extroverts prefer to work in noisy environments. Markets may also be affected by politics – an announcement from the Chancellor – or by the war in Kosovo, or by good or bad company results. With so much noise it may be hard to be sure just why a stock performed well or performed badly. This makes it easier to devise excuses of the sort 'My strategy would have worked if the finance minister hadn't resigned.'

O'Creevy and his team studied 488 traders and managers. They used three methods: interview, computer-game experiments and personality data.

The team developed a game as part of the RAT. Subjects sit in front of a screen. The screen has a line which represents a fictional stock-market index; the line can grow or shrink at two points per second. Depending on the particular condition, the line can grow as a result of random variation or the subject's strategy. Its score can go from minus 2,000 to plus 2,000.

The subject sits in front of the computer screen which presents the index line and has a box with three keys, Z, X and C. The subject is told that the keys either increase the score, decrease the score or increase the random variation. Subjects are asked what they think the effect of each key is and are told that they can press each key as often as they like.

The psychologists devised a number of tasks for the subjects:

▨ To work out the function of X, C and Z keys.
▨ To bet on the final score of the index and set confidence limits. If therefore someone bets the index will end in the range 1,100 to 1,140, say, he will win more points (if he bets right) than someone who had bet the index will end between 1,100 and 1,180.
▨ To bet again, this time with the promise of a sure gain which can be increased by having smaller confidence limits, say between 1,100 and 1,200.
▨ To bet on a sure loss which can be limited by using the confidence limits.

O'Creevy and his team also got subjects to fill in a Risk Propensity Scale to test for any links between their scores on the RAT and attitudes to risk taking in the rest of their lives. The scale looks at health risks, career risks, social risks, personal financial risks and social risks. Each subject also had to fill in a 240-item questionnaire about their personality. The questions covered five different scales or personality traits:

▨ E scale – extroversion versus introversion. High E scorers are warm, gregarious and seek excitement.
▨ N scale – emotional versus unemotional. High N scorers are hostile, depressed, impulsive, vulnerable, neurotic.
▨ O scale – open as opposed to conventional. Those who score high are more open.
▨ A scale – those who score high value trust and modesty and are straightforward.
▨ C scale – conscientious versus casual. Those who score high are self-disciplined and ordered, and value competence.

In the best tradition of scientific psychology the team made a num-

The better the performance, the less powerful illusions of control.

ber of predictions. The more optimistic and the more unrealistic a trader's perception of control the more likely he or she would be to underestimate the risks of his/her actions. Traders who showed a high degree of illusion of control should perform less well than traders with low to middling illusions.

The subject is sensitive. The London Business School promised not to reveal the names of the firms who gave them access, but only one firm provided data on how well individual traders had done to match their performance in the real market with psychological scores. O'Creevy and his colleagues correlated the illusion-of-control score individual traders got on the RAT with their real contribution to desk profits. Both the traders and their managers related that individual contribution to the company's profit. As the graph shows, the higher the profit the less the illusion of control.

The traders' performance was rated from minus 10 to plus 110. The higher the illusion of control the more discrepancy between how much control dealers really had and how much control they perceived they had. The more control dealers thought they had the less good their real performance was. These 'bad' traders were also most likely to overestimate how much they contributed to overall profits. O'Creevy and his colleagues suggest that traders with a high illusion of control may not be sensitive to feedback and will therefore not learn intelligent lessons when they made losses. These traders were also likely to flatter themselves when it came to judging how well their managers thought they handled risk.

The personality data also showed a clear link between how traders handled investment risk and their propensity to take life risks. The detailed findings were:

- There was a simple and robust link between extroversion and risk taking.
- There was a more complex link between neuroticism, emotionality and risk taking. Neurotic traders were likely not to take financial or career risks but they were more likely to take health risks, such as drinking too much or smoking. This suggests they were having to cope with high levels of anxiety.
- Conscientious traders were less likely to take financial or health risks.
- Traders who scored high on agreeableness were less inclined to take risks of all kinds.

O'Creevy and his colleagues argue that managers need to keep an eye not just on the profits and losses of traders but on their psychological reactions as well. Apter would argue that these can change from day to day in response to pressures. The environment in which traders operate is stressful and, day in day out, traders have to make guesses about uncertain prices and trends. The stress will lead some traders who have a high desire for control to overestimate how much control they have.

I have not mentioned cognitive dissonance in this chapter but it is plausible to argue that this theory (which I described in Chapter 2) can help us to understand what is going on in the minds of traders and investors. The inconsistent realities we have to handle are:

a. the truth that the markets cannot be controlled or predicted;
b. the truth that as a trader or an investor we have to try to predict market movements.

The solution to the insoluble for some is to believe:

c. most people cannot predict markets but I have more control or insight so I will get it right.

As we saw, one way to cope with cognitive dissonance is to pay particular attention to evidence that confirms proposition *c* and to discount evidence against proposition *c*. So the profits on Glaxo are down to my skill; the losses on Marks & Spencer are the failure of the market to see the truth in the interim. In the end the market will see the truth, Marks will rise and I will be proved right, since legend tells us confidence is key to good trading.

Fenton O'Creevy and his team make it clear that three factors are central in understanding attitudes to risk. Extroverts are more likely to take financial risks. Traders who have a high illusion of control are also more likely to take risks – and they will underestimate the size of the risks they are taking. As a result, they will perform less well. The implications for recruitment are considerable. Companies should be wary of employing high extroverts as traders. There is also evidence which suggests that, while introverts learn from their mistakes if they are punished, extroverts do not. They respond better to praise. This evidence comes from a study of children learning mathematics so it does not directly apply to financial professionals but it is suggestive.

Risk-taking investors are more likely to feel proud of doing something and regret omissions – why did I not buy – more than commissions. Kahneman (1998) argues that risk-taking investors focus on the positive, do not attribute much to luck and resist short-sighted strategies for not taking risks – the market has to fall drastically before I'll invest. These characteristics seem more typical of extroverts. Patel (1997) has found some traders have what he calls 'long loss tails' and are much more willing to let losses run. In the next chapter I look at why some individuals seem so unwilling to sell.

There are two further issues – the personality of gamblers and whether there is any evidence that suggests we can modify our financial behaviour.

The gambler is, of course, the greatest of all risk takers.

The gambler as masochist – spirals of risk taking

Freud argued that the chronic gambler is a masochist who wants to lose. Freud also argued that the gambler is a child who can never stop masturbating and that he is doomed to gamble as a result of childhood experiences. Both the biographies of gamblers and the histories of financial scandals show, however, that individuals do change – especially under pressure. The conventional clerk becomes the big player. S/he starts to take risks s/he would never have contemplated. What pushes them may be vanity, getting away with it, fear, a desperate attempt to cover their tracks or something we do not understand. But they do change, as Nick Leeson did, turning from a moderately successful trader into the man who broke the bank.

We do not yet have all the details of how ex-partners in Phillips & Drew, mostly very experienced City players, lost some £20 million entrusted to Hugh Eaves, who had been their finance director. On 19 April 1999, Eaves confessed to his clients that he had lost all their monies in a series of high-risk trades. In a catty editorial *The Times*'s business news section wondered why the Phillips & Drew partners had entrusted money to a man with a not very distinguished track record and show-off spending habits. But Eaves too probably changed from sober trader to gambler.

It seems useful, therefore, to look at the life history of a gambler to see what pressures and lures can turn someone into a compulsive gambler. Marvin Zuckerman (1991), who has done much research on sensation seeking, claims that gamblers come to see taking risks as the answer to all their problems – financial stress, boredom, depression and even sexual hang-ups. One case history shows how life is more complex.

Gary the gambler

Gary was born in a small Midwestern town. He was the youngest of three boys. His father was killed in the Korean War when Gary was

5 years old. Gary's mother was religious but her three children were often in trouble at school and even with the law.

The only man Gary saw much of was his Uncle Howie. Howie was a local character, famously lazy and laid back. He liked to bet on horses and often took his nephews racing. He fantasized often about big payouts, long shots and getting rich without doing much work. The psychiatrists who eventually treated Gary were sure that Howie's influence had turned a wild, insecure fatherless boy into a compulsive gambler.

When Gary was 16, he left home and worked, putting insulation in houses. He was part of a crew of builders – tough young men. He drank and lost his virginity. After a few months, Gary joined the Navy. Tests found him capable of college and the Navy paid for him to go. In his first year Gary thrived and met Joyce. She was a fervent Christian. Gary decided to ditch his bad habits and became a born-again Christian.

After a year, however, the Navy withdrew its students from the college and sent them to a small military academy. Gary was now back in a world much like that of the insulation crew. The lifestyle was very jockish; the young sailors held drinking parties and played lots of poker. Gary discovered that he had a talent for the game.

At first, Gary sent most of his winnings to Joyce. They were going to get a house together. Gary knew Joyce would hate it if she knew he was making money by gambling, so he lied. The lie had a nice touch; he said he was working for a local evangelist; the faithful were showering him with money and Gary got a cut. Joyce believed Gary, now her fiancé.

The longer Gary stayed away from Joyce the more gambling became his life. It affected his studies. He spent less and less time working. Later he told his therapist he experienced a strong build-up of excitement before playing cards. He only felt a release of satisfaction after a protracted bout of gambling. Gambling was like sex – only it cost much more.

Gary's grades fell but he managed to scrape a degree in mechanical engineering. He and Joyce married and he was posted in Germany. Joyce believed at first that she was a Navy wife leading a normal married life. She knew nothing about Gary's secret, his compulsive gambling.

For about 2 years Gary managed to keep Joyce in the dark, even though he was under more and more stress as a result of gambling. When he lost badly he did extra duties and the overtime helped cover his debts. But the gambling became more compulsive. Gary took larger and larger risks. Partly he craved the excitement. Partly he needed the money to cover his losses.

Gary lost far more than he won. He started to borrow to pay off his debts. He soon owed thousands of dollars to loan sharks. Joyce noticed that money was missing from their accounts. When she asked him questions he accused her of nagging. Gary now forged a number of cheques. He was soon caught, court-martialled and dishonourably discharged.

Gary always promised Joyce that he would go into therapy, re-form and somehow manage to kick the habit. Every time he tried, however, it did not work out. The marriage slowly disintegrated. That failure made Gary gamble even more. He gambled to pass the time; he gambled to pay his debts; he gambled for consolation.

Gary started to work for other betters at horse races. He would accept money from friends to place bets and then use their money to pay off his debts. Some of his friends found out and beat him up. He had his ribs broken.

Gary's story suggests it was when he started to mix with men who gambled and when he discovered he was good at poker that he started to become 'addicted'. This version seems to support the theory of Walker (1995), who claims that Freud and the analysts are wrong. Gambling is not a response to long-term psychological stress or too much or too little nipple. Gamblers gamble because they think – mistakenly – they will make money at it. They feel they can control the odds.

One idea in psychoanalytic literature that offers an eerie echo to some of the research I have been discussing is 'total control'. The Hungarian analyst Sandor Ferenzci (1930) suggested that the gambler has the feeling of a omnipotent baby, the feeling of total confidence and control babies have when they have no under-standing of how the world works. The baby cries and mother gives him the breast; the baby howls and his nappy is changed. Total control.

Total control of the markets is unrealistic but it is the feeling you have when you are a master of the universe on a winning streak or a master of the universe who thinks he is about to hit a winning streak. For most investors it is dangerous feeling.

All the studies I have reported so far assume that attitudes to risk are deeply entrenched in personality and thinking style. There is only one study with adults I have come across which, however, has really tested this – and its results are surprising.

Can we learn?

Wärneryd (1999) reports a Swedish experiment from the 1970s and notes that it is not widely known because it was never published in English. Julander (1975) studied the effect of feedback on saving. He carried out detailed interviews with 215 young women aged between 24 and 28. They had no academic training but they worked full time. Julander asked them about their saving habits, spending habits and personalities. He also asked them to keep detailed diaries and gave the experimental group books in which to note their expenditure. He first found that the more people knew about how they were spending their money the more satisfied they were. When the subjects started to keep detailed records of their expenditure, however, there were some interesting changes. A number of subjects who had never bothered to track their spending were upset by how they were using their money. Those who discovered they were spending too much of their disposable income tended to change their habits – and saved more; those who discovered how little they were spending and how much they were saving tended to increase their spending. Julander argues this shows how knowing about your finances in detail can change patterns of saving and spending. This interesting study suggests we all need detailed self-knowledge of our financial habits.

We have seen that there is a pattern to the personality types that take risks and that this affects how they perceive certain situations. One of my aims is to offer readers a chance to better understand their own attitudes. The following questionnaire is based on the different areas of research I have outlined.

Not recommended for those who hate risk!

Risk questionnaire

Try to answer the following questions truthfully. Some questions are followed by a box. Tick this if you think you would have answered the question differently at any time in the last 5 years.

1   You have an unexpected week off work. Would you rather spend it

   a   reading a good novel? ☐

   b   decorating? ☐

   c   going scuba-diving? ☐

2   Do you drink wines and spirits

   a   every day? ☐

   b   two to three times a week? ☐

   c   never? ☐

   d   at Christmas and other special occasions? ☐

3   You are not happy in your present job. Do you

   a   look for another job? ☐

   b   quit – and then look for another job? ☐

   c   try harder to negotiate with your bosses so that the present job satisfies you more? ☐

4   You are in a car whose driver is going at 100 m.p.h. Do you

   a   sit back and enjoy it? ☐

   b   look out of the back window to see if the police are on your trail? ☐

   c   warn the driver that he or she is going much too fast? ☐

5   Have you been stopped for speeding?

   a   never

   b   once or twice

   c   more than three times.

6   A rich uncle offers you £1,000 to invest. Do you choose to invest either

   a   in a small biotechnology firm? ☐

   b   in a tracker fund? ☐

   c   in a building society? ☐

7   Someone you fancy but do not know well suggests you go away for a weekend together to see how you'll get on. Do you

   a   accept at once? ☐

   b   suggest you might go on a date first to see how you get on? ☐

   c   turn them down? ☐

8   Do you smoke

   a   over 20 cigarettes a day? ☐

   b   between 10 and 20 cigarettes a day? ☐

   c   not at all? ☐

9   You go to an expensive restaurant and find the steak that you ordered blue has actually been served up pretty well done. Do you

   a   politely point out the steak has not been cooked to your instructions and wait for the restaurant to replace it? ☐

   b   say nothing? ☐

   c   summon the head waiter and make a scene? ☐

10   Your boss announces that your company is going to devote all its resources to project X and that for the next month all efforts must be concentrated on it. You happen to disagree. Do you

   a   say nothing?

   b   ask for a private meeting where you express your reservations?

   c   raise the questions at an open meeting where other members of staff are present?

   d   resign in disgust?

11 Would you describe yourself as

a a safe driver because you never go very fast?

b a safe driver because you can handle the speed?

12 You play the lottery every week. Which of the following stakes is typical of you?

a £2 ☐

b £5 ☐

c £30 ☐

d you join a syndicate and pay £10 a week so that together you gamble £120 ☐

13 Many television programmes now have a welter of fast whizzing images. Do you find these

a interesting? ☐

b irritating? ☐

c amusing but they distract from the message of the programme? ☐

14 You are sitting alone in your room. There is total silence. What do you do?

a start to meditate ☐

b do nothing ☐

c put a record on ☐

d start to feel anxious. ☐

15 In your daydreams do you ever imagine that you are a completely different person?

a often

b hardly ever

c enough to know your unconscious is trying to tell you something

d never.

16   Someone offers you £100 if you will

    a   drive your car so that it breaks the speed limit ☐

    b   take off all your clothes in front of a group of friends ☐

    c   break a window that will cost £20 to replace ☐

    d   drink 12 pints of beer or three bottles of wine in 2 hours. ☐

How many of them do you accept? Which is the most difficult?

17   Two friends reveal that sometimes they pretend one of them is someone completely different. It spices up their sex lives. Catherine, for example, calls herself Angie. Which of the following statements represents most closely what you think?

    a   this is extremely weird and suggests their normal sex life is lousy ☐

    b   you hope your lover will want to try it ☐

    c   in theory this sounds fun; in practice it's a bit silly ☐

18   Do you find that you get anxious

    a   rarely? ☐

    b   often? ☐

    c   when you have good reason to be? ☐

19   Your company wants to cut white-collar crime. Employees are asked to fill in a questionnaire and admit if they have ever stolen small items like stationery from the company. What do you do?

    a   tell the truth and admit you have sometimes done it

    b   tell the truth – you have never done it

    c   refuse to answer and suggest it is an abuse of civil liberties

    d   worry because you have stolen a few stationery items in the past 6 months and decide to lie.

20 A friend returns from a holiday in Africa and says they had to eat camel meat. Which of the following best describes your reaction?

   a you utterly disapprove of anything so barbaric

   b how can they be sure they weren't eating camel dung?

   c it sounds disgusting but shouldn't you have a few disgusting experiences in life?

   d you immediately ring up Harrods and ask if they're stocking camel.

21 You receive an unexpected inheritance from an uncle. Before you decide what to do with it, do you discuss it

   a with your bank manager?

   b with your partner?

   c with no one?

   d with an astrologer – it's play money anyway.

22 You reckon this inheritance is

   a a gift from the gods

   b disappointing, you expected to be left more

   c a nest egg to pass on to your children

   d a worrying responsibility.

23 List your favourite sports.

24 How many of the sports you have listed do you actually play – and how often?

25 You are on holiday and at the end of the beach there is a casino. Do you

   a go in every night?

   b go once during the holiday just to see what it is like?

   c decide to risk £200, which represents 2 days' earnings, but rigidly stick to the rule that you won't play after you've lost it

   d never enter?

26 You find that you have turned your £200 into £1,000. Do you

   a bank it?

   b decide to carry on playing and hope to win even more?

   c bank £500 and keep on playing with the other £500?

   d buy something extravagant you've always wanted?

27 You read a description in the papers of how City workers are getting huge bonuses. Do you

   a envy them?

   b wonder about the stress and the fact that their personal lives are shot?

   c think money is less important than job satisfaction?

28 You find that a confidential e-mail has arrived on your computer. Do you

   a squirrel it away?

   b wait a day and then tell your boss it has turned up on your desk?

   c copy it and then erase it from your hard disk.

29 How often during an hour when you're working at a screen do you tend to look out of the window?

   Make a guess if you do not know or, if you prefer, test yourself by getting a friend or partner to watch you and observe your looks.

30 It is 6 p.m. on a Saturday evening. Which of the following is typical of your social life?

   a you have made your plans well in advance

   b you have no idea what you will be doing, you usually wait till the last moment

   c you have no special plans because it's always the same – going down to the pub.

31 How would you rate yourself?

   a usually confident

   b hardly ever confident

   c I know I can get carried away if I think something is right but I try to control that.

32 Compared to other people do you think you are

   a less anxious? ☐

   b averagely anxious? ☐

   c more anxious? ☐

33 Compared to other people do you think you are

   a a bit of a hermit? ☐

   b a good mixer? ☐

   c a good enough mixer if people don't seem intimidating? ☐

34 Compared to other people do you think you are

   a impulsive? ☐

   b a good calculator of risks? ☐

   c cautious? ☐

   d extremely cautious? ☐

35 Which of the following statements best reflects your feelings?

   a I enjoy making my own decisions ☐

   b I find it agonizing to make decisions about my future ☐

   c I always discuss decisions with my partner but in the end I make the decisions. ☐

36 Your boyfriend/girlfriend throws a surprise dinner for you. Do you

   a enjoy it? ☐

   b find yourself taken aback but then get into the spirit? ☐

c wish they had asked you about it, they should know you hate surprises? ☐

d wish you'd been dressed for the occasion? ☐

37 Which of the following statements reflects your views most accurately?

a as an adult I have to take my responsibilities seriously ☐

b inside I often feel I'm still only 10 years old ☐

c people who can't let off steam and have fun are sad.

38 Which of the following reflects your views most accurately?

a I do not like influencing other people's decisions, it makes me feel too responsible ☐

b I can give people good advice but only in some subjects where I have a lot of experience ☐

c I enjoy influencing other people's decisions. ☐

39 Which of the following statements reflects your feelings most truthfully?

a it's much better to have everything planned in advance ☐

b I like to improvise ☐

c Sometimes I like doing things on the spur of the moment, but not often. ☐

40 Which of the following reflects your views most accurately?

a I prefer situations where I take the lead

b I can take the lead in some situations but I have to be sure it will not create a conflict with other people

c I would rather be one of the crowd.

41 'Taking financial risks is something I am comfortable with as long as ...

a the potential rewards are big – over 20 per cent ☐

b it is possible to be well informed about the risks ☐

c my horoscope suggests it's a good time ☐

d I know other people are taking similar risks. ☐

Which of these most accurately reflects your views?

42 What is your attitude to spending a whole weekend doing no work and just having fun

a I try to do that every weekend anyway ☐

b It worries me if I can't show I've spent my time profitably ☐

c sometimes, bunking off is good but you can't do it too much. ☐

43 Which of the following statements is most true about you?

a I find that I often cannot do anything

b I am frightened of committing myself to a course of action

c I would rather make a decision.

44 You find yourself on a date. You are not really sure whether the your date wants you to kiss them.

a you try it on any way ☐

b you never make a move unless you are totally sure you are wanted ☐

c you laugh nervously and say you don't really know if they want you to kiss them and, what with political correctness, you think it's wiser to ask. ☐

45 Which of the following statements is most accurate about you?

a financial security is desperately important to me ☐

b No one can plan for every eventuality ☐

c I like the idea of being financially secure but I refuse to have no fun now because of what my pension will be like. ☐

46 You are given the information that a company you work with has just concluded a deal with Microsoft which will make their shares very valuable. You are the company's banker, solicitor, broker or accountant but you know enough to know they were foolish to give you this confidential information. Do you

   a invest £1,000 in it?

   b worry about being accused of insider trading?

   c borrow £10,000 on a personal loan and use it all to buy shares?

47 Have you ever done any of the following?

   a cheated in an exam

   b cheated on a partner

   c told a lie on a questionnaire.

48 Which of the following statements reflects your attitudes most accurately?

   a I often wish I could push decisions on to someone else

   b I never want someone else to tell me what to do

   c It depends on the specifics of the situation.

49 Did you answer this questionnaire

   a after reading the chapter?

   b before reading the chapter?

   c having sneaked a look at it but then read the chapter?

   d having started by reading the chapter but then decided to take a look at the questionnaire?

50 Someone suggests to you and some other people that you each put up £1,000 to start a part-time business.

   a you go for it if you think the idea is good

   b you can't be bothered, you know most businesses fail

c   you don't want to admit that you're nervous about the idea so you say you want time to study it.

51   Which of the following activities would you rather spend £40 on?

a   two seats at a concert

b   a four-course meal in a five-star restaurant

c   going up in a balloon which gives a good view of London.

52   Which of the following activities would you rather spend £500 on?

a   a trip to Paris

b   adding to your building society account

c   paying off a credit-card debt which is incurring 20 per cent interest

d   acting on a hot tip for a share.

The answers are on pages 162–164. Attitudes to risk are part of our core psychology, but we are not necessarily conscious of what they are. It is not easy to be certain that we can change how we respond to risk, but Julander's work needs following up. Readers certainly need to be as aware of their own attitudes to risk as possible. One of the tasks of therapy, Freud suggested, was to make the unconscious conscious. Look at your results and see what they tell you about yourself.

Answers to risk quiz

(C = liking for conformity; P = liking for power and dominance; RA = risk averse; see page 165 for full details)

1   a 1   b 1   c 3

2   a 3   b 2   c 1 plus *RA*   d 1

3   a 2   b 3   c 2

4   a 1   b 1   c 1 plus *RA*

5   a 1 plus *RA*   b 2   c 3

6   a 3   b 2   c 1 plus *RA*

7   a 3   b 2   c 1

8   a 3   b 2   c 1

9   a 2   b 1   c 3

10   a 1 plus *RA*   b 2   c 2   d 3

11   a 1   b 3

12   a 1   b 2   c 3   d 2

13   a 3   b 1   c 2

14   a 2   b 1   c 2   d 3

15   a 3   b 1   c 2   d 1

16   a 3   b 3   c 3   d 3 – each of these is a high risk.

17   a 1   b 3   c 2

18   a 2   b 3   c 2

19   a 2   b 1   c 2   d 3

20   a 1 plus *RA*   b 1   c 2   d 3

21   a 1   b 1   c 3   d 3

22   a 3   b 2   c 1   d 1

23   You have to use judgment here. Some sports are definitely high
      risk – skiing, waterskiing, motorcycling, racing any kind of car,
      hang-gliding, parachuting, mountain climbing, diving, pothol-
      ing, light aircraft flying, gliding, marathon, roller skating in
      any form. Score 3 points for each of these. I don't claim my
      list is exhaustive so use your common sense.

24   Score 3 for each sport you do regularly.

25   a 3   b 2   c 2   d 1

26   a 2   b 3   c 2   d 2   e 1 plus *RA*

27   a 3   b 1   c 2

28   a 2   b 1   c 3

29   The higher your score – the more times you look out – the
      higher your sensation-seeker disposition.

30   a 1   b 3   c 1

31   a 2   b 1   c 3

32   a 3   b 2   c 1

33   a 1   b 3   c 2

34   a 3   b 3   c 1   d 1 plus *RA*

35   a 3   b 1   c 2

36   a 3   b 2   c 1   d 2

37   a 1   b 3   c 2

38   a 1 – this is essentially a trick question but score a *P* if you answer c as this suggests a liking for power.

39   a 1   b 3   c 2

40   a 3   b 2   c 1 – score a *C* also if you answer c

41   a 3   b 2   c 3   d 2 – score a *C* if you answer d

42   a 2   b 1   c 2

43   a 1   b 1   c 3

44   a 3   b 1   c 2

45   a 1 plus *RA*   b 3   c 2

46   a 2   b 1   c 3

47   Score 3 for answers a and b, score 2 for c unless you are lying on this questionnaire, which is meant for your eyes only and as a tool for helping yourself, in which case chastise yourself for being silly.

48   Score a *C* for a and a *P* for d. The other two answers are not relevant.

49   a 1   b 3   c 2   d 2

50   a 3   b 1   c 2

51   a 1   b 1   c 3

52   a 2   b 1   c 1   d 3

This questionnaire examines attitudes to risk, but, in order to stop those who answer it getting too familiar with the issues, I have also included questions that relate to conformity and power seeking. The answers marked C indicate a liking for conformity and those marked P a liking for power and dominance.

The highest possible score is not certain. If you answered all the questions by choosing the high-risk option and took part in two high-risk sports (see question 23) you would score 165. Theoretically though, someone might be a roller skater, skier, glider, etc. and so their score with 3 points for each high-risk sport could be well into the 200s.

The higher your score the more of a risk taker you are.

Anyone who scores above 130 will be a person who enjoys risks and feels comfortable with them. This is not necessarily a good thing because it may indicate a disposition to like situations which are nothing other than sheer gambles. Anyone who scores over 160 would be well advised to take a deep breath, pause and ask themselves why they like such a high-risk lifestyle. Investment decisions will not be the only adventurous ones.

Anyone who scores in the range 110–130 will be fairly comfortable with risk and would seem to have a reasonably balanced attitude to risk.

Anyone who scores between 85 and 110 will be cautious and rather anxious about taking risks.

If you score lower than this you are likely to be risk averse. You should note how many items you marked RA because these stand for Risk Averse. Score more than 3 of these and you can be sure that taking financial risks is quite problematic for you.

The questionnaire can tell you what you are like. There are no right or wrong answers. If you feel you are either too cautious or too risk-inclined, what can you do if you think you would like to modify your attitudes?

This is a complex question and there are no magic solutions. First don't do anything sudden. Talk about what the questionnaire seems to say with your partner and/or close friends. Do they agree? Is this how they see you?

Those who are cautious will usually find it easier to change their investment attitudes a little by imagining and thinking what it might be like to take greater risks. The next step would be studying either

If you're risk averse, imagine doing this if you want to change!

shares or unit trusts thoroughly because for many people fear of risk is fear of the unknown. You can begin to make some sense of the world of financial risk taking and build up to changing your investment behaviour. This is a rational answer to what may be in part an emotional problem, but there is nothing wrong with a dash of rationality. Being cautious about money is probably a learned habit rather than a phobia.

More problematic are those who are in love with risk taking. They may have more problems in changing their behaviour because the evidence suggests that there are real psychological depths involved in gambling – and therapy has a very mixed record.

The curious traditions of British stockbroking do offer one possible solution, however which only requires one moment of self-discipline. You can, especially if your behaviour has led you to lose money in risky investments, think about handing over your portfolio to a broker authorizing him to deal in a more cautious way on your behalf. You will only have to steel yourself not to gamble on stocks and shares for as long as it takes you to sign that mandate. I am not a major fan of brokers, as this book makes clear, but here they may finally find the therapeutic role some of them seem to want.

If you have ticked more than 20 answers as answers you might have given differently 5 years ago you should note that you have obviously been through good or bad life changes and be especially aware if these made you more dramatically inclined to take risks.

And financial institutions do keep tempting investors with delectable not-so-risky seeming risks. Not even in the small print does it say 'only have a punt if you don't mind losing 90% or even the lot.' Today, analysts and salesmen in Britain are pushing Venture Capital trusts which offer small investors the chance to back new companies at an early stage of development. The trusts also offer a chance of getting tax breaks.

Once it was only the rich or very experienced investors who would seek out such opportunities; now these risk are being parcelled up and marketed for the ordinary investor. Roll up, roll up, ladies and gent, nice fresh risk to buy, you've got noting to lose ... except, as always in history, your pants not to mention the elastic that keeps them up especially if you don't know your risk profile.

six

Going for broke – the secret art of broking

In the last chapter we looked at the dangers of illusion of control. Stockbrokers often have real control over other people's money. Paul O'Donnell of Brewin Dolphin told me that the real fun of broking was running discretionary accounts, accounts where once a strategy has been decided on the broker operates without having to ask the client for permission to do particular deals. Hugh Priestley spoke affectionately of private clients whose main personality trait is inertia. The inert are not known for their fear or greed. I am not suggesting that either O'Donnell or Priestley take any advantage of this situation but both have been so long in the City that it does not seem remotely odd to them.

Commentators like Robert Haugen (1996) contrast the broker–client relationship with the doctor–patient relationship. No one would dream of giving a doctor total discretion over their body; and doctors have been criticized throughout the 1980s and 1990s for not talking to their patients properly. Yet people give brokers total discretion over large amounts of their money. Indeed, controlling other people's money is perhaps the oldest tradition in the City. It shows how psychologically unaware most brokers are that no one has even raised this issue or pondered its problems or psychological consequences. Tom Basso (1994), as we shall see, writes of his clients as if they were unfortunate delinquents whose poor financial habits have to be healed. The broker is really a therapist!

And these therapists have their hands on ever-rising sums of money. One Liverpool broker who did not want to be named told me he still had on his desk his commission book from 1959. Then a deal for £200 was normal. 'If you did a deal for £1,000 it was big money. Today £10,000 is nowt. £20,000 is a more appropriate level to deal in.' Paul O'Donnell of Brewin Dolphin suggested that £50,000 was a reasonable sum to start dealing in the markets.

Despite all this, many brokers are worried about their future. It's an indication of the strains many in the City feel that Hugh Priestley, investment director of Rathbone, told me that he had recently been at a conference where the headmaster of Marlborough College said they were recruiting teachers in the City because many graduates could no longer work there. For many of them the Square Mile was paved with angst, not gold.

All these anxieties are understandable given what the evidence suggests about brokers' skill and their relationships with their clients. There is more research on the performance of brokers than ever before; pension funds especially demand that. This research has also led to work on the optimism of brokers, on their poor record at picking stocks, on how they respond to conflicts of interest and some aspects of the broking personality. The interviews I have carried out also give some indication of how brokers think they select shares – and these descriptions are psychologically interesting.

City traditions aren't just picturesque; they help reinforce the status and power of brokers. These traditions allow brokers to pretend that it has been normal for over 250 years for perfectly sensible persons to hand control of the day-to-day management of their money to others, if not to the kindness of strangers then, at least, to their good sense.

The bizarreness of that struck me particularly in March 1999 when I had lunch with Mark Sanders, art editor of the cool bible *Dazed and Confused*. Mark is amused by the stock market. Two friends from his art college went to work for brokers. One had to be moved after turning up with too much cocaine on his face. The other regularly clocked £400,000 bonuses but developed weird sexual habits. His £400,000 prick could only have sex in a stretched white limo, for example. No one cared as long as he was doing the money, Mark said.

Mark's friends would not have aroused much curiosity in the 1980s. Paul O'Donnell of Brewin Dolphin told me, 'Then it was no secret that the gents was known as the powder room.' No secret perhaps in the City, but it just makes you wonder how clients in the shires might have felt if they knew they had entrusted their money to the well-known firm of Smack and Crack. Many clients may have imagined their money was in the hands of the classic Brit stockbroker, old public school, respectable brolly in respectable hand whose worst tipple was Glenfiddich!

The brolly broker thrived from the middle of the 19th century to Big Bang in 1986. Social connections mattered; commissions were easy pickings; clients were rich. Paul Ferris (1961) in *The City*, describes an eternally Tory world where the old-school tie waltzed with the regimental sword, but controlling clients was a feature of that world too. Long liquid lunches were quite normal. Sometimes partners of large houses fell down dead drunk in City watering holes and they were allowed to snooze the booze off. No one minded too much if they didn't turn up for the afternoon. Finance was fun for the privileged.

Matthew Orr, managing director of Killik & Co, told me that when he started to work in the City in the 1970s 'To get a stockbroker was impossible. You might inherit one from Mummy and Daddy or you might meet someone at Oxford or Cambridge who became a stockbroker or run into one at a dinner party.' Orr remembers diffident army majors asking him to become their broker and apologizing for the fact they had only £300,000 to invest. 'I normally said we can probably manage to fit you in,' Orr smiled. You had to be rich to get rich by investing. The market was not for ordinary people; they could stick their money in the Post Office. Orr put his finger on an important psychological truth – brokers have power over their clients.

Psychologists know that if you want to exercise control, the setting in which you work and see clients matters. In researching this book I was greeted at Cazenove (set up in 1792) by two immaculately groomed men dressed as butlers. I restrained myself from calling them Jeeves. At Brewin Dolphin I admired a very public display of the copperplate-filled ledgers used when Dickens was still alive. Paul O'Donnell said they traced their ancestry back to 1749 and a market trader called Alfred Brewin and so Cazenoves were johnny-come-latelies. Rathbone in New Bond Street claims to be even older than Brewins. It was set up by a Liverpool merchant, William Rathbone II. His ledger book of 1742 beats Brewin by 7 years. Even an arriviste upstart like Panmure Gordon, founded in 1876, displays its historical trophies – the clipping from *The Times* announcing the setting up of the firm in 1876, when Mr H. Panmure Gordon opened for business, a letter from the 1880s offering Chinese government bonds to a select few and a red box with more 19th-century cuttings.

Such displays of antiquity trumpet the soundness of these firms. If you are a client you should feel privileged. Until 1986 the organization of most stockbrokers reinforced the gentlemanly image; they were not limited companies but partnerships. Important clients had their own individual partner. The partners owned the enterprise and were entitled to a share of the profits. Ian Francis, a boisterous man, was in his early twenties when he went to work for Phillips & Drew. The annual declaration of who was being made up to partner was a major event.

'We knew something was up in 1985,' he told me. 'There were perhaps five or six people who were very good and who would normally have become junior partners but, when only one did, we knew something was on the cards.' The next year the partners sold out to the Union de Banque Suisse.

Francis now runs the convertible bond section of West LB Panmure. He misses the partnership arrangements. 'You went in, you worked hard for 10 years and, if you were good, you could expect to become a partner. You were investing your hard work in the firm.' A partnership was not just a question of earning more money; it was also serious status. Goldman Sachs considered becoming a public company in 1986 and 1996, but one factor that dissuaded partners was having to face people who had spent years working their way up and telling them they were never going to be partners. Now Goldman Sachs have gone public.

The demise of the partnership means that time horizons, that favourite City phrase, have shortened, Francis thinks. It is not just that 'loyalty means nothing, but that people focus on immediate rewards,' he explained. 'In practice, that can mean conflicts between making money for your clients and making money for your firm.' Brokers are faced, he suggested, with this conflict more often than they like to admit or investors like to know.

Today, conglomerates such as Merrill Lynch and Goldman Sachs rule and they have even less subtle ways of impressing clients. The conglomerates have concentrated power as never before. They can make markets, sell shares, provide stockbroking services, advise on takeovers, fix corporate finance, arrange flotations, run pension and investment funds, and offer a bewildering variety of unit trusts. These operations are divided by Chinese walls which means that they are kept utterly separate, and that separation is supervised by compliance officers. It is called providing an 'integrated service'. But this integrated service may not be the best service. Some recent American research suggests there are serious conflicts of interest between brokers and their clients and that brokers are put under pressure to make money for their institutions even if, for example, that means giving clients bad advice.

One of the skills of brokers was finding interesting shares, picking unlikely winners. Now, though there are still many smaller company funds and recovery situations, many think the safest way to make money is to regard most shares on the stock market as too small, too uncertain and too much hard work to follow. And where does that leave the broker and his expertise? As redundant as Arthur Scargill's miners? They fought a long battle not to be replaced by robots who could dig underground, and lost. The great advantage brokers have is that many of their clients rely on the same and seem to be magnificently, supinely, loyal.

The Internet has even created a new animal, day traders. Roger Yates of the giant fund manager Invesco told me, 'One of the things that is happening now are so-called day traders who use the Internet and make maybe 500 trades a day and work on tiny margins. They're happy if they make 5 cents a share and they trade frenetically. It's just not a business I recognize. ' In Britain, however, day trading was slower to start than in the States. But it is now taking hold with many companies such as P&O and British Airways offering facilities to investors. Very unlikely people go into it. I met Charles Jones who is in his late thirties. Jones had been working in a restaurant when he decided to try his luck at investing. He insisted he was making better money than ever before, though he refused to tell me his secret. In early January 2001 he told me 'I'm bullish' ; he did not think the fall in high-tech shares would last long. I asked him what he based this on and he smiled knowingly at me. He had information, instincts, intuition that the rest of us lacked.

The inertia of clients

In theory, brokers should provide some of the best evidence for the motivation of clients. They talk to them all the time and so we might expect them to develop some insights into their aims. Almost to a man, however, brokers told me that the psychology of markets was simple; markets are driven by greed and fear. 'Human nature doesn't change,' Priestley told me. But I soon found out there was a paradox. Somehow they – and their clients – are not so predictable or crass, even though, of course, it is brokers and clients who make up the markets.

'Greed is good' is not a mantra you find spoken or, perhaps, even believed. Many brokers say that they offer a uniquely personal service, that they are about preserving wealth, not taking risks and throw up their hands in horror when talking about evil and greedy speculators – you'd almost think they were Marxists.

Paul O'Donnell of Brewin Dolphin gave a virtuoso display of 'the guff', stressing the difference between stockbrokers and investment funds. 'They provide a product, we provide a service,' and then he smiled – as if he realized he was uttering marketing speak.

Many brokers claim, as Paul O'Donnell does, that the real fun is still in handling individual accounts. Accounts are either *advisory* when the broker suggests but the client makes the final decisions, or *discretionary* when the broker runs the account in the best interest of the client but does not have to get approval for every deal. Brokers prefer discretionary accounts.

Brewin Dolphin has 70,000 clients, most of whom are discretionary. 'My own clients range from some who have £5,000 to some who have £17.5 million,' O'Donnell told me. 'I wouldn't recommend being in the market if you didn't have £50,000.' O'Donnell went so far as to say, 'We don't see ourselves in the business of wealth creation but of wealth preservation.' It is surprising that brokers divide clients into worthy long-term investors and evil speculators only out to make a fast buck, but this particular piece of 'guff' was constantly mouthed at me.

A more unflattering view came from Priestley. He said, 'If you have private clients they tend to stay with you and not to leave till death overtakes them. I spend my time in a gentlemanly way looking after gentlemanly and ladylike investors.' What Priestley savours is time to make decisions, which dealing with individual clients or running a unit trust allows. 'It's much less frenetic than dealing with pension funds.'

'The average private client is a dear,' Priestley told me. 'As long as the dividend cheques come in on time and they're the right amount and the administration is fine, they're happy.' Inertia rules. It is an interesting addition to the view that markets are driven by fear and greed. That is not utterly so in middle England whose inhabitants are content with a middling dividend in mustn't-grumble shares. Priestley said that it was no good investment experts telling someone who had bought Marks & Spencer shares when they were 89p that there was a disaster – they had lost momentum and were only 340p. 'And many older investors are like that.' Since my partner's mother keeps share certificates in a sock and is far from sure what she owns in what, I know Priestley has a point. It is telling that when Marks & Spencer held their annual general meeting in 1999, their most troubled year, out of 307,000 shareholders only 2,600 turned up. Yet the company was shocked so many put in an appearance – and there was standing room only. Slightly more turned up in 2000 when the share price was below 300p.

The best private clients (from the broker's point of view) are undemanding and grateful. The worst, though few brokers will say so publicly, are those who are on the phone all the time, wanting advice, needing a chat, those who actually insist on a relationship and demand to know more than every 6 months how brokers are handling their money.

Pension funds and pressure to perform

I pointed out earlier the relevance of the Yerkes Dodson law, which states that people perform best when they are under pressure but not under too great pressure. In many interviews brokers, like analysts, stressed the pressure that being constantly measured caused them.

The most troublesome customers in this respect, as far as the brokers are concerned, are pension-fund trustees, who are afraid that they will be criticized if their fund is not doing well. Trustees threaten to move their funds if performance is not tip-top.

Priestley put on a surprisingly convincing Yorkshire accent imitating the gruff pension-fund trustee who carps 'quarterly figures were 3 per cent lower than last year ba gum and thy performance's down 3.2 per cent. What you going to do about it?' While the trustees say they are only interested in the long term, they expect something to be done in the sharpish short term. Or else.

Priestley told me that he was glad to have escaped that constant pressure. 'With the insurance funds there's pressure to do well on an annual basis and pension-fund trustees say they look at the record over 3 years but actually they get very wound up with the quarterly figures. Unit trust comparisons are monthly. You can be put in a situation where you do something to look good in the short term.' He has known recent instances where people have bought telecom shares for two reasons. First, if the pension fund quibbles, you can say everyone else also has telecoms. Second, telecoms have been having a good run. But, by focusing on the quick fix, fund managers and brokers can miss better long-term opportunities. Cabot (1998) noted that fund managers become especially frantic at the end of quarters when 'they pull out all the stops including high portfolio turnover and excessive risk to keep up with and surpass the index. They also use end of quarters for window dressing.' The idea is to show better figures when their performance is compared.

Priestley believes that the tendency of big houses to go in for a company strategy or so-called 'direction to investment' is the result of fear of criticism by pension funds and their advisers. It is a reaction to pressure and offers a way for individual brokers to avoid feeling ultimately responsible. Investment is by committee.

'What critics don't like is if company Fund *A* is up 20 per cent while Fund *B* is down 5 per cent. They like to see the movements in the same direction. So at Schröders, for example, you can buy any food retailers as long as it's Tesco,' Priestley said. If big houses have well-defined investment policies, which exclude much of the market, it should give smaller fish the chance to weave in and out.

Having argued that unconscious motives seem to affect the behaviour of investors – and having looked at some of the methods analysts use – I wanted to see how brokers themselves explained their strategies for picking shares. These explanations come down to a mixture of judgements based on financial statistics and subjective criteria. It is the interplay of these – and the different emphases different brokers give them – that is psychologically interesting.

Blue bloods inspect the management

Cazenove is the most exclusive stockbroker in the City. The Queen is one of their private clients.

David Mayhew, a gaunt man who is one of the long-serving partners, was, like many people I talked to, worried about the fact that I am a psychologist. His two children read psychology at university, 'and they say that allows them to understand why I do things,' he smiled.

Mayhew is proud that his company has managed to retain its independence in the face of American competition. 'I think that's because we have no ambitions for global domination. We think we provide a useful service for some clients.'

Mayhew advises companies on investments and takeovers. He insists that the fundamental issue in whether or not to buy into a company is that of assessing its management. I asked him how he judged the quality of management, but he could point to nothing either very systematic or scientific. 'I don't really know how you do that. My judgement is born out of being exposed to a lot of situations. You get very close to people in some situations like takeover battles.' His experience made it possible for him to have sound judgement. It was a question of knowing people, of knowing their track records. More than that he could not say specifically.

I was surprised that Mayhew hardly tried to justify how to judge management – perhaps because it seems such a quaint view and he is a man who, despite his age, loves the new technology. He was the broker who had praised his tiny screen which gave him instant access to all the deals in all the markets in the world. Yet, like Lenhoff discussing sentiment, he was nebulous on discussing judging management.

Mayhew added that he would miss the young people he works with when he retires and that he will miss 'the competitive, adversarial nature of the business.' 'You need to be highly aggressive,' he smiled and in that honest self-analysis showed some of the truths beneath the traditions.

It's a sign of continuing changes in the City that late in 2000 Cazenove announced that they would float on the stock market in 2002. The historic partnership had to do it because it was the only way of generating the monies they needed to drive their business forward and to keep their team together.

Unbalanced markets

Charles Clark has worked all his City career at West LB Panmure. He is a nervous man who worries a great deal about why he is doing things and prides himself on being different. He controls about £250 million of money and a small unit trust. Clark was very eager to explain his philosophy. 'I don't just focus on equities. I like to think of myself as a three-dimensional investor with money in equities, bonds and currencies.' He is particularly known for handling the funds of a few very wealthy people – some who entrust over £50 million to him. His clients come by word of mouth. 'I get recommended. My track record is good.'

'I don't meet them often,' he says,' and I don't really talk to them much. I work to their mandate. There's an annual meeting. They're very bright people and they often give me ideas.' Clark thought this gives him an unusual – and gratifying – degree of freedom to follow his fancies. One client has £17 million with him and they speak just a few times a year.

Clark prides himself on having thought through a philosophy of investment. After going into the Army and serving in the Gulf and in Northern Ireland, he got an MBA (Master of Business Administration) in the City. 'I did it part time and I loved it. It made me think. I usually have a book going – Popper, Soros – people who are much cleverer than me.' Suddenly he reminds me of a diffident general who admits he did win the battle, but thinks he didn't deserve to. The other side had better tactics, better weapons, but, happily, shot themselves in the foot.

As a result of his studies, Clark thinks he understands the risks of following what he calls 'the herd'. The herd is under pressure. Most fund managers are, in fact, working for pension funds. Clark even thinks we may see investors suing pension funds that have not given good returns. So the tracker funds seem wonderful to pension funds. 'No one can complain if you put money in the Footsie Index. They can all sleep soundly.'

Clark rejected this intellectual caution. He did not want to sound conceited. 'I'm trying to distance myself from the market and analyse the process of behaviour of the market, so I position my funds to try and take the benefit of flaws in the market.' The word flaws often came up. He thought the market is flawed; many of his fellow investment managers are flawed; he's flawed himself.

'The market isn't balanced. If it were perfectly balanced, I wouldn't have a job.' Clark excludes some sectors of the economy completely. 'There are areas I wouldn't touch with a bargepole because the economics don't work. We've got, for example, far too many firms providing chemicals. In the car industry we've just got massive supply chasing too little demand.'

One way in which Clark fights against becoming part of the herd mentality is to introspect. 'In my mind I'm after a certain reflexivity. I try to dislocate myself from the market.' He thought this helps him spot situations which can be exploited rapidly. There is nothing wrong with a dash of profitable short-termism. He divides his funds into 70 per cent for long-term investment and a more speculative 30 per cent with which he will dip in and out of the market when he sees good opportunities.

To cope with information overload Clark specializes, for now, in six different areas – technology, outsourcing, global franchises, utilities, transport and health care. Those areas carry less risk, he argued. He did not think there is a mystique in assessing risk. 'A lot of what is needed is sheer hard work and many people in the City don't believe in that.'

Sheer hard work means not just going through the company balance sheets, but also visiting companies. Here again we have this strange paradox. The computer rules, and firms are hiring more and more mathematicians and physicists; yet many of those who make major investment decisions rely on a sniff and hunch about the quality of management. Is he a sound bloke at Incorporated Widgets?

Clark admitted that there is no real science in picking stocks, but he felt there ought to be. Some brokers make fun of the very idea.

My Liverpool broker told me, 'What I do is stick my fingers up in the air, feel the wind, take a pin out and then stick it on any of FT shares. It works too. No, I like being facetious.' His rules turned out to be simple. Go for shares in big companies and trust in history. The index may be high in the short term but in the long term equities win out. 'Timing is essential, of course,' he added. But time is on the side of the investor.

Like Mayhew and many others, Clark believes judging management is key. 'If I can do it, I meet the management. I think I'm quite good at recognizing honest management – the chief executive who looks after his shareholders and not just himself. I think you can spot a management team who believe in what they're doing and who are totally sold on their product. I believe that if you want something badly enough you'll find some way of getting it.'

When I explained that I was interested in speculative bubbles, Clark ran with the phrase. He likes to think he can spot bubbles 'and the skill is to see how much further the bubble has to go.' A sense of when the market in a particular share is out of equilibrium is partly a matter of crunching the numbers, 'which is very boring but it's a discipline.' He gave me two examples of times when he reckoned he did well for his clients.

A few weeks before we talked the telecom company Nokia said that by the year 2002 there would be 1 billion handsets in circulation. 'I did a calculation on the back of an envelope and I reckoned that that meant that everyone on the planet earning more than £20,000 would be the proud owner of a handset. I just thought that was balls.'

Clark turned out to be prescient in the long run. By the end of 2000 it was becoming clear that the mobile-phone market was more limited than dreamers believed. Nokia had to report slower sales than expected and the company came under some criticism for allegedly massaging figures so as to make its market share look bigger. Other mobile phone makers like Motorola did worse.

In 1999, Clark also saw a position in a company called Alcatel. Alcatel make engineering and telecommunications products. 'Alcatel had issued a profit warning.' One of the large American institutions decided to sell 40 million shares – 'that was about 10 per cent of the company and they were selling at any price. I looked at the fundamental values and they seemed perfectly good. If we were working together now, we'd look at some numbers and we would talk.' Someone's fear that Alcatel would lose and lose became his opportunity for profit. For Clark that's the skill of picking the right time as much as the right share.

Momentum trader

Priestley also likes the new technology. When he gets into his New Bond Street office the first thing he does every morning is look at the screens. 'And I make a mental calculation about whether I'm ahead or behind and if something is doing well or badly. I look particularly at those shares where there seems to be a lot of movement.' He smiled as he said that he did not watch much television at home, but his favourite viewing was the financial screens and their changing prices.

But Priestley's approach is very different from Clark's. 'I'm what the Americans call a tape trader, someone who keeps an eye on the tape crawling at the bottom of the screen.' Priestley is convinced that the screens form a real network. The screen allows one to keep in touch, to feel the pulse of the crowd. 'The market is a crowd – we like to feel we are part of a crowd and not going against it.'

'By instinct I'm a momentum investor,' he told me. 'So I buy stocks that are going up and I sell stocks that are going down.' He agreed that it sounded a recipe for disaster but said in fact it was not so. If you stayed with the herd, you were likely to do well most of the time. He came close to saying that he saw himself as one of the herd – and liked that. 'I take the view that if there's a lot of movement in a share, somebody out there knows more about it than I do.'

Momentum trading has been boosted by the tracker funds. Priestley gave me an example. 'We know that Vodafone is buying Airtouch. At present, Vodafone represents 4 per cent of the value of the Footsie 100. When it owns Airtouch it will represent about 5 per cent of the Footsie. Therefore all the tracker funds will have to buy more Vodafone. So we might as well buy more Vodafone now.' This decision has nothing to do with judging the value of Vodafone shares, but is a logical deduction based on the fact that demand for the shares will rise in the short term.

I asked Priestley if Rathbone had the kind of scorecard of 'good', 'bad', 'promising' and 'do not touch' shares that Lenhoff described in Chapter 4. He smiled and shook his head. 'No. We're not so far advanced. We've just got a recommended list, but if someone wants to buy breweries there isn't a direction of investment policy which says, "Thou shalt buy Bass, thou shalt not buy Whitbread".'

Priestley understood why Clark ruled out some sectors because the numbers did not crunch. Priestley told me he excludes some areas for personal reasons. For example, he would not touch textiles because someone can 'always make anything four times as cheap as we can here. I'm also not very good on Australian gold shares and I seem to be bad at buying housebuilders.' He offered no explanation for this strange mix of failures.

'I prefer the financial sectors – banks, insurance – though I know there will always be good stocks in unloved sectors.' (That is a lovely phrase, 'unloved sectors' – wallflower shares no one wants to tango with.) Priestley has also been a fan of telecom shares.

Priestley also advises the University of London Pension Fund, which has some £800 million. The experience has forced him to revise his view that active investment will make more money than passive. The pension fund has found that tracking a number of indexes – including indexes abroad – has done far better than it would have ever expected. That worries Priestley for the obvious reason: why should clients pay fees to fund managers or brokers if a computer does it better? Priestley never trotted out the 'brokers provide service' guff. He argued that active trading does work, but that it tends to work best when a broker is dealing in his own domestic market that he understands.

Accounting instincts

Paul O'Donnell of Brewin Dolphin said that his experience as an accountant is still with him. He believes that you should look for value. He told me the way that Brewin Dolphin choose shares is complicated.

Brewin is now made up of three different companies. One of them, Wise Speke, is very structured, Brewin is pretty much *laissez-faire* and the other is a mixture of the two styles. He suggested they are rather less structured than Capel Cure Sharp, whose methods Mike Lenhoff described.

'We have a morning meeting,' O'Donnell told me, 'which is open to all. There isn't the exclusivity of Capel Cure Sharp, where decisions are handed down by seven or eight senior executives and the rest have to execute. As Brewin has 22 offices, the meeting is broadcast on the tannoy, 'which means it has a certain Orwellian flavour.' The meeting is led from London and Edinburgh. They report on overnight news, talk about any company reports 'and what we think of them', and set the parameters.

O'Donnell compared the situation to playing in a sports team. 'I used to play rugby and I think it's very much like rugby. You can take risks within certain parameters. If you want to go beyond those parameters, you talk to your captain.' If a dealer in Marlborough wants to make a riskier or unusual investment, the rule is that he or she should talk it through with the Centre.

'We want the Centre to provide a coat hanger. We do have a list of stocks, but you don't have to buy from the list. The Centre provides the research that justifies the deals.' Handling the sheer weight of research is a major undertaking. 'We have secondary analysts who get all the stuff from outfits like Merrill Lynch and we have some rather well-known technical analysts. But we take the view that the client isn't going to want to wade through 60 pages of reports, which include the colour of the socks the chairman wears.' Advisory clients 'want it given to them in *Daily Mail* speak,' O'Donnell said. 'I hope that's not doing them down.'

O'Donnell insisted that stockbroking is a very personal business and that often when a broker joins a new firm, 'if he's a half-decent broker, his clients will come with him.' Yet while 70 per cent of his clients have become friends, he was not dewy-eyed about that. 'Some investors are very sophisticated and some know nothing at all and, then, there are those who think they know a lot. In the stock market a little knowledge is a dangerous thing.'

Patrick Marvin of Capel Cure Sharp, who manages the accounts of a number of clients, saw his job as being one of reassurance. 'We very much try to give them confidence by explaining the firm's approach,' he told me.

I put it to O'Donnell that what investors really want is brokers who make money for them. He countered that private surveys commissioned by stockbrokers reveal what clients value is, first and foremost, honesty, then broker knowledge, then performance and only last is that vexed question of how much brokers charge. In other words, clients did not care that much about how brokers handled their money as long as the personal relationships were good.

I cannot help being a little sceptical, especially because psychologists know that you can interpret and reinterpret survey evidence. Such surveys, of course, currently provide brokers with much-needed comfort. If investors rate relationships above performance they will never leave you to do business through a computer.

One of oldest traditions in the City is that of restrictive practices and one of the strongest was that brokers had to be in the City and certainly not on the high street; you could not buy and sell shares like fridges or cheese.

'Please call in – we're a shop'

Matthew Orr, who told me the story about the retired major who apologized for being able to invest only £300,000, is the managing director of a chain of share shops called Killik & Co. Their main office is by Victoria Station in a rather grand building.

At reception, a girl said, 'Do you have a broker you deal with?' A middle-aged woman in jeans turned up and said she had an appointment with her broker. Every 2 or 3 minutes there was another call – someone else wanting to speak to their broker.

Orr is a lean sinewy man who enjoys smiling and is obviously a good salesman. He is also passionate about what he does. He told me, 'I suppose I'm a serial entrepreneur.' He started in the City in a conventional stockbroking firm but was a little restless. In 1985 he opened share shops in Debenham's department stores. 'They worked in 1985 and 1986 but then 1987 happened and it all went horribly quiet.'

Orr then teamed up with Paul Killik, who had been his boss in the traditional stockbroking firm, and they started a shop in Chelsea. Matthew's nanny was at a loose end so she answered the phones and did the typing. 'We both passionately believed in making stocks and shares available and we were fed up with some of the historical baggage of stockbroking, the companies like Capel who, if you say you have £50,000 to invest, will tell you, sorry, but come back when your capital has increased.'

One of their first clients was an aristocratic old lady who was a compulsive gambler and who always lost money but consoled herself because brokers 'always give me a free glass of champagne'. Not surprising, Orr suggested, when they made so much out of her.

'When we first started we were completely ignored. No one in the City thought we could make a go of it or make money out of it. And it was considered that we were tacky or mad.' They had a point to prove. Orr described himself as very competitive – he used to row at university – so he relishes the fact that Killik & Co. now have 11 shops and 25,000 clients 'and hold on their behalf £1.1 billion of assets'. In 1999, the company made profits of over £3 million on turnover of about £13 million.

'One of the things I like about being my own boss is that you can make decisions. In big firms you can't. If you have a good idea it has to be approved by half a dozen different committees and here I don't have those constraints,' he said.

Killik's shops are in upper middle-class areas like Hampstead, Battersea and Chelsea, where people have income rather than assets. 'But I'd much rather have as a client a 40-year-old man who is making £60,000–£80,000 a year, can save £10,000 a year and is interested in growth and a little risk, than a major who just wants to be in blue-chip companies,' Orr said. Over his lifetime those savings will be significant.

Orr denied that money was his overwhelming motive. Now that they were successful, companies were offering them large amounts of money to sell, but he did not want to. 'I'm unemployable,' he smiled.

A key skill of his business is to cultivate relationships. 'People don't immediately trust you. A typical first call we get is from someone who wants a PEP, has £6,000 to invest and says he wants to put a toe in the water. Then a few months later, the PEP is going well and he rings up again and says, ''By the way, I've also got £10,000 in the building society. What do you think I should do with it?" A new client entering into the world of the stockbroker fears both that it is elitist and that they will cheat him.' Orr did not deny his clients wanted to make money, but many also wanted to understand the workings of the market and the opportunities it presented.

Killik recruit men and women who are good at building relationships. 'The minimum requirement is that they have a degree and that they're PSDs, which stands for being Poor, Smart and with a Deep Desire to be rich. We don't go for the traditional public-school types. Very often the people we recruit are career changers. We have a few people who went into the forces on short-term commissions, for example. We also have people who trained to be engineers, but who got fed up with the fact that there is no money in it. And accountants who got bored. We also take people who have run private clients.'

Every client gets their own 'dedicated broker', Orr said, 'and we do call people. Nine times out of ten when a broker rings it's a good-news call to say those BT shares have risen or might you be interested in this share.' The purpose of the contact is twofold – business and human.

Orr argues that, in a bull market, investors may feel they can do without a broker and deal through American-style 'execution only' brokers. But 'it's different when it crashes. When the market wobbled in September 1998, for example, Charles Schwab got 2,500 calls from people who used them to buy and sell. They were asking what was going on, and should they buy or should they sell.' Schwab could not give advice, however, since the company's service offers only the execution of trades. The moral is simple. Clients need brokers, but well-trained brokers.

Once Killik has trained its brokers, 'We give them the basis on which they can give advice. And they can have their own opinions – otherwise they would be just mouthpieces. I can see situations in which quite legitimately one of my brokers would be recommending to a client to sell Glaxo and another would be recommending to another client that they sell Glaxo.'

Sometimes, Orr admitted, the broker–client relationships did not work. 'I get phone calls from clients who say that they just don't like a particular person, and usually we change the person who is the dedicated broker.'

The fuzzy logic of investment decisions

Unlike Adam Smith's rational man, Orr knows that investments can be driven by personal enthusiasms. He gave me an example of journeys he has taken into some investments.

'I'm a real anorak,' Orr started. 'And I bought one of these hand-held organizers called Psion.' Through Psion he got interested in what else the company was doing and found they that were involved with Sindism – an operating system used to send e-mails. Orr asked himself what microchips are needed to run this. He discovered that they were called risk processors, and so he became interested in a company called ARM. ARM's chips sit inside most mobile phones, but part of the next-generation technology is made by a small company in Sweden called Sendit. Their technology allows people to get e-mails on mobile phones. Sendit are a small company capitalized to the tune of $30 million. Though most brokers currently shy well away from small shares Orr bought into Sendit.

Orr then started to look at other companies ARM was involved with and found that 29 per cent of the company was owned by Acorn, who used to make the BBC computer. 'The basic assets of Acorn are worth 300p a share, but their price at present values them at 186p a share,' he said. No one had spotted this. Most of Acorn's value comes from its share in ARM. (In late April 1999, a month after I talked to Orr, Acorn was effectively bought up by ARM, with its shares valued at 254p.) In May 2001, ARM has grown and now is the 74th ranked company in the FT-SE 100 and has weathered the tech fallout better than many others.

This kind of free association and fuzzy logic seems very much like the thinking style Cottrell and Weaver used in the Cow & Gate coup.

Brewin has an additional technique. Using its status as one of the City's oldest companies, the brokers invite the managers of large companies to be interviewed by them. O'Donnell stressed that this was not a presentation, but an interview whose aim is to grill the CEO of major players.

'For example, we'll invite the chief executive of Boots to see us and he'll sit in a room with maybe 20 people and be asked questions. The questions may be very varied. They include things about ethics too.'

O'Donnell told me his wife worked with psychometric tests and he was well aware of their imperfections; and he knew the limits of what interviews can reveal. Nevertheless, he had no doubt that one of the best ways to test the management skills of a company and its growth potential was to cross-examine chief executives.

The impression the chief executive makes becomes a crucial part of the equation that decides whether or not Brewin recommends the shares.

Lenhoff's downplaying of the role of management – an issue I explored in Chapter 4 on analysts – seems a little bizarre to O'Donnell. 'If you're manufacturing widgets maybe management matters less because what counts is the process, but in service industries like advertising, finance or PR management is everything.' Like most brokers, O'Donnell specializes. 'Pharmaceuticals and retail are my areas but that doesn't mean I won't buy something else. But I can get advice.' Colleagues cover every sector in the stock market.

Judging management seems to him more and more important these days because of the state of the market. 'Given the volatility of the market I don't think technical factors are as useful as they used to be. If someone says to me, forget about what the company does, forget about the management, look at the charts, then I'm sceptical,' O'Donnell told me.

Focusing on possible choices of shares remains a key skill. O'Donnell says that Brewin Dolphin has a call list of the FT 350 and, within that, the brokers look at all the fundamental values, the assets of the company, its earnings, its track record. Like Clark, he recognizes the essential discipline of number crunching.

Throughout our talk O'Donnell was at pains to emphasize how mundane much of what he did was. Yet he was more willing than anyone else to admit he sometimes worked on sheer instinct. 'There are one in ten, perhaps one in fifteen, times when I decide we really ought to buy that.' He believes too that the older he gets, the sharper that instinct is, though he could not give any rationale or justification for that.

O'Donnell talked a lot of 'the fun' of doing it 'by the seat of your pants'. And sometimes, his humour gets the better of him. In one panic an investor asked him what to do and 'I said put your money on the 3.30 at Kempton. And the horse won. I gave him the race, he picked the horse. We make a great team.' O'Donnell's views are interesting compared to those of Robert Haugen, professor at UCLA. Haugen suggests that brokers' recommendations are influenced by the social situation they find themselves in *vis à vis* their clients. They have to have something to talk about with them so brokers 'produce news to impress and as a result they are attracted to stocks which have interesting and exciting prospects upon which they can build captivating stories.' Extroverts, in particular, will behave in the way Haugen describes because they like to please and to be the centre of attention.

Such factors may help explain aspects of the increasingly detailed – and mainly American – research which points to the fact that brokers tend to be poor at predicting the market's movements.

Brokers' recommendations and conflicts of interest

David Dremer and Michael A. Barry (1998) looked at earning forecasts made for 1,200 companies between 1974 and 1991 by American brokers and analysts. Some 73 per cent of these forecasts were out by over 5 per cent. The industry whose results were best predicted was the tobacco industry. There were a large number of forecasts which were out by over 15 per cent. Nearly all analysts tend to be optimistic on average. Dremer and Barry found that analysts and brokers were roughly 40 per cent worse than executives of the companies in forecasting future profits. In essence, the brokers and analysts often ignored what the company forecasts themselves had said in the previous year or quarter and, then, produced more optimistic predictions. The authors accuse analysts of ignoring important issues and conclude: 'few recognise the persistent nature of large scale forecasting errors or have the ability to make adjustments to them.' Womack (1997) found similar patterns with new issues. The situation is worse in the States with New York firms which tend to be more optimistic than regional brokerage houses.

An interesting cross-national study compared the accuracy of forecasts with how much information had to be disclosed to comply with that country's accountancy laws (Higgins 1998). Hung Higgins found that the more disclosure was required the more accurate were brokers' forecasts. The worst countries were Switzerland and Japan. What is especially worrying, however, is that even in the two most 'honest' countries – the United States and Britain – brokers' forecasts were significantly over-optimistic. The optimistic bias was found by Hung Higgins to be 29 per cent.

The failure of analysts and brokers to predict well is, in the final analysis, best measured by the bottom line. A study of how well brokers and funds did in 1997 found that only 5 per cent of brokers and 11 per cent of mutual funds did better than the Standard & Poor's 500 shares index.

British studies suggest that only 18 per cent of investment funds consistently outperform the FT-SE 100. The discovery that in the mid-quarter of 1999 Schröders funds beat the FT-SE Index by just under 2 per cent was seen as big news and merited an editorial in the *Sunday Times* Business News, so poor is the reputation of brokers currently.

If stock picking is a true skill, we would expect certain brokers and analysts to consistently do better than average. Another study looked at how 1,500 US domestic equities were recommended between 1978 and 1998. They found that the brokers and managers who did best were those who had the widest spread of shares. The top firms tended to hold an average of 70 shares at the same time whereas the worst tended to hold just 45. The idea that brilliant brokers can spot a few wonder shares and coin extraordinary profits seems to be quite simply wrong. Beckers (1997) sweetly suggests that we should not underestimate the role of luck. He divided brokers into aggressive, skilful and lucky ones and complacent, unskilled ones. He re-analysed thousands of their recommendations. He found that 35 per cent of aggressive and skilful brokers still ended up in the red after 36 months. Admittedly, the unskilled brokers did worse. Another study suggests that brokers in America who have an MBA will consistently do better than brokers who do not.

Perhaps most worrying is evidence that brokers' recommendations are often influenced by their role as brokers' for particular companies. Carleton et al. (1998) have also looked at this conflict of interest when brokers are the brokers for particular companies. They claim that in a study of 250 companies they found the company's brokers were significantly more optimistic than other brokers about the prospects for that company. In a number of instances, they found that, when other brokers recommended selling, the company broker much later just switched to a HOLD recommendation. In one case Joyce Albers, an American analyst, resigned because she felt this 'pressure to be positive' was unethical.

Carleton's findings mean in essence that the broker who is closest to a company, and who one might expect to provide the most accurate forecasts, may actually be providing the least accurate forecasts despite all the Chinese walls which are supposed to protect investors.

Stockbrokers often talk about fear or greed driving the market, but they are more reluctant to talk about their own vulnerabilities. Pressure to be positive will particularly affect extroverts who want to please their group. Extrovert brokers will also admit less anxiety about pressure to perform and will find it harder to learn from their mistakes. Suggestible and extrovert brokers are likely to be least skilled at understanding risk and resisting the case that analysts put forward for buying certain shares. The weight of this research is worrying, of course. It suggests that brokers and analysts are poor at telling their clients the nature of the risks different shares involve. One of the sectors where brokers read the market especially badly are oil and gas shares.

Clark's colleague at West LB Panmure, Ian Francis, blames the obsession with performance not merely on tracker funds but on the electronics that make it possible to update the Index constantly. 'In the 1970s you used to have the Index updated every hour and jobbers looked at the boards to see deals being done. Then it was every 30 minutes and they glanced at it, but still looked at the boards where deals were done. Then the Index was updated every 15 minutes, then every 5 minutes. Now you can see a deal the moment it's being done. The time horizon has tightened.' It all adds to the short-termism everyone condemns and everyone is affected by.

Haugen (1996) summarized these findings and claimed 'these results are going to be very hard to explain by those who theorise under the paradigm of the rational economic man.' And if brokers are irrational in a consistently optimistic way, then that means, of course, that most are better suited temperamentally to bull markets.

No fun in bear markets

William I. La Tourette liked bear markets because they gave him the chance to outsmart the opposition. But I found no broker today who liked them or who admitted enjoying the situation in early 2001. Only the older ones had experience of a sustained period of falling. Both the 1987 crash and the August/autumn 1998 decline were very short term – lasting less than 6 months. No one is clear whether the reverses in the NASDAQ in late 2000/early 2001 constitute the start of a deep bear market, as opposed to a fall in an important sector which had previously gone far too high. We still have not seen the catastrophic fall Andrew Smithers predicted.

O'Donnell said the 1987 crash 'taught me more in 2 days than in 10 years about personal relationships. I grew up. This was serious stuff. Clients didn't know what to do. I learned more about investor behaviour – I saw the panic that is inherent in any client, no matter how cool or controlled they seem to be. People were seeing their own personal savings going down. They could see losses of 40 per cent and they were counting on that money to retire and they were retiring next week.' It highlighted for him the fact that people were driven by greed and fear. 'And curiously you end up making more money for the fearful investors.'

Charles Clark echoed the point, on the basis of personal experience. He had lost a great deal of money on a deal and found the experience agonizing. It taught him what his clients can go through.

Priestley remembered the bear markets of 1972 and 1974, which he found depressing. 'Every day you came in and you adjusted yourself to the market being lower. Then you went home and you came in and it was still lower. It was horrible.' He seems to have taken it personally, which is perhaps how bear markets hit optimists.

He says that while the 1987 crash was a blip, the late summer and autumn of 1998 felt like a bear market again – 'and stressful'.

Priestley said the French have a word '*anomie*, meaning things have no bottom – and that is how it felt then.' The short bear market of late 1998 is well behind us, however. In May 2001, the high-tech bubble burst but the Dow Jones got over 11,000 again – just. Trackers still attract money and worry. Why does someone need the advice of a broker if all they need do is buy into a tracker fund, which will offer them a good return without too much trouble?

Many stockbrokers point out that trackers only do well in a bull market. The Liverpool broker, for instance, had recently counselled a client against a tracker fund. 'I told my client he'd be a fool to do that. At the moment the market's up but what happens when tracker funds have to cope with a falling market?' It is a view that was often repeated.

William Cabot, who is scathing about analysts and brokers, argues the long bull market has also made investors unrealistic and too demanding.

One effect of the success of the tracker funds has been that it is harder to be a contrarian – an investor who goes consistently against the trend. Clark, whose investment philosophy comes perhaps closest, has still picked six sectors to invest in which are currently fashionable. The success of tracker funds of all kinds is only increasing the strength of the group mentality and making it riskier to go against it because in the 1995–2000 bull market there were short-term profits to be made by mimicking trackers or just staying in fashionable sectors like telecoms.

I came away with the feeling that the one consistent fact brokers told me was not to invest in textiles or engineering, the unloved stocks, and otherwise different brokers tended to stress different aspects of share-picking skills. The momentum traders did not care too much about value; the value traders were slightly frustrated by the lack of bargains, but thought their ideas were basically right. Current prices mean it is hard to find 'forgotten' shares in any but rather small companies. Many brokers are pessimists about the market, but they see that the real pessimists, who have been saying for years that the market is too expensive, have been wrong so far.

There's nothing wrong in such diversity of views, of course, but it does signal that perhaps the broker does not know best – and that investors should be careful about how they handle their relationship with their broker.

How to handle your broker

Institutions are becoming more assertive in their relationship with the companies they invest in. While as a small investor you cannot expect the companies you invest in to listen to you, there is no reason why you cannot be firm with your broker and expect him or her to listen to you and your investment needs. Don't get into the apologetic pattern Orr found, apologizing for having only so much to invest. If you have a broker on an advisory basis get and use his opinions, but do not be ruled by them. Brokers, as I've shown, have their own enthusiasms.

My talks with brokers makes it clear that clients should be careful to retain the initiative in talking to them. Brokers clearly prefer discretionary accounts where they do not have to justify every trade they make, especially as private clients are on the whole much more forgiving about judging performance. Killik was the only company where I got the feeling that talking to clients might be seen as a real essential – partly I suspect because Killik sees educating its clients as part of their mission and their business.

If you are a discretionary client ask yourself why you do not want to take day-to-day responsibility for your money. There is nothing to stop you negotiating a relationship with a broker where he will ring you if he has interesting ideas, but still need you to approve them. If a broker has good reasons for going into a particular share he can explain that to you.

Keep the psychological high ground. Find out the personality of your broker. Try this test. Offer him or her a boiled sweet. If he sucks it slowly, fine. If he crunches it and eats up the little pieces, beware: he is an impatient oral type and may lose you lots of money. (I do not claim total reliability for this test, but, of course, to try it you have to meet your broker face to face. For many clients, the broker is just a voice on the phone.)

Ironically, at a time when brokers feel under pressure, many stress the quasi-therapeutic nature of their relationship with clients. Psychologists know that in such relationships the expert has – and feels he has – real power over his clients. This makes sense, and is acceptable, if the expert is someone you have gone to in order to be healed. It does not make sense, and is not acceptable, if the expert is someone you have gone to for financial advice. But this strange power relationship suits brokers and financial advisers in the seemingly more democratic investment climate of today. With thousands of clients, professionals like to make sure clients know that when they bother the broker they are being a bit pushy, a bit of a nuisance; most like to make you feel that you must not bother the doctor. This doctor, the broker, will be doing very nicely out of you thanks – and all of them know it.

Turn the table on your broker. Given what I have said about the Yerkes Dodson law, inquire how stressed he feels. If he responds by turning your question into a joke, worry. That kind of joking is likely to be a defence and would suggest he is truly stressed. Do not take the advice of a stressed broker.

Be canny. Many brokers – especially small brokers but not execution-only services – will give you free advice if you ring to discuss a specific deal or a choice of deals. You've got £5,000. Do you buy Dixons or British Airways?

It is also important to get a sense of whether the person you are talking to is generally an optimist or a pessimist – and how stable that trait is. A good way to open that discussion – and incidentally a sensible question for brokers and other financial professionals to ask them themselves – is to ask:

- Have you always been an optimist? If so, can you remember a time when you were pessimistic?
- Have you always been a pessimist? Why have you clung to this belief in a long bull market?

Psychologists who offer hard and fast rules are unwise, but generally speaking, I would worry about permanent optimists, because they will deny the existence of a bear market until it is very late. Pessimism was a reasonable response between December and April 2001. I would also worry about permanent pessimists. They may have read the fundamental value of shares correctly, but they are not much good at reading 'sentiment' or at understanding the herd.

While it is true that in the long term markets have gone up, as Priestley said, we should not forget Keynes's less famous remark, 'The long term is a succession of short terms' (which may be of more practical advice than the famous 'In the long term we are all dead').

Do not be frightened of brokers. They should be there for you – not you for them.

seven

Inside the markets – dealers and traders

On the Stock Exchange today Nathan Rothschild would find no pillar to lean against, no floor to dominate. His personality would probably make itself felt in screen-to-screen trading, but he would not have the audience waiting on his every move. The shift to screen-to-screen trading has made the psychological qualities that allowed some men to dominate the floor much less important. Standing six foot three and having a voice that can boom impressively across a crowded room does not help much if all the deals are being done on computer.

In 1999 when I started this book two specialized London markets – the London International Futures Market (LIFFE) and the International Petroleum Exchange (IPE) – as well as the Chicago futures market still had trading floors so it was still possible to glimpse what these old exchanges were like, and how psychological factors affected success and failure. LIFFE and IPE are both open outcry markets where traders meet and bargain, bid and sell face to face. Everyone I talked to insisted personality was a key factor in successful trading. Simon Rubins, who manages traders for E. D. & F. Man in London, said 'traders need to be astute and assertive', for example. Others said they needed stamina and, less kindly, that they needed to be obsessed, quick and greedy.

Traders on the commodities, futures and foreign exchanges, it has been argued, are under more pressure than any other City professionals. They can't fall back on intangibles; mo one cares whether

195

they have good relationships with clients or how much they know about technical aspects of markets. A trader is judged by profit and condemned by loss. Are they good or bad? The bottom line tells all.

I have argued that today a major cause of pressure on market professionals is information overload. Traders are particularly likely to suffer as they have little time to make decisions. Robert Laughlin of GNI, a company on the IPE, told me customers often asked him for advice, advice about the way the market would go in the next 10 minutes or 30 minutes. Traders have to decide, to take the risk of being proved wrong. Characters who ponder deeply, weigh the pros and cons for a long time, probably would be better off seeking alternative employment.

A number of traders interviewed did not want to be named because they felt traders had already got a bad 'greed is good' – or should that be 'greed is god' – image. They complained they had the worst press of all the groups involved with financial markets. They were mocked as Porsche-pushing barrow boys, testosterone-high spoilt brats who were overpaid and addicted to the non-Coca Cola kind of coke. At the IPE one of the first questions Dr Nigel Glen, vice-president of market services, asked me was if I intended to do a hatchet job. Traders were nervous about their image, he said. Nervous and yet a little in love with being bad boys. Some like being seen as rough trade, the opposite of the sober old brolly brigade. Rough trade is energy, a real love of risk, the buccaneer spirit. A film made for Channel 4 about a LIFFE trader showed him taking drugs as a matter of routine and he made no attempt to hide it.

Simon Rubins told me that when the LIFFE Exchange was opened by the Queen, one trader warned he had every intention of mooning Her Majesty or, if not providing her with a full moon of his buttocks, at least showing off his patriotic Union Jack boxer shorts. LIFFE was terrified of the bad publicity and issued dire warnings to the individual and his firm if he did anything of the sort. 'In the end he didn't show up for the opening,' Simon told me. Many traders found this disappointing.

LIFFE dealers didn't behave any better when Prime Minister Tony Blair visited them. He was greeted with yobbish behaviour till one trader came up to him, all smiles, and asked for his autograph. A relieved Blair signed only for the trader to below-the-belt him shouting 'it's not for me but for a friend. I don't think much of you.' Which got cheers all round from the traders.

It is hard not to see such behaviour as, among other things, a response to intense pressures including class pressures. On the old Stock Exchange such behaviour would have got you hammered but then all the brolly brokers had been to the same public schools and they did not have to survive in such a cut-throat world. Today, the situation is very different though. The bottom line – are they making or losing money? – is the only thing traders are judged by.

The dying pit markets

In 1999, LIFFE and IPE were still operating as 'open outcry' markets. Today LIFFE is an electronic market but IPE has stayed with the tradition.

Ironically, LIFFE and IPE are actually the newest financial markets. LIFFE was set up in 1982. IPE was set up in 1980. Both deal in options and futures. You walk to IPE through St Katharine's Dock near Tower Bridge. The exchange itself is in an unremarkable office building but it is one of the hubs of the world's oil trade.

The IPE allows people to buy and sell oil and gas futures. 'These are all paper transactions,' Nigel Glen conceded. But the daily amount of paper is huge. On an average day 60,000 lots of oil are traded. The daily production of Brent Crude is 70,000 lots. Two-thirds of the world's output is handled here.

You wouldn't think it was anything as important. From the gallery I looked down on to a floor that was smaller than expected. Traders stand in small hexagonal metallic pits. In one pit they deal in Brent Crude; in another pit they deal in natural gas, a much smaller business. The pits dominate the floor. Behind them there are desks, booths and telephones where dealers take orders from their clients. Hanging down from the roof are screens which give the latest price, the latest trades and, crawling along the bottom, the latest headlines.

Traders wear different coloured jackets. The rhythms between them are mysterious. At times they lounge around the pits, doing nothing much. Observing the scene are officials from IPE, referees almost, whose job it is to monitor the trades. Suddenly the quiet shatters; in its place a hubbub of noise and gestures as people shout bids and buys. Dealers make frantic hand signals that owe much to the hand signals bookies make at race courses.

Dr Nigel Glen smiled 'You need a really loud voice. It's not a very nice place down there. There have been women traders but ...' Glen's voice trailed off, suggesting the raw sweaty place was no place for women. As I looked down on the floor I saw none in the pits at all though there were one or two dotted around. (It's ironic, of course, that the new head of the London Stock Exchange, Clara Furse, made her reputation at LIFFE where she at first defended the open outcry system, but then came to see the exchange had to switch to electronic trading).

Roger Laughlin at GNI, a company on the IPE, who is 40 years old, has been working on the market over 20 years. He got in 'through connections, like most people. My Dad was a commodity broker, dealing in sugar. It's very much a question of who you know. As a small boy I visited the commodities exchange. Then I started pretty much as an apprentice when I was 16. About 2 years later I came on to the floor.'

When he first started work, Laughlin told me, 'I wasn't intimidated. I felt the thrill of it, the excitement.' Over the years the amount of work has increased dramatically, but the basic principles are much the same. 'Our idea is that it's a little bit like an auction, with buyers and sellers of a commodity that moves. It may move for political reasons or technical reasons.' As long as it moves, there's a market.

Laughlin's company deals for many major players on the market including petrol retailers and oil producing companies. The market exists, Laughlin stressed, because there are some 60 companies trading on the floor – brokers, oil retailers, banks, oil producing countries. And he made one surprising admission. Instability was good for business and so he had to confess he had to 'be a fan of Saddam Hussein because he is so unpredictable that he creates business.'

Ironically, Britain's largest oil retailer BP Amoco who could trade directly on the Exchange does not. Nigel Glen who used to work for BP told me he thought that was because they would be such a dominant presence – and many traders would mimic their traders. So BP Amoco deal through different companies which gives it a better chance of keeping the markets guessing about its strategies.

Both IPE and LIFFE argue their markets are not about speculation but have a serious economic justification. They were set up to help to manage risk. The rationale for setting up the IPE was clear. Large companies have to buy petrol, oil and gas. In the past 10 years the price of oil in particular has been very volatile. Between January 1999 and April 1999 the price of Brent Crude moved from $10 a barrel to $14 (a rise of 40 per cent, after all) to over $34 and then down again to the $28 level. Earlier in the 1990s the price had hit $40 a barrel. In 2001, oil was trading between $28 and $34.

In a paper in *Pipeline*, the official quarterly journal of the IPE, Jason Perl (1999) argues that volatility in oil prices has been greater in the 1990s than in most decades. Perl argues that IPE has helped because 'oil futures and options have introduced an element of stability and security in an environment which had previously been inherently erratic and unpredictable.' His argument supports the justification that IPE has a role other than out and out speculation.

Though investors buy and sell the right to buy or sell a real physical product, futures trading still causes some nervousness among investors, even sophisticated ones. A study in 1995 by CIBC Wood Gundy asked organizations that did not use derivatives why they did not. A total of 45 per cent answered that the level of their exposure did not justify using derivatives. But 17 per cent also said that they didn't have enough knowledge to do so, and that lack of knowledge made them anxious about the risks involved.

Creating new risks

Unlike stock markets in the past, which offered an arena to which companies could bring their shares to sell, LIFFE and IPE see their role as creative. IPE, for example, has a product development unit which looks for new kinds of risks and vehicles to market. This has uncanny echoes of Michael Lewis's coup at Salomons which I described in Chapter 5. The development team at IPE is planning a pilot on trading emissions. The British government is likely to announce schemes by which companies will be given permits for the amount of emissions they produce. Company *A* and Company *B* will both have to reduce emissions to 85 per cent of current levels. Company *A* finds it easy to reduce emissions to 50 per cent, so it will sell on the pilot exchange the 35 per cent of emissions it still has available.

The product development unit is also looking at whether the Exchange should launch a weather based derivative contract. The idea started in November 1998 when Scottish Hydro Electric and Enron announced an agreement. Under the deal Enron would compensate Scottish if the temperature fell below a certain level over a period of time; on the other hand, Scottish would pay Enron compensation if the temperature climbed higher than this specified level.

The kind of risk product IPE are thinking of launching would allow a gas utility to hedge against good weather, for example. A gas company will expect to sell a certain volume of natural gas in the winter. If the weather is warmer than usual, consumer demand will fall and so the gas company will not sell as much. So the company can insure against that, as it were, by buying a derivative linked to temperature. If the winter is warm the company may sell less gas, but it will offset those losses against profits it makes on the derivative.

I can see the form of the market in the future. Derivatives will be based on temperatures in Brighton. Gas companies will punt for the weather to be warm. Suncream companies will buy the opposite risk. If it is cold, sales of cream will fall, but sales of gas will rise. There are already trades of this sort in the USA, so companies can hedge against snow, hail, tornadoes and, probably, thunder. Individuals also do it, but it is a very risky form of trading.

LIFFE is perhaps even more anxious than IPE to prove that it does not exist to encourage speculation, but to provide respectable companies with means of hedging against their real risks. Its glossy brochure trumpets that it provides hedges against risks, especially risks of currency changes, and not vehicles for speculation.

But while the futures in oil and gas are not that hard to understand, the main risks traded on LIFFE often look to be essentially speculative. (If you really believe in free choice and free markets there is nothing wrong with speculation, but it has had a bad press ever since Walpole accused stockjobbers of ruining industry.)

A sight of the markets

Given that these markets are public institutions it's surprising how hard it is to see them in action. You can't just turn up as you could to the galleries on the stock market when there was a floor. You have to make an appointment and it helps if you know someone who knows someone. IPE were very helpful, but with LIFFE I had to find a trader prepared to show me round.

Luckily my accountant's son-in-law had been a trader on LIFFE. The first time I went to visit Simon Rubins of E. D. & F. Man Locals, he apologized the moment I arrived at his office. Simon is 29 years old and very amiable. He wears short-cropped hair and is slightly gawky in a suit which could be an undertaker's. This very sober look is totally wrecked by his brazen yellow tie. Simon's small office near Cannon Street is dominated by a trading terminal.

Simon did not get into LIFFE through connections. He studied law, but found it hard to get articled as a solicitor. So, he became a legal adviser to a company that executed trades on LIFFE. 'I checked with the Law Society. As long as I carefully told people I wasn't a qualified solicitor I was doing nothing wrong. I sent the Law Society copies of the contracts I was doing.' Simon was thrown in at the deep end very quickly and had to sort out a dispute with a big client. It was the kind of dispute, which often happens in a fast-moving market where much depends on hand signals and other gestures.

Simon worked as a trader and eventually became part of team that managed a group of 16. He firmly believes in the importance of psychology in making good traders. When I first went to visit him to observe LIFFE, I turned up in a leather jacket – and no tie. Simon was very apologetic. There was no way my leather-jacketed self would be allowed to view what was going on, even though I would be tucked away in a room looking down at the trading floor from behind a glass screen. Maybe it's because its members have a rough trade image that LIFFE insists no one can even look at their work unless they're formally dressed.

Simon thought we might as well make use of the time so he sat me down in front of his screen in his office. He said 'I'm going to talk to you about ticks.'

'Ticks,' I repeated – blankly.

On the screen Simon showed me a graph that tracked the price of the German bond index. The price changed minute by minute. At 10:00 a.m it was 116.48, at 11.00 a.m it was 116.61. Each single number was called 'a tick'. So the difference between 116.48 and 116.61 was 15 ticks. Each tick was worth £10. If you had bought one unit at 10 a.m. and sold it at 11 a.m. you'd have made £150. A small deal could easily make you £2,000, or lose you £2,000. This is not a game for the faint-hearted. If your trades have done badly during the day you will be asked to put up more margin on deposit. Simon didn't think it was a good idea to trade on LIFFE unless you could afford to lose £10,000 without any real pain.

The trading tribes

I returned a few days later wearing my best suit and tie, fit to view LIFFE. Simon and I wandered over past Cannon Street Station into a modern building. After Security checked we were expected, we went up an amazingly long escalator. 'It's very quiet,' Simon apologized. The quiet reflected the fact that many traders had already decamped and were doing electronic trading from their homes, offices and mobile phones some months before all trading on LIFFE would become electronic.

The floor of the exchange was also quiet. From the viewing gallery, the LIFFE floor stretches away like a set in a sci-fi film. Screens that flash the latest prices, the latest trades and headline news hang over the floor as at IPE. There are again hexagonal metallic pits where men – and it is nearly all men again – mill around. During the hour I spent watching, most of the time nothing much was happening. Then occasional manic outbursts of energy, shouting, waving, gestures, hands on foreheads, fingers flashing, flexing, counting – trading.

What makes it feel even more surreal is that traders from different organizations wear different strips. E. D. & F. Man are in red and white, Paribas Futures are in lurid orange, Prudential Bache in black. Traders who deal on their own account wear red jackets. They look like brightly coloured fish in a metal aquarium. The official explanation is that it is important for people to know who they are trading with. The different colours make recognition easy. But one has the feeling this could be a sports area with different teams in different kits.

Through the glass screens at LIFFE you can't hear what's being said so, with Simon, I watched a dumb show, with traders occasionally coming to manic life. At the IPE either the sound is louder or the glass less thick. As I stood peering through the glass partition with Nigel Glen, I could always hear a murmur; suddenly, that murmur would well up. Traders would scream, gesture, fling themselves into total animation.

On both exchanges, traders use sign language to make deals. There's something primitive about non-verbal language, so when traders snap into life, I had the feeling I was watching a tribe of apes. At LIFFE you use your hands to gesture the price, how many you're buying or selling. The fingers dance.

'The price is forward,' Simon told me, 'so you gesture the price you're dealing with on the fingers of your outstretched hand.'

'You signal the actual amount on your face,' he added, so that would indicate the number of lots you are dealing with. The traders signal in frantic rhythm and nod or shake their heads as well.

What makes this activity seem even more like children or animals at play is that the trading floor at LIFFE looks a complete mess. Paper is littered all over the trading pits. The mess is swept away at the end of the day. So around noon, when I was looking down, there was a carpet of discarded paper scraps. The IPE is marginally – but only marginally – more hygienic, probably because there are fewer actual trades. I was reminded of the fact that German slang for securities is toilet paper.

To the side of the pits at LIFFE, as at IPE, are little kiosks, literally telephone booths where brokers speak to their clients. They take orders, dispense advice. In these booths at LIFFE there were finally a few women. Traders usually start on the phones and then graduate to the pits, where they can make huge profits for themselves and their companies.

Simon pointed out some of the characters on the market including a trader from Merrill Lynch who had started his professional career as a a a boxer.

What struck me was how quickly dealers had to react. Laughlin told me he reckoned the qualities any traders needed were 'aggression, numeracy and experience in that order.' He now manages traders and he wasn't interested in academic numeracy. 'It's more a question of being able to keep in your head figures from 1 to 100. A good floor trader may have to keep 6 to 7 trades going at one time. He'll need to know that he's buying 6 lots from one person and 24 from another to put together what a client wants. He has to think on his feet.' And he has to think quickly. Nigel Glen argued sheer physical presence counts for a lot – and made yet another comparison with sports – almost like in a rugby scrum.

There are referees whose job it is to keep an eye on the market, to report the deals that are made. Since everything is initially done by using sign language, there are disputes as to what was intended, what the price or the amount was. A signal to sell 1,000 German bond index options at 115.03 can be misread as buying them at 115.13. You just have to forget or misread one finger. As each tick is worth £10, the difference on the deal would be £10,000.

Sorting out one of these disputed cases was Simon's first job because a large customer maintained a trade had been done at a different price from that at which it had been agreed. Eventually, since the customer was a large bank and a long-term client, they split the difference and the traders bore 50 per cent of the loss.

As an observer of these markets, Nigel Glen is less sympathetic than Simon Rubins. 'These are markets of pure short-termism' Glen told me. He had worked at BP and he had been involved in business plans that projected results 15 years ahead. 'What dealers are interested in is whether they make money today. If you say to one of these guys but you're going to lose money in a year, they say they don't care.'

Robert Laughlin of GNI disagreed. Companies and individuals trade for different reasons – hedging future price changes, making sure that they did have oil to deliver and speculation. 'That's what

Markets at work.

makes the market. You'll have the local contingent trading on their own account and you'll have companies who use the market more strategically to hedge,' he said.

In both markets, there was long controversy about going electronic. Glen said that many traders loved the feel of the daily market. Many at LIFFE regret the move to screen-to-screen trading (by 2000 all trading was screen to screen) but not just for nostalgic reasons. They like person-to-person dealing for all its hardness. Simon added that, 'The trades have to be honest because people work eye to eye.' Once computer trading was the only form of trading, you could ask your mate at Merrill Lynch to tell you what the positions Merrill Lynch are going to take. The sheer importance of Merrill Lynch means it would be almost certainly profitable to mirror their trades.

Simon also told me in 1999 he was worried that, with LIFFE changing to a screen exchange, many of the traders were going to be trading on their own account. He suspected many of them would start to lose significant amounts of money.

Simon thinks he was not such a good trader. You need to be totally assertive and instantly assertive – and he thinks he just wasn't assertive or loud enough. It's instant assertiveness that's wanted. It's also important not to brood. Laughlin believes the over-academic are at a disadvantage. 'You don't want to think too much about the job. I don't want someone to tell me that they're not sure this is a good time to buy because I have to do what clients tell me,' he said.

Laughlin has seen a great deal of burnout among traders. 'The hours are immense. I know there was a lot of attention in the 1980s to yuppies making huge salaries, but what people don't realize is the sheer hours people work; you have to literally live and die the job.' Laughlin starts at 6.30 every morning and doesn't usually finish till 9 in the evening. 'There's no respite. There are many people who just wouldn't consider doing it. You're on the phone all the time. It's very tiring.' Yet he told me 'I love it.' And then he added he couldn't think of anything else that he could do for living. It's precisely for that reason that many LIFFE traders are now planning to trade on their own account.

Through the weariness you have, Laughlin insists, 'to keep a level head. That means you have to keep off the vices of the world.' Clients look to traders to advise them on the state of the market. 'The advice we give is very short term. We're looking to see what the market is likely to be 10 minutes or 30 minutes ahead.'

Laughlin added that he had been lucky. In 22 years he had worked for only three companies. He had many colleagues who had worked for three companies in 5 to 6 years. 'Once there was loyalty and companies always traded through one firm, but loyalty has changed over the years. Companies use a number of brokers so it's very competitive. We've become mechanical tools for doing deals.'

'It takes a lot of physical stamina, of waiting just standing around for something to happen.' Nigel Glen added he knew of one trader who was 27 who had had three heart attacks. 'I think that says stress,' he added. Simon pointed out LIFFE is brutal. It is not just financially brutal, it is also psychologically brutal. Other dealers soon know if you are doing well or badly. Failure is very public – and failure means you've failed to understand the market at that moment.

At the age of 40, Laughlin told me, he was in no position to retire.

He was looking ahead to working for another fifteen years. He had no wish to speculate on his own account. 'I get enough grey hairs from the stress as it is.'

The stress to deliver

This thumbnail sketch of trading supports many of the findings made by Howard Kahn and Cary Cooper (1993) in *Stress in the Dealing Room*. They studied 225 dealers in foreign exchange, swaps, Eurobonds and gilts. Rather unfortunately they lumped these results in with studies of analysts in 10 City institutions. Nevertheless a fairly worrying picture of traders and dealers emerges.

Dealers are young. The average age was 32 and predominantly male. Many of the things they like about the work reflect macho values. One of them said: 'There's the risk. The risk of who can make most money. It's an ego trip. It's legalized gambling; the adrenaline surges.'

Kahn and Cooper found that City dealers are more stressed than the general population. They reported far more depression and other mental health problems than comparable groups of workers. One-third of dealers drank more than 30 units of alcohol a week – and some drank up to 95 units a week. They were very much computer potatoes and took very little exercise. Half the dealers were concerned about their weight. Many reported getting home after 9 p.m and often it was their families who bore the brunt of the stress they felt. Some said they were ashamed that they took it out on their families.

Kahn and Cooper were worried that many of the dealers showed the kind of behaviour typical of those prone to having heart attacks. This is not a health manual for City workers, but the Yerkes Dodson law shows people perform at their peak when they feel under pressure – but not too much pressure. Kahn and Cooper also found that many dealers complained they were under additional pressure because they were badly managed and had to deliver relentlessly. In many ways that's not surprising. Traditionally, good traders move up to become managers but the assertion and aggression good traders need – the ability to make a short-term kill – are not good qualities in managers who have to nurture and motivate staff.

You would expect badly managed dealers to feel the opposite of 'well-being'. Unfortunately Kahn and Cooper made no attempt to link a sense of well-being and/or levels of stress with performance, but it has to be a possibility that it harms their performance. That would fit the London Business School work covered in Chapter 5.

I want now to look at the life and work of a trader who works for a bank. He and his employers insist he remains anonymous.

Pressure and the anxious trader

Alex's day starts very early.

Wapping 5.30 a.m. A mile from the edge of the City, there are cobbled streets.

The alarm screeches. Alex hardly moves. His head hurts. A heavy night. He downed too much booze and some weed. The clock radio clicks on the LBC Financial News. He doesn't want to know about Tokyo Financial Futures. Or Third World pharmaceuticals.

He goes on automatic. Shower, shave, suit. The City expects smartness. Alex can't face cycling in to work. The minicab firm he uses tells him he can't have a cab for 20 minutes. He should have booked last night. He tells them he'll take his business elsewhere.

The moment he's snapped at them he feels sorry, but calmer. He pours two glasses of apricot juice down his throat. The streets are quiet. He reckons he'll get a black cab coming in from Bow. He doesn't want to go into work feeling stressed. He gives himself five to look at the river. Alex has a hobby. Pirates. He lives 50 yards from where Captain Kidd swung from the gallows.

Captain Kidd swept down the Thames in 1697 in the *Adventure Galley* on the way to the East Indies. On the high seas he captured argosies of treasure, fleets of gold, boxes of rubies, emeralds, sapphires. He was the finest pirate of them all, Alex reckons. Kidd never revealed where he hid his treasure. Some 3 years later, betrayed by his backers, Kidd sailed back on the Thames. In chains.

Bound for Newgate. Headed for the gallows. Execution Dock. You can still stand there at Wapping.

Alex is diffident about his fascination with Kidd or maybe he thinks he ought to serve me up something psychologically interesting. He says he likes to think of himself as a latter-day buccaneer, taking big risks for big rewards. Someone told him when he first started in the City 'bankers are dreamers.' He dreams of becoming rich enough to get involved in backing expeditions to salvage treasure.

Alex walks away from the dull, brown river, through a web of canals and pretty modern bridges. He hails a cab and 10 minutes later he's at Liverpool Street.

Alex buys and sells shares mainly for the bank's big clients, but he also trades for the bank. Alex was recruited from Warwick University and paid the princely wage of £27,000 in his first year. In the good years that followed his base salary went up to £75,000 and bonuses usually topped £100,000.

Alex grabs an almond croissant from a cafe. He walks into the bank's imposing marble halls and takes the escalator up. He likes the sense of belonging to a bank which can afford to follow the Victorian tradition of showing off to the depositors with fine halls.

Matthew Orr, founder of Killik & Co, told me: 'Stockbroking does have a lot of historical baggage. When people enter the grand halls they're impressed. They seem to forget that the Bank is doing this with their money. But it does impress people.' The marble pillars worked their psychological magic on the £300,000 majors; they felt grateful such grand brokers would look after their little fortune.

In the last few months Alex has started to worry he'll never make the money of his dreams. He heads for the coffee machine because he needs caffeine to unglue his brain. He sits at his screen. He wishes he hadn't hit the booze last night, but he knows why he's been hitting it. He seems to have lost the trading knack. Last month, he lost his bank £750,000. Another bad month and he'll be sacked. Human resources give no warnings here. They log each deal, each profit, each loss. The £750,000 down is as black a mark as you can get unless you're Nick Leeson. In the City they call human resources inhuman resources. They've been trained in how to sack people sensitively.

Sensitive sacking amounts to being told you're a failure. You had the chance to get rich. Alex was one of 15 graduates chosen from

3,000. If he blows it, the axe will be quick. Human resource will sensitively call him in and tell him to clear his desk. If he behaves, they'll give him a reference for a second-string house like The Minor League Bank of Kansas or the Consolidated Bank of Nepal.

There is a pecking order of financial institutions known to all those who work in the City. At one end, the Goldman Sachs, Salomon, Merrill Lynch; at the other end, the bit players. Someone has to buy and sell for the Bank of Mozambique in London, Alex supposes, but he would rather it was not him.

Alex knows he has to focus on the screens. He has access to 20 windows, but windows don't deliver inspiration – just the guilty feeling that he ought to be able to spot something. He knows what he wants. A stock no one has noticed which he can trade in on behalf of the bank – preferably a stock that has not been recommended by the analysts because then he can claim all the credit for a brilliant trade.

Alex scans the price of stocks in Tokyo where it's 2 p.m. The Nikkei is up 24. He looks at the index in Sydney, 2 hours ahead of Tokyo. There is even an exchange in New Zealand though it doesn't make many waves.

Alex notices something interesting as he flicks through his windows. In Sydney, which is closing, the shares of the Alexandria Corp – he wouldn't give me the real name of the company – are trading at 12.22 Australian dollars. In Tokyo shares in the same company are at US$7.95 Given the rate of Australian dollar, to the US dollar, if he can manage to sell these shares now in Tokyo and buy them the same instant in Sydney he will make 2 US cents a share.

Global markets throw up anomalies and sometimes the computer programs designed to catch them, miss them. Sometimes the human eye is quicker. Alex knows he has to move fast. He contacts the broker who deals for the bank in Tokyo and places an order to sell 100,000 shares.

Alex immediately contacts Sydney with an order to buy 100,000 shares. He's careful to quote the price in Australian dollars because he doesn't want anyone to compare the prices in Sydney and Tokyo.

He gets a trade in Sydney at 12.21 Australian dollars which is a cent better than he hoped.

The transactions are confirmed. He has made £13,000 for his bank. He's done the trades just in time. Someone else has noticed the differences between the quoted prices in Sydney and Tokyo and the prices are now coming closer together. The 0.3 per cent difference has disappeared. Someone may have spotted the deal Alex made. He had perhaps 5 minutes to spot and make the trade.

Alex grins to himself. He used to believe in his own unique skill at trading. Now, at 27, he's less sure. His girlfriend who left him because he drank too much, kept on sniping he was not as smart as he thought. Maybe she's right. She wanted him to go into therapy, he eventually told me, but for him Freud is psychobabble.

Alex hates doubting himself. Having made £13,000 means he's ahead by £83,000 this month and there are eight more working days. Not brilliant, but it might convince inhuman human resources not to dump him yet.

Alex feels more confident now. Confidence is vital. If you have confidence, it shows, it glows. You can turn it into profit. He summons up the latest headlines for more inspiration on one of his 20 windows. The smartest trades are not the obvious ones. You don't follow the news, let alone what the papers say. Rather, you try to imagine oblique consequences. Psychologists call this lateral thinking.

Pigs now become part of Alex's lateral thinking. When I first met him in the spring of 1999 the papers were full of the misery of Britain's pig farmers. The price of pork was falling drastically. One pig farmer had announced he was going to turn his land into a cemetery as there was more money in burials than in bacon. If they were going under, pig farmers would have to sell their farms, Alex tells himself. One unlikely consequence – demand for large-scale agricultural machinery would increase as small farms went bust. Bigger firms would handle more production. They'd need more machinery. Smart, thinks Alex. When he scans the price of options on the shares of companies that made heavy machinery, though, he is disappointed. The shares are already expensive; future options on them even more so. He was obviously not the first person to have had that lateral pig idea.

It's just his luck – not to be lucky twice.

The pressures Alex works under are supposed to motivate him to do his best, to work all hours. They do that, but at a price. As with

Kahn and Cooper's subjects one has to wonder if individuals under these pressures perform most effectively.

E-trading

Some of the sharpest pressures from day trading

In America there are 100 online brokerages, but in Britain the business is still in its infancy. Charles Schwab have about 14,000 online customers, but they expect you to have funds of at least $10,000. In May 1999 the first British all-Internet broker Etrade UK took a step closer to opening its doors for public business. It joined the Stock Exchange and then it got recogniton from the Securities and Futures Authority to provide both execution and advisory services. Etrade is not an established broker going online, but a company which will be the UK's first Internet-only trading company and its research services will be the first to use the Web as the only way of communicating research.

Since 1999 many more British investors trade on the Net for themselves – and that creates enormous pressures. The behaviourist B.F. Skinner would have been intrigued by the phenomenon of day trading. Investors sit at a screen and buy and sell stocks and commodities for long periods. Day traders use their own money and some do 2,000 deals a day. Like Skinner's rats, they get instant reward or instant punishment, profit or loss.

Skinner found that as long as the rats sometimes got a reward, food pellets or sugar, they would go on pressing levers thousands of times. A rat might get only two or three rewards in a hundred presses but this intermittent reward schedule would keep him pressing for days. It's interesting to compare this with the situation that day traders find themselves in. Skinner could not, of course, interview the rats about their levels of frustration; all he could do was observe the link between their reward schedule and their willingness to persist. Intermittently rewarded rats were endlessly persistent – and day trading creates just such a pattern of reinforcement.

Day traders seem to show some similar traits – and, sometimes, as in the case of Mark Barton in Atlanta the frustration leads to extreme violence. Barton was a 44-year-old chemist who collected $600,000 insurance when his first wife was killed in 1993. He then became a day trader – and one who kept on losing. On Thursday 29 July 1998, he killed his second wife, their two children and nine workers in Atlanta brokerage houses.

If investors lose and become violent, they have till now turned it inwards as John Gay did after he lost out in the 1720 South Sea Bubble. The murders committed by Mark Barton may be a one-off case, but his actions may also suggest that changes in the operations of markets are having an impact. Certainly there never seems to have been a case like it before. There are no recorded instances in 1929 of desperate investors shooting their brokers before jumping off Wall Street ledges. Bill Campbell, the mayor of Atlanta, said that one of Barton's many suicide notes expressed 'some concern about market losses.' Campbell insisted the killings weren't just a reaction to market fluctuations.

In his lethal rampage Barton killed four people at All Tech and five at Momentum Securities. These firms were the gurus of day trading who sold investors not just the old snake oil – that they could get rich – but that they had real power. All Tech has just been banned from soliciting trade for 2 years in Massachussetts because its ads were misleading. Advocates of e-trading promise that you can 'sit at the screen and be in control'. Barton discovered it didn't work for him and I suspect reacted not just to losing his money but also to losing his sense of power and control. Till now investors had to deal through brokers. You had 3 weeks to settle your account. It was anything but instant. Now trading is faster and more direct – and this is bound to have psychological effects. Traders feel more in charge. You hit the keys, you make the deals. Intense. And you feel the losses perhaps even more intensely. The sheer intensity of day trading may also have contributed.

Barton's case was tragic. The breakdown of Peter Young, a fund manager for Deutsche Bank, was less violent, but in the destruction of a promising career just as tragic. Young had been charged with embezzling huge amounts of money and turned up in court dressed as a woman. Psychiatrists argued that he had suffered a schizophrenic episode and some attributed this to pressure of life in the

City. In the end, Young has been found unfit to stand trial. Most dealers cope with the pressures in a socially acceptable way, but there are real casualties too.

Imagery and the traders

At various points in the book I've reported that market professionals often compare their experiences in the City with earlier experiences on the sports field. Sports psychologists are regularly used by high-class tennis players, footballers and other performers to help them tune up. David Hemery, the 1968 Olympics 440 metres hurdles champion, has spoken of the way he used imagery to prepare for that competition. I think there may be something in this for all individuals who trade under pressure.

Sports psychologists recommend that you relax and then play in your mind the images of success. For their clients the key images include:

- getting a good start to a race;
- leaping high over the hurdles;
- making a maximum effort over the last part of the course;
- being declared the winner;
- standing on the podium and collecting the trophies.

Is there anything here that individual traders can learn? I would suggest there is. The two key factors are:

- relaxation;
- imagination.

The pace of electronic trading encourages people to trade too quickly when they sit at their screens. Extroverts will be especially vulnerable to this. A good way to deal with this is to discipline yourself to relax for 2 to 3 minutes. Switch on your screen. Surf it. But do so without feeling you have to make a deal at this second.

You may occasionally miss a deal but, overall, it will pay off. What is good tactics for sports champions should be good tactics for you.

Once this 2–3 minute period is over – and you feel relaxed – imagine what a good deal will mean. Imagining success can take different forms:

- imagine the graph showing the rise of the stock;
- imagine what the profit you make might look like on your bank statement;
- imagine telling your partner – yes boasting – of the success you've had;
- if you have been having a bad run lately, imagine the pleasure you'll get by reversing it;
- then, with these images well in mind, look for the opportunities on the screen.

This method may sound childish but it's a way of feeling in control and feeling confidence. The relaxation exercises are also an excellent way of combating the stresses I've described throughout this chapter. In the next chapter I describe the investment strategies of a number of gurus. What is noticeable about each is that the guru feels in control, not of events, but of his own choices. S/he doesn't panic into action. S/he keeps, as Laughlin recommends traders must, 'a clear head.'

The signs are that the information overload will only get worse with more new markets opening and new instruments of risk being created.

When I first started writing this book in 1999 there was a plan to set up a new stock market in the Emirates. The promoters argued the world did not yet have genuine 24 hour trading worldwide. There was a gap in the 24 hour clock. What were traders to do after the Frankfurt market closed – roughly at 7 p.m. Greenwich Mean Time (GMT) – and the Hong Kong and Singapore markets opened at midnight? Could they content themselves with punting on the puny Tel Aviv exchange or playing Bombay? Surely not. And even then there was a 3 hour gap when no international market was open. Today, the Emirate Exchange is working so, workaholics rejoice, obsessives relax. There is now no second on earth when some financial market isn't open, when some index isn't moving either up or down – and so offers the prospect of trades. The market never sleeps and all too many traders deep down love that, I suspect.

eight

Psychology and the great gurus of investment

Psychology students can buy textbooks which explain and compare Freud's theories with those of B.F. Skinner, the behaviourist who argued consciousness did not matter. Everything was learned. Skinner's triumphs included training pigeons to play ping-pong. To psychologists the question of whether Freud or Skinner is right is vital. It cannot be true both that human behaviour is largely determined by internal unconscious motives and childhood experiences (Freud, 1900, 1905) and also that human behaviour is largely the product of external forces *and* rewards and punishments a person has received shape him or her (Skinner 1953). Only one of these stories can be true. Searching for such absolute truths has its murky side. One of the great psychologists of the post-war era, David McClelland, once explained to me that psychologists were motivated by power (Cohen 1977). They wanted to prove their ideas were right and other peoples were wrong.

With investment theories, however, there seems less obsession with achieving total theory triumph. Value theorists, momentumists, chartists and noise traders seek to prove their claims, but they seem less fervent about proving themselves right and others wrong. Their main aim is more practical – to do well in the market. As long as their ideas allow them to make a profit, they tend not to feel they have to batter their rivals into the ground.

In a way this theoretical tolerance is paradoxical. Financial professionals are very competitive. Most of those I talked to, however, were acutely aware of the fact that grand theories of how the markets work remain unproven. In this chapter, I want to look at the ideas and psychology behind a number of investment approaches including:

▨ The ideas of Benjamin Graham, commonly reckoned to be the first and greatest of investment gurus and co-author of *Security Analysis*, one of the ultimate text on equities.

▨ The ideas of Warren Buffett, the world's greatest investor. Most material has to be gleaned from texts on so-called buffettology (Train 1986, Lowenstein 1995) because Buffett himself tends to publish wise sayings, amusing anecdotes rather than the specific ideas that have made him the only man to become a billionaire just by investing in stocks.

▨ The ideas of Phillip Fisher. Warren Buffett has argued his ideas are 85 per cent Graham and 15 per cent Fisher.

▨ The ideas of Jim Slater developed in *The Zulu Principle* and *Beyond the Zulu Principle* (Slater 1994, 1997).

▨ The ideas of the world's other greatest current investor George Soros (Soros 1988, 1995).

I will also look briefly at the ideas of some lesser market 'wizards', particularly Tom Basso (1994) because he takes such a psychological approach to investing.

None of their theories really deal with how the markets work in any lofty sense. Rather, they explain how to pick shares which will do well, unexpectedly well: many also deal with the crucial questions of nerve and timing.

I want to look at the background of some of these 'gurus'; the evidence indicates their childhood experiences have influenced their investment strategies. Supreme examples are Warren Buffett and George Soros. Both have suggested that their investment ideas and ideals owe something to their experiences before they became professional investors. Both have impressed commentators with aspects of their personality – Buffett the small-town sage, Soros the philosopher and philanthropist.

Train (1986) in *The Midas Touch* repeatedly calls such great investors 'fanatics' who are driven by a 'ruling passion' just as solving the riddle of the Universe was Einstein and Newton's passion. The evidence suggests great investors past and present are unusual beings. Buffett and Soros created empires based on their investment skills. Just like great musicians and scientists are often totally dedicated and obsessed, great investors live for the market. It is part of the meaning of their lives.

There has been little research on the personality of great investors as opposed to the personality of other highly talented people. Nevertheless, it seems likely they share some of the traits of the very talented – persistence, intelligence, the refusal to be beaten by adverse circumstances and dedication to their craft. Research on geniuses (Steptoe 1998, Eysenck 1996) suggests they often pay a high price for their gifts. Painters like Van Gogh and Richard Dadd, Nietzsche, Schumann, the dancer Nijinsky, the great comic playwright Georges Feydeau and the poet John Clare are only a few of those who spent time in the asylum. Anthony Storr (1999) has argued that something like 40 per cent of creative geniuses have serious mental health problems.

I am not suggesting either that Buffett or Soros are geniuses like Van Gogh or need therapy, but a little speculation, as it were, on the psychology of high achievers suggests we should be wary of assuming that we just have to imitate them to get rich. Yet investment books are often ready to suggest that, with their text in hand and some part-time number crunching, you too can be like Buffett or Soros.

How ridiculous this is becomes clear if we think about our aims when we study Einstein or Freud. Of course, we want to learn about psychoanalysis or relativity, but we don't expect to produce insights such as theirs by imitating the great ancients.

So why do people feel they can so easily learn from investment gurus? I suspect we are susceptible to this flattery partly because of unconscious attitudes, including the feeling that making money out of the markets is easy – perhaps even a bit disreputable. Both Britain and the USA are still to some extent ruled by the 'Protestant' work ethic. You work; you earn. Playing the stock market is not working, so success is more a matter of luck than merit.

No reasonable person would say it's a matter of bad luck they're not Einstein, but some do say it was bad luck that stopped them buying shares in Microsoft or Body Shop or Buffett's investment partnership when these first started. If they had been there, had the luck of being in Omaha or Brighton at the right time, if they had had $50,000 spare instead of having to fork out for the children's college fees, they too would have been millionaires.

You don't have to be a master of psychology to spot the insidious mix of flattery and self-delusion.

Like many very talented people, many great investors have a certain vanity which can manifest itself in a lofty philosophical tone – whether it's the homespun à la Buffett or Popperian à la Soros. Just after the Second World War, Soros was a student at the London School of Economics. One of his teachers was Karl Popper, author of *The Open Society and Its Enemies* and one of the leading philosophers of the mid-20th century (Popper 1995). Soros has remained deeply impressed by his teacher – and keeps trying to impress him in turn. Buffett has done nothing to stop people calling him the Sage of Omaha and tends to draw comparisons between how the markets and God treat individuals. This is not the kind of approach you generally find in self-help books.

The ideas of Jim Slater

Jim Slater is probably the guru who is most realistic and accessible – partly because he feels he has a mission to convince the British middle class of the joys of intelligent investment. He argues that small investors can become experts in one or two sectors of the market; and if they do so, they can not only profit from exceptional growth in equities but also enjoy themselves in the process.

In *The Zulu Principle* Slater recommends wannaberich investors should make themselves an expert on one sector of the market. This is the Zulu Principle, which Slater admits he owes to his wife. One day Mrs Slater read an article on Zulus in the *Readers Digest*. After a few minutes, she knew more about Zulus than Slater did. It then occurred to him that if she read all the books in the local library about Zulus, Mrs Slater would have the unlikely distinction of being the leading expert on Zulus in Surrey. If Mrs Slater then went to South Africa, spent 6 months at Johannesburg University and some time on a kraal, she could soon become one of the world's great experts on the Zulus.

It does not take that much to become an expert, Slater argues. A person who spends an hour a day studying different companies who make microchips will soon understand the essentials of the industry. That person will be less likely to make basic misjudgements and more likely to analyse well the financial information about companies in that sector. S/he will be better placed to spot which companies have promising products and ideas. Becoming an expert requires work and effort, but not that much work and effort. Aware of the risks of information overload, Slater suggests most people can develop expertise in one or two areas.

Do not aim for total knowledge of all sectors of the markets.

As we shall see, it is only after Slater has prepared this ground, by making readers feel he is asking the possible, that he requires them to understand the quite complex mathematical formulae needed to put his ideas into practice. It is also interesting that Slater should emphasize the need for sector knowledge because Warren Buffett's own career is, we shall see, a good illustration of this.

The childhood experiences
of investment gurus

Warren Buffett was born in 1931 in Omaha in the Midwest. He grew up around farms. His father was a stockbroker and then became a congressman. Buffett grew up in a household where there was always an eye on Wall Street. He was interested in the market before he even went to high school. When he was a teenager he set up a small newspaper.

Warren Buffett learned one of his key lessons at the age of 11, it is claimed. He persuaded his sister to invest her entire fortune – just over $100 – in buying three shares in a company called Cities Services. They were $38 when he bought them. The shares fell to $27 which led to family rows when the not yet teenage market wizard told his sister about the $11 a share loss. She became anxious she was going to lose all her savings. Finally, the shares started to rise and the relieved young Buffett sold them at $40, netting a grand profit of $5 after dealing charges. What upset him was that the shares then charged up to $100. The young Buffett had succumbed to client pressure, but he learned from the experience. The mature Buffett rarely tells his clients what he is doing with their money because it will only worry them – and make it harder for him to make cool decisions for their benefit.

I want to compare Warren Buffett with another famous American 'country boy', the therapist Carl Rogers. Rogers (1965) pioneered humanistic therapy and was in the early 1980s mentioned as a possible candidate for the Nobel Peace Prize (Cohen 1997). Rogers grew up on a farm outside Chicago. He was made to work on the land from the time he was 10. Like Buffett, Rogers set up a small newspaper when he was in his teens. Again like Buffett, Rogers was interested in making money from his teens.

Rogers went to China when he was 18 as part of young people's Christian mission. China impressed the young man enormously: he also saw the chance of making serious money and started to import Chinese artefacts into the USA. He developed this into a small but successful business. Among his papers in the Library of Congress is the bank book he used for his profits, a memento he kept for the rest of his life.

By the time Rogers went to Union Theological Seminary in New York his Chinese business was thriving. His main aim, however, wasn't really to make money, but to become independent of his wealthy father who ran a construction company. When he had enough money never to bother his father again, Rogers dropped the Chinese artefacts and focused his intense energies on becoming a therapist.

Buffett's interest in making money, however, seems never to have flagged. Before he went to university he had managed to make and save enough to buy 40 acres of land in Nebraska as an investment. While he was at the University of Pennsylvania, he was corresponding with Benjamin Graham, the co-author of *Security Analysis*, suggesting ideas to him and offering to work for him.

Benjamin Graham ran a four man investment business, perhaps the first ever 'investment boutique'. He was a pioneer of the concept of looking for hidden value. Two keys indicators for Graham were the ratio of inventories to sales and the ratio of debt to equity. Graham was against investing in companies which had more debt than equity. He also believed it was possible to find companies whose net worth was not reflected in the equity value. That was easier then than it is now, when everyone is well aware of Graham's ideas, as Graham himself admitted in an interview in 1976, shortly before his death. Luckily for him, there was less press interest in finance in the 1940s, 1950s and early 1960s, so Graham only started to become famous in the 1960s well after he had first published his magisterial *Security Analysis*.

Buffett absorbed Graham's ideas and also those of Philip Fisher. Fisher was as interested in the competence of management as in dissecting accounts and inventories. But Fisher made a point Buffett has never forgotten. The investor needs to back good managers, but he must not manage companies himself.

By the time Buffett was 25 he had persuaded neighbours in Omaha to invest $100,000 with him. That was a considerable achievement for a young man. Adjusted for inflation it means his 'fund' started with about $1 million. Buffett promised his partners a return of at least 6 per cent on their money and the deal was that he took 25 per cent of profits made above that. In a letter to his partners Buffett wrote, 'I cannot promise results to partners, but I can and do promise this:

a. our investments will be chosen on the basis of value;
b. our pattern of speculation will attempt to reduce permanent capital loss (not short-term quotational loss) to a minimum.'

Buffett did more than deliver his 6 per cent return. All these first Buffett investors made millions. There are said to be at least 52 Buffett millionaires in Omaha who had invested with him in his first few years.

In 1969, however, Buffett decided he was out of tune with the times and with the long bull market of the 1960s which left many shares looking expensive. He got out of the markets and coped with his frustration at dealing less. The result was that Buffett did not lose money in the 1973–1974 bear market and was in an excellent position to take advantage of the low prices towards the end of 1974. When Buffett came back into the market, he said it was like being a sex-starved man in a harem. There were so many opportunities.

Many of the first shares Buffett purchased for his new investment vehicle were media shares. Buffett bought 0.7 per cent of Knight Ridder newspapers at $8 and 5 per cent of Ogilvy and Mather, the advertising agency. Both investments were very successful. Much later he bought into ABC TV.

Buffett was, in fact, working the Zulu Principle (even though Slater had not yet discovered it) because his family had real roots in the media business. As a student his father had edited the university newspaper, the *Daily Nebraskan*. Warren Buffett's grandfather on his mother's side was a professional newspaperman. He owned and edited the *Cuming Country Democrat*. Buffett noted one of the best American monopolies is a local newspaper in a town which has only one paper. Every local business has to advertise in it.

Many of Buffett's ideas also appear to reflect these small-town roots. He dislikes companies which change what they do and how they do it often. Stability is a plus. So are great American names. Two of Buffett's successful investments have been in Coca Cola and in Walt Disney, both American icons.

This very homely approach to investment is a little romantic, of course. To cynics it seems to reflect a carefully crafted image – the great investor as a regular guy.

The psychology of buffettology

The basis of Buffett's approach is what psychologists call a gestalt. The gestaltists were German psychologists who showed that when we look at patterns we tend to perceive a meaningful whole. Show subjects a series of dots which vaguely form the shape of a face and subjects will see a face, not a collection of dots. We see the whole, not the parts.

Buffett is 'at heart' a gestaltist. He stresses that you need to focus on the merits of a company as a whole rather than, for example, what price you could get by splitting off and selling the different assets. Buffett has often been critical of portfolios which have constant turnover. One of the most successful funds in the 1970s and 1980s was Sequoia which was run by a colleague of Benjamin Graham. The portfolio was quiet, little trading was done. Yet, because the shares had been intelligently selected, Sequoia showed excellent returns year after year, as Buffett has pointed out.

One example of Buffett's gestaltist approach was buying into American Express. In 1982 American Express shares suffered a large loss because of a scandal connected to salad oil. The shares fell from $62 to $35. There was a feeling American Express was on the run; the press were highly critical. Buffett stayed calm. He looked at the basic businesses of American Express – travel, credit cards, travellers' cheques. These were not damaged by its troubles with salad oil. As a whole, as gestalt, the company was good. The market had panicked and exaggerated the scale of the disaster. Buffett bought American Express heavily and within a few years the $35 shares were standing at $189.

We have seen that one of Buffett's mentors, Philip Fisher, insisted on investing only in companies with first-class honest management. Managers should also not be the sort who make money for themselves at the expense of shareholders.

Buffett has always been careful to differentiate between being able to spot good managers and being able to manage companies. When Buffett bought a huge stake in ABC TV in 1985, he went on to the board of the company. But he did not want to influence day to day management. So he promised he would vote with the management as long as the same two individuals stayed as Chairman and President. He had faith in them and he had no wish to show them how to run the company better.

One of Buffett's key ideas is that eventually the true value of shares will be reflected in the market price. The trick is to spot the value before anyone else, buy cheaply – and then to be prepared to wait. To find such value is not, however, that simple – and he has never revealed the detailed mathematics he uses to assess the true value of a company and to predict how well companies will do.

Buffett has his idiosyncrasies too. He has said that his experiences on the farm have made him worry about agricultural shares because farmers have to carry far too large inventories, something Graham was always against. Buffett also suggested that he has 'bad luck' in certain industries. He has never done well out of retailing shares. Here we're again reminded of the usefulness of the cognitive dissonance perspective. Rumours of Buffett's interest in M&S helped boost the shares in the spring of 1999. It is well known that he distrusts retailing shares, however, but those who wanted M&S to go up forgot this fact, bought on the momentum of his possible interest and lost money when the rumours faded away.

As he has become more famous Buffett likes to emphasize his very ordinariness. He lives in Omaha in the house he bought in the 1950s. He seems the antithesis of the mover and shaker. He has become known for some of his quotes. Two of these have the requisite sage-like properties. There is the rule quote:

- Rule No. 1. Never lose money
- Rule No. 2. Never forget Rule No. 1.

And there is the religious quote:

> The market like the Lord helps those who help themselves. But unlike the Lord, the market does not forgive those who know not what they do.

These are both memorable quotes which also reinforce the image of Buffett as an all-American regular guy. Yet, it's obvious that at some level commentators know this is a slightly misleading image. It is no accident that Train calls his book on Buffett *The Midas Touch*. Midas was granted his wish; everything he touched turned to gold and his obsession ruined his life. The principles of buffetology seem simple enough but making them work requires total passion, commitment and concentration on the market, a very high degree of numeracy and access to information that is denied to those who are less well connected.

The philosopher manqué

George Soros's background is far more cosmopolitan than Buffett's and Soros has played commodity and foreign exchange markets far more. His most famous coup which netted him $958 million was going short on sterling in 1992. He gambled and made in that throw of the dice more money than Nick Leeson lost.

Soros also has major intellectual aspirations. He was born in

Hungary. His father had survived as a prisoner of war in Russia during the First World War. When the Nazis took over Hungary, he managed to get his son false papers which concealed the fact he was Jewish. Soros, like Robert Maxwell, had to survive the Nazis. The young Soros, however, showed none of Maxwell's early gifts as an entrepreneur. While Maxwell started in academic publishing and other forms of wheeler-dealing as soon as he reached London, Soros came to study at the London School of Economics.

Soros was financially poor as a student in London and, at one time, a Jewish agency refused him help. Post-war London was full of gifted Hungarian refugees like Andre Deutsch, the publisher and Tommy Balogh, the economist. Soros does not seem to have frequented these circles, however. He had to take a variety of menial jobs including selling shoes and being a waiter at the Gay Hussar instead. Soros probably waited tables on Deutsch and Balogh because the Gay Hussar was the only Hungarian restaurant in town and a favourite of both émigrés and socialists like Michael Foot.

But the London School of Economics marked Soros for ever. He has always remained a little the philosopher manqué. For example, Soros sent the manuscript of his first book to Popper. It was very much influenced by Popper's famous *The Open Society* and it described the horrors of life under a dictatorship. Popper first enthused because he thought the author was an American and his arguments the product of imaginative reconstruction. When Popper discovered Soros had lived through the Nazi occupation of Hungary, he was less impressed. Soros was affected by Popper's reaction; he shelved the book and it has yet to be published.

At first, too, Soros showed much less fierce financial ambition than Buffett did. He did eventually get a job in the City. By his mid-twenties he had got together $5,000. With that he went to New York.

Soros brought one great strength to America. At the time there was little interest in European markets. Soros understood Europe and its markets probably better than anyone on Wall Street – and that led to his first investment coup. He had the insight to realize that the German insurance company Allianz was worth far more than anyone realized. He wrote a paper recommending it. Two clients of his Wall Street firm were impressed. The directors of Allianz were outraged because Soros's analysis suggested they did not realize the value of their own assets; they wrote a long letter rebutting Soros's arguments but Soros was proved right. His clients bought into Allianz and made spectacular profits.

This triumph started to make Soros's reputation. He started his fund in 1969, but soon after he became immensely wealthy, he focused a good deal of his energy on the kind of work Popper would have approved of – helping fund projects in Hungary which helped foster an open society and, eventually, democracy. Ultimately you get the feeling Soros would rather be remembered for his ideas and what he did with his money than for the brilliance of his investment decisions.

When studying Soros's ideas it is important to realize that he is a survivor and the son of a survivor. He would seem to be more willing than Buffett to take risks; Soros's family had to take risks to survive the Nazis. It's no accident he should be more willing to gamble, to go into a situation, make a killing and then get out. This high-risk approach has meant that he has also made large-scale losses. He would not seem to subscribe to the principles Buffett outlined in 1956, that investment should reduce capital loss.

Soros's strategies also reflect the sociological and psychological ideas from the London School of Economics. He argues what is crucial is not judging the value of shares or commodities, but judging perceptions of an asset and realizing when that asset and perceptions of it are changing. Soros also argues markets help shape values and perception. Value is not something there in a company for a skilful accountant to spot, but a much more fluid, changing entity.

Summing up his ideas, Soros has argued there are six different stages in the development of an investment position.

The first is an as yet unrecognized trend in the market.

The second is when the trend becomes reinforced. The fall in American Express shares in 1982 from $62 to $35 is an excellent example of this. The market in its panic reinforced the pattern of the shares falling. Another example, very pertinent to Soros, was the British policy of trying to shadow rates in the Exchange Rate Mechanism (ERM) in 1992. The target of keeping the pound to DM rate at around 2.95 DM at all costs was exactly this kind of self-reinforcing manoeuvre. It distorted the British economy and did not reflect the economic truth.

The third is a successful test of the market. It could be argued that in 1992, a few weeks before the British were forced out of the ERM (see Major 1999), the foreign-exchange market was tested by the lira. Italians, who were having problems keeping the lira within the ERM bounds, had to devalue by 7 per cent. That devaluation was the maximum allowed by the ERM rules and it did not really calm jitters about the stability of the ERM.

The fourth stage is growing divergence between reality and perception. The efforts of the British to keep the pound in the ERM were an attempt to sustain an illusion – and the British paid the price. It is in this kind of situation that Festinger's theory of cognitive dissonance is highly pertinent, for many investors will seek information to persuade themselves there isn't really a divergence between reality and public positions.

The climax is the fifth stage – and you can hardly ask for a more dramatic climax than that of Black Wednesday – 13 October 1992. Books by John Major (1999) and Norman Lamont (1999), then the Chancellor of the Exchequer, differ in details, but the basics are clear. In the morning sterling was in deep trouble. By noon, interest rates had been hiked up by 2 per cent. Lamont describes how he watched the screens but, despite the big increase, sterling did not blip into recovery. At around 2.15 p.m he increased interest rates again – something which had never been done in any sterling crisis. Lamont argued that staying in the ERM was vital to the British national interest. Kenneth Clarke, then the Home Secretary, said he had always been a believer in the power of markets in theory, but he had never witnessed their sheer brutal power before that day. Lamont's second hike worked no more than the first one. The British government was powerless in the face of the speculators and had to withdraw from the ERM. It was the frantic climax of the policy of trying to keep the pound in the ERM at an inflated rate. Soros had sold $10 billion sterling short and had contributed significantly to the crisis. He had shaped the market as well as understanding it. Soros calls Black Wednesday 'White Wednesday' incidentally because the disaster for the British was his triumph.

The final stage in this boom/bust cycle is what Soros calls 'the reverse mirror image' when the trend reverses itself so that the assets which have been driven down to exaggerated levels start to recover. John Meriwether put that idea spectacularly into practice in 1987 when he saw the opportunities in bonds discussed in Chapter 5.

At the heart of these principles is the difference between image and reality. The crucial difference between Buffett and Soros is that Buffett, true to the principles of Benjamin Graham 40 years on, calculates – or says he calculates – on the basis of the hidden value of assets, whereas Soros is much more an inspired trader.

For all his psychological sophistication, just as Buffett believes he has bad luck in some sectors, Soros is also prey to idiosyncrasies. He has said there are days when he knows there is something wrong with the market because it gives him a backache. That, however, is as close as he gets to Buffett's homely touch. After the 1992 coup Soros lost billions on different stakes – particularly on backing the yen. He remains a very successful investor, but he has recently said he will concentrate much more on his philanthropy.

Slater's advice

I argued earlier that the guru who probably has most useful advice for ordinary investors is Jim Slater. Slater set up Slater Walker Securities. He was the first British investment guru to recommend seeking out shares with low-price earnings ratios. Slater (1997) argues that investing in shares is both lucrative and also an interesting hobby from which you can derive intellectual pleasure. He is a fan of investment clubs where a few individuals pool resources and expertise. Slater too, however, flatters small investors. He points out they have some key advantages over professionals.

First, they have less money to invest and so they can invest with great effect in smaller companies. Second, they are unlikely to invest in more than 10 companies which means they can choose the very best 10. By comparison, Slater suggests, professionals will have a much larger portfolio and inevitably, it will include many less than tip top shares.

Slater admits many investors will be depressed by opportunities they feel they have missed. He points out that £10,000 invested in Racal in the 1970s would now be worth £1.5 million. But nil desperandum. There are always good growth companies for sharp eyes and calculators to spot Slater insists. You get the feeling Slater is perfectly willing to share most of his secrets. This may be a bluff or it may reflect the fact he does not seek to walk the world stage as much as Buffett or Soros.

Much of the advice in *Beyond the Zulu Principle* is common sense. Slater recommends investing in companies which have a competitive advantage. This can come from having a good brand name like Next or intellectual property rights such as pharmaceutical companies have in certain drugs. Once investors have established a company has this competitive advantage, he urges them to look for growth companies. Slater does not worry about making certain intellectual demands of investors, but he does provide a detailed model.

Slater defines 'great growth companies' as companies which can increase their EPS (earnings per share) at an above-average rate. He suggests finding companies who are increasing their EPS by at least 15 per cent a year. He claims – and this clearly derives from Buffett's faith in franchises – that companies which can clone an activity like a shop, a restaurant, a nursing home have exceptional prospects. The success of Pizza Express was a good example for a while. Analysts are now waiting for the sandwich chain Prêt à Manger to come to the market because that appears to be a good franchise.

Slater accepts it is difficult to judge the calibre of management – and perhaps exceptionally so for small investors now that every aggressive company employs spin doctors. So he recommends starting with the arithmetic. The key rules are:

- Each of the last 5 years' results must be profitable. None can show a loss.
- Where four periods of growth follow a previous setback, it must have achieved its highest normalized EPS in the latest period. This suggests the company is really motoring.
- Property shares are eliminated because they are asset situations rather than growth ones. An asset may grow in value, but if it does so it may not be that much the result of management skill.
- There have to be broker forecasts – and, in effect, positive ones. The merit of this approach is that investors can use other people's research. The Buffett and Soros technique of spotting what no

one else has spotted – either hidden value or an as yet un-recognized trend in the market – requires in-depth research, at least, and possibly access to information small investors may find hard to get. Slater recognizes these limit the independent re-search small investors can do, hence the usefulness of broker forecasts.

- Slater is wary of companies in cyclical sectors like building and construction. To qualify as a growth share, shares in those sectors still have to meet the criteria he has set out.
- Finally, Slater advises looking at price/earnings growth (PEG) factors. The traditional price/earnings ratio (PER) is a measure of how much an investor is being asked to pay for future growth and how much investors have paid before. Slater claims this measure is 'one dimensional'. He prefers PEG. To calculate the PEG you divide the forecast PER by the forecast growth in bearnings per share. Say a company is growing at 11 per cent per year and has a prospective PER of 11 then its PEG is 1. Slater argues that companies with a PEG of under 1 are especially attractive. He recommends looking for companies which are growing at between 15 per cent and 25 per cent a year as this is a sustainable level of growth. On the basis of this in 1996 he recommended JJB Sports and Psion, both of which have performed well. JJB seemed to peak by summer 1999 when it acquired Littlewoods, but it has proved robust into 2001.

Analysing the FT-SE indices in 1996, Slater concluded there were 50 shares in the FT-SE 100, about 90 in the FT-SE Mid-250 and 160 in the FT-SE SmallCap Index which met his criteria. In the fledging index of 700 shares, Slater estimated there were perhaps 60 which again met his criteria. The small investor has plenty of choice.

Another of Slater's suggestions makes equally good sense. He argues it is best to avoid companies whose chief executives live 'in an overtly flashy way'. Personalized car number plates are a bad sign. It is probably fatal if a chief executive acquires a substantial interests in a football club. Big ego, small profits.

There is another kind of investment guru whose ideas I want to examine briefly – the psychological guru who recommends inner investing.

Tom Basso is one of the market wizards who takes this psychological approach. Like many others, Basso makes many sensible points. He argues investors need to have a good understanding of themselves and especially of their tolerance of risk. He then develops a curious line of argument based on his case histories (Basso 1994).

Basso also warns against too much ego – and suggests that this gets in the way of rational decisions. He pokes fun, for example, at a big-shot provincial doctor who was always certain he was right, right about everything and thus ignored what his broker told him. The result of the big ego; the doctor lost money. One case history doesn't prove or disprove a theory. Many good investors are aggressive and self-confident; in fact, traits that often go with a well-developed sense of ego.

Insider knowledge

There have been many recent scandals about insider trading and investors using privileged information. Small investors rarely have the chance to commit this crime. But insider trading is often more subtle.

One of the difficulties facing small investors when they read the now mountains of investment advice is that while some financial information is publicly available in company accounts and brokers' circulars, it is much harder to access some key facts about companies. When Buffett bought over 30 per cent of ABC TV, for example, he went on to the board of the company. He promised, however, to vote with the management for the next 11 years as long as the current Chairman and President stayed in their jobs. This policy of non-interference was obviously a great vote of confidence in the two men. Unlike most investors, Buffett knew the two men very well. He had seen them at work and they were members of an elite circle who met with him once a year to discuss the markets. He had insider psychological knowledge without being unethical.

Few investment gurus really reflect on the very different situation of insiders and outsiders. In discussing how to use the lessons of the great investors, for example, Train recommends:

- getting to know the people running a company;
- talking to the company;
- studying the kind of fanaticism great investors show.

These are not options open to most people. Furthermore, when he suggests ways of coping with these problems, Train seems to me to illustrate a rather typical lack of realism. If you do not have access Train recommends:

- talking to a friend who works for one of the large players in the industry;
- and if you are so badly connected that you have no friends in the relevant industry talking to a friend who is a corporate banker who is involved in lending to that particular industry.

For most small investors these are impossible aims. The only contact most will have with a company is if they go to the Annual General Meeting, rituals which are massaged by financial PR consultants. In Britain large institutions try to influence the management of companies more – this is so-called shareholder power – but those who try to wield it are in a powerful position and own 1 per cent or more of the company.

Train also argues investors need originality and that the person who does the opposite of what the market trends suggest may often do well. In theory we should absolutely agree and, in the era of increasingly powerful tracker funds, I sympathize. But for the small investor being original means running risks because it is not easy to have all the information the big boys have.

In sum, the psychology behind the ideas of investment gurus is interesting. What we know of their strategies often seems sensible and provides a good check against rash 'I do it by instinct' investing. It is simplistic, however, to suppose small investors can easily imitate the gurus. Certainly you can learn by studying buffettology or soros-ology, but their strategies are harder to imitate than the many texts on them suggest. Slater, a highly successful investor and an accessible writer, recognizes this implicitly. His psychological insights into how small investors operate make him, I suggest, the most useful of these gurus. You should certainly study the ideas of great investors, but only as part of a strategy of being better informed. Copycatting their moves is less easy than most texts make out for the reasons I have suggested.

nine

Case histories

'The sheer hard work and discipline' of number crunching, as Charles Clark put it, is usually the basis for predicting whether an equity will move up or down. The gurus, whose views I looked at in the previous chapter, all focus on fundamental value or growth. Yet Clark speaks of the importance of 'sentiment', of 'expectations' and of so-called 'noise traders' who follow them and we have seen that these factors influence many others in the market.

At the start of this book I pointed out that political pundits claim voters in the Western world are more volatile than ever while analysts claim investors are more volatile than ever. The 18 months from mid-1999 to the start of 2001 have seen the markets zoom up and plunge down. Internet, high tech and e-shares produced many wonder stocks which hit statistical stratospheres. On 23 June 1999 ARM Holdings traded on a price/earnings ratio (PER) of 299! By October ARM was trading at a PER of over 500. With many e-stocks like, Lastminute.com, it was impossible to calculate the PER because the company had earned so very little. Internet stocks were often scoring PERs in the 100s and even 1,000s in the spring of 2000. Yahoo employs just 386 people and is valued in billions.

Meanwhile, ordinary stocks like Bellway, a decent construction company, or Great Universal Stores stayed becalmed on PERs of around 8 in Bellway's case and 11 in GUS while the average PER on the Standard & Poor's 500 Index (the second division USA index after the main Dow Jones) was 35.

Differences in PERs are supposed to reflect what *the market believes and hopes*. In 1999–2000 there was more promise in electronics than in frozen foods, and the future, once Orange, had turned e – that is, E for Exciting and Electrifying profits. Then in autumn and winter 2000 the high-tech stocks began a long retreat – in effect, the start of at least a partial bear market.

The NASDAQ Index which used to promote itself with television ads that boasted of its role in high technology fell from over 5,000 in early 2000 to around 1,700 in April 2001.

Baltimore Technology, a favourite share of Killik's, reached the dizzy heights of £14 in April and then fell back to a series of lows – first 250p, then 150p, then as low as 61p. Another fashionable stock, Autonomy dropped from 2,480p to 235p. Lastminute.com floated at 340p and went up to nearly 600p. Some 7 months later it trades at around 50p. In such volatile times fundamental value seems to matter much less than image.

Wonder stocks have come in all shapes and sizes during the history of stock markets. In the 1920s it was radio shares than ballooned towards infinity. But sometimes the wonder is not high tech but high calorie. One item I came across in my research referred to 'struggling sausage skin maker, Devro International, once a wonder stock'. If a company which produces sausage skins can become a wonder stock, no enterprise, however eccentric, can be excluded.

There were, as we shall see, many sceptics about high-tech all puff and no profit shares. The frenzy always left some 'great' investors cold. For instance, it has been said Warren Buffett has stayed clear of them and that his lack of enthusiasm is an example of masterly caution. Some commentators saw in the insane rises, in the search for Urquhart's 'ten banger' (the share that went up ten times in value which was true of Baltimore and the now-suspended Money Channel) not just greed but decadence. Real markets peopled by real investors did not, should not, behave like that.

The anatomy of enthusiasm

In fact, the 1990s had seen an earlier craze – for biotechnology stocks. Stocks like British Biotech reached their peak in 1994–1995. It was not just old heads like Buffett's who saw a parallel. In an e-mail published in 2000 a 15-year-old reader of the *Investors Chronicle* had the historical sense to compare the e-frenzy with the biotechnology boom of 1994–1995 when stocks like British Biotech promised genetic miracles. The miraculous profits never materialized, of course.

We have seen that markets have often behaved irrationally, but the reasons are perhaps more complex than financial analysts believe. In this chapter I am going to discuss 13 different shares whose recent history illustrates some more hidden aspects of market movements.

Go back to the phrase *'the market believes and hopes'*. If you start to analyse its meaning you begin to see what philosophers like the late Gilbert Ryle, author of *The Concept of Mind*, called 'a category mistake' (Ryle 1949). Markets can neither hope nor believe; only human beings can do that. It is the sum total of the beliefs of those who play the markets that matter. If we are to understand those beliefs, understanding number crunching is not enough; we also need to look at the psychology of shares – and of particular shares.

Psychologists don't have perfect measures of hopes and feelings, but they have at least developed scales like Kelly's Repertory Grid (Bannister and Fransella 1977) and the Edwards Personal Preference Schedule (Edwards 1959) which offer useful approaches to studying emotions, beliefs and expectations – and how intensely they're held.

Let's take a fictional share, Middlesex Railways. The tabloids hate Middlesex Railways because their services run late and the carriages are overcrowded. Middlesex need to invest in new stock, but its board has shied away from decisions. Profits today, problems tomorrow. The new chairman is bringing in a new management team but many doubt they will have the vision needed. Forecasts suggest more people will be forced to use railways in the London area because of congestion and sky-high parking costs so the rail management is tempted to do too little.

Wet shares and dry shares

I want here to introduce what seem a strange concept – dry shares and wet shares. 'Dry' shares do not arouse emotional associations easily; wet shares do.

Table 3   Financial performance of Middlesex Railways.

Turnover	£350 million
Expected profit	£35
Cash flow forecast	£8 million positive
Price earnings ratio	11

Middlesex Railways is mainly a dry share. The company provokes a mixture of feelings; anger from commuters; ridicule from the tabloids; hopes that new management will get their act together; fears that the Rail Regulator may slam them; fears the unions will become strong again; irritation from many commuters who don't just dislike its bad performance, but the very fact of commuting. These feelings, however, are essentially surface feelings. The only 'personal' feelings and associations Middlesex arouses centre around anger at commuting. As Middlesex has avoided any major accident, the anger is not deeply felt: it does not trigger the personal and, sometimes even, unconscious feelings and associations wet shares evoke.

You can draw two pictures of the company. The first conventional picture (Table 3) projects its financial performance but we need to look at less conventional measures too.

Associations evoked by Middlesex

▨ Expectations in brokers' reports: seven brokers expect profits to rise and the dividend to be increased. Five criticize the company's failure to invest in new rolling stock. Three worry about how well the dividend will be covered. Three also think the company will not meet its profits forecast. The unions are also showing more muscle which scares four brokers who have memories of the bad old days of union power before Mrs Thatcher handbagged them.

After the Paddington crash and the Hatfield disaster, everyone knows the railway companies will have to invest more in railways, but there is a cynical view that the government can be made to pay for this.

- Sentiment: more brokers suggest buying than selling, but many have anxieties because of the issues above.
- Press comment: generally very poor.
- Public attitudes: suspicion of railway companies was widespread before Paddington and is only getting worse. Their managers are seen as fat cats. A total of 45 per cent of commuters are fed up, with the poor performance and 66 per cent of people are aware of the frequent criticism and constant trashing by papers, and that hurts. The public is also worried as unions have a track record of calling strikes and stoppages which could damage both the image and the earnings of the company.
- Brand identification: the public in south-east England know who Middlesex Railways are but no one loves the brand in the same way as they love Nike.
- Personal associations: many commuters resent the time they spend travelling. It's uncomfortable. These negative feelings are associated with the company. None of these associations deal with childhood or sexuality. There is nothing deep about any of them. That is why the railway is mainly a dry share.

Now try to combine Table 3 and Circle 1. It's not possible. This sum is a mathematical non-starter. You cannot add cash flow, turnover and profit and loss figures to public feelings or to a risk analysis of the likelihood of unions coming out on strike.

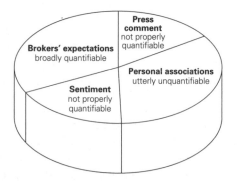

Circle 1 Attitudes towards Middlesex Railways.

But there is a solution. Convert all the measures into points on a series of scales set, say, on the basis of 1 to 10. Excellent cash flow would be 10; calamity cash flow would be 1. A similar scale could then rate very positive public attitudes as 10 and very negative ones as 1.

You can then add up scores on the scales and compare Middlesex with other railway shares:

	Middlesex Railways	Superior Railways
Cashflow	5/10	7/10
Public attitudes	4/10	6/10
Timetable	8.9/10	9.2/10

Measures for public attitudes differ from cash flow and other financial calculations, however; they are far less easy to quantify solidly. It's because many financial analysts realize these problems exist that it often seems easier to rely on precise number crunching and vague babblings about sentiment.

Most market professionals are so used to repeating that markets are about fear, greed and the herd instinct that they don't really think about measuring sentiment in any sophisticated manner. I want to suggest the market value of many shares also reflects these 'emotional' associations.

Do shares have personalities?

The question seems silly. Shares are impersonal objects. Yet human beings have invested objects with life and personality since the ancient Greeks. Modern marketing creates cognitive and emotional associations.

The Porsche was once the smartest car until too many upwardly mobile executives bought one and the marque lost some of its cachet. Other recent marketing triumphs include making us associate Yorkie, a bar of chocolate, with toughness, Jaguar, only a car, with elegance and individuality and sanitary towels with the freedom to climb mountains. And the marketeers start young. The first edition of *The International Journal of Advertising and Marketing to Children* (1999) analyses how the chocolate biscuit Penguin had a personality makeover. Transformed into a cheeky chocolate biscuit, Penguin pecked off the competition from less buzzy chocolate products. Sales rocketed.

Consumers are affected by the identity of products, so why should investors, who are consumers and collectors of shares, be immune?

In 2000 I made a series of films for the Victoria and Albert's *brand.new* exhibition which looked at the brands different people loved and hated. One of the experts I interviewed, Ralph Ardill of Imagination, speaks of the changing 'brandscapes'. He argues that in the 1980s and 1990s brands tried to create relationships with consumers. Ardill thinks brands find this harder now because consumers were not just more critical but very media savvy. Eight-year-olds understand that brands like Nike try to be cool in order to sell them more stuff. Nike, Nestlés, Red Bull, Coca Cola and MacDonalds devote millions to making consumers feel good about them and feel good if they buy the brand. Given the huge resources the companies spend on creating such feelings in consumers, it's hardly surprising that share values should be affected by both conscious and unconscious emotional factors.

Stock-market analysts and fund managers may resist this because, while punters may be taken in by the mysteries of marketing, number crunchers like them, sophisticated financial wizards like them, aspiring masters of the money universe like them, are just too smart to be taken in like that.

I want to suggest that shares do have images or a psychology and that this affects how most investors see them and deal in them. What I call 'wet' shares are shares where the business arouses complex emotional associations usually linked to family memories, history, houses, food, children and often sexuality. Such shares have a number of interesting characteristics. These 'wet' stocks are stubborn survivors even in tough conditions precisely because complex associations – even though investors will often not be aware of them – create a certain resistance to selling them.

For example, it may be harder for most individuals to sell shares in Marks & Spencer than in Pilkington Glass not just for financial reasons but also because investors have more emotional associations with M&S. They used to go there with their mothers to buy clothes – and were sometimes given a chocolate as a treat. It felt safe, part of the family experience. Glass, however excellent, can't evoke parallel associations. So Pilkingtons are a dry share.

Associations may well be unconscious. Marks & Spencer have been suppliers of underwear to the nation for decades. Freudian stockbrokers (a small breed) realize M&S will evoke unconscious associations. These will be different for different individuals. One man may associate M&S knickers – his wife has always worn them – with nice but dull marital sex. Another may associate it with his mother who used to take him shopping. Happy childhood days.

As we saw in Chapter 2, Freud was heavily into word plays. I believe that if he studied these issues today – and especially given M&S dominance in the knicker markets – the following would not have escaped him. What do you get if you reverse M&S? S&M? Is this an accident? Certainly. Does it have meaning? Certainly. Accidents can reinforce a certain image. If you want S&M or erotic cutting edge sex, M&S is not the store.

Given its traditions and history, many Britons will associate M&S with warmth, safety, affectionate sex and going there as a kid with parents to buy clothes. The most exotic associations will come from the food department which in the late 1970s and 1980s started to offer delicious and unusual sweets.

As a wet share, M&S can evoke strong associations of security and happiness – associations the most high-tech company could never dream of. I want to suggest these cognitive, emotional and unconscious associations help make up the intangible sentiment market that professionals want so badly to define.

Dry shares don't have this hinterland. They operate more on the traditional greed and panic model. Investors can be very enthusiastic about dry companies, but, if things go wrong, they enjoy far less emotional support so that the price goes down sharply in response to negative number crunching. High-tech shares are classic examples of dry shares and so, when a reaction sets in, there is not much to bolster their value other than rigorous analysis of their prospects. This prediction was made in early 2000 in the first version of this book.

I'm aware that some market professionals will think these ideas bizarre. Nevertheless, try the following.

The share association test

This test really does give you a chance to pick companies by closing your eyes, using a needle and pointing.

And please don't cheat.

Sit down at a comfortable table. You need a pad, a clock that ticks seconds and a pencil.

Open the FT or The Times. Now using the 'point with a needle' method, choose one company from the FT-SE 100 Index.

Write down the name of the share at the head of a column.

You now have 10 seconds.

Write down the first three words that come into your mind when you think of that share?

If you only have 10 seconds your most immediate associations will come out.

If you struggle to find any associations and are taking more than 10 seconds it suggests the company doesn't have any very memorable identity. Certainly its branding is poor.

If the associations are to impersonal rather than personal words, you have hit on a dry company.

Now repeat the exercise with nine other companies that you choose by sticking a needle on the page. Ideally choose four companies from the FT-SE 100 and five from the FT-SE Mid-250 Index, the index that covers the 250 next largest shares called Mid Caps for middle capitalization.

Every time you should just take 10 seconds to write down your three associations.

Once you have finished the exercise go back over your associations. See if the wet/dry distinction makes sense to you.

I'll give you some of my associations:

- HK Land – property, Hong Kong, . . . no memorable associations.
- Tate & Lyle – white sugar, Silvertown, Tibbs. I hate white sugar and think of one of the Tate & Lyle sites I came across when I was researching a film on a gang called the Tibbs gang.
- Hoechst – chemicals, no clear picture emerges.
- Elsevier – science, Dutch, dull but important books.
- Safeways – peanut butter, creche and sex. When my children were small they loved peanut butter and endlessly nagged me to buy it at Safeways and elsewhere. Later, I lived in Camden and noticed they had an attractive creche. All these positives are countered by memories of their campaign in which toddlers had adult attitudes, flirted and asked if there was 'any chance of a snog'. The campaign has been axed but it left a bad taste. Clearly a wet share, but one which caused some offence.

This 'test' will not tell you what shares to invest in. But it's quite useful to do before you buy shares, because if you turn up three negative associations you should be careful. That would be a little bit like deciding to buy into a hotel chain, turning up in the lobby of one of their hotels and discovering the receptionist was very rude to you.

The sentiment index

There have been few attempts to objectively measure sentiment either in the market as a whole or in particular shares. One attempt to, at least, include sentiment comes from Merrill Lynch who have developed an assessment of shares which includes newsflow and sentiment as factors. In Merrill Lynch's approach sentiment is defined entirely in terms of brokers' recommendations and whether they suggest buying, selling or holding.

I think this is a too narrow and inward-looking definition of sentiment. A proper measure of sentiment has to include:

- brokers' recommendations;
- press comment;
- some attempt to measure how investors perceive the company;
- associations of the sort I've described.

The distinction between 'wet' shares that evoke particular rich emotional associations and 'dry' shares that do not, does not mean investors can't get excited about them or that they will be not be profitable, but it does mean the main irrational element in the value of 'dry' shares will be the degree of enthusiasm they create. Hope for huge profits will be the emotion they evoke and, if their prospects change, they will have less support.

Thirteen case histories

To test my ideas I analysed 13 shares. I chose most of them when discussions of the book were in progress. I say this because 14 is a small sample on which to test some of these ideas and there is a risk of my choosing shares to fit my hypotheses. At the point when I had just developed an outline of the book I had not developed my hypotheses in any detail.

Initially, I thought 10 shares would be enough but I ended up adding Barclays Bank, Baltimore Technologies and ARM Holdings.

I believe these case histories illustrate how curious the relationship between the price of shares, their fundamental value, experts' recommendation and 'sentiment' is – and the contrast between dry and wet shares. The results show that many brokers are much worse predictors of how wet shares move than of how dry shares move.

The shares whose movements I've examined are:

- Body Shop
- Laura Ashley
- Vodafone
- Sainsbury's

- Marks & Spencer
- Allied Carpets
- British Biotech
- BP Amoco
- Barclays Bank
- Amazon.com
- Manchester United Football Club
- ARM Holdings
- Baltimore Technologies

The specific ideas I look at in an attempt to develop a more precise sense of sentiment and expectations are the following:

- What is the impact of general newsflow on share price?
- What is the effect of economic news on the share price?

How does 'sentiment' affect prices? I suggest we should look at two ways of measuring sentiment. A narrow measure based on brokers' and press recommendations. A broader measure based on public attitudes including the emotional and unconscious associations I've discussed.

How does enthusiasm for a product or a technology affect price?

Political newsflow

Between 1997 and 2001, the major UK and international developments included:

- the British Labour Party general election victory of May 1997;
- the handing back of Hong Kong to the Chinese;
- the saga of President Clinton and Monica Lewinsky which led to his unsuccessful impeachment;
- continuing war against Iraq;
- endless tensions in the Middle East;
- instability in Russia;

- war in Serbia and Kosovo;
- dismissal of the European Commission after allegations of corruption;
- hostilities between India and Pakistan, both nuclear powers;
- the coup in Pakistan in October 1999.

Historically, stock markets have reacted to political news. Napoleon's defeat at Waterloo gave Nathan Rothschild the chance to dominate the market. The 1973 Yom Kippur War and the rise in oil prices triggered the last long bear market. The Gulf War of 1991 had a much smaller impact.

By contrast, the war of 1999 against Serbia did not have any effect on worldwide stock-market prices even though it produced the worst East–West confrontations since the end of the Cold War. Two incidents stand out. The Russian President Boris Yeltsin threatened to stop co-operating with the peace process and the fury of the Chinese when their Belgrade Embassy was bombed.

I want to examine the impact of two events which we might have imagined would have an effect on prices.

The handing back of Hong Kong to the Chinese in June 1997. We can see that over the next 6 months what really mattered were problems with Asian economies.

	27 June	31 December 1997
Hang Seng Index	15,128	10,722
Dow Jones	7,654	7,908
London FT-SE 100	4,657	5,135
Nikkei 225	20,624	20,129
Frankfurt DAX	3,805	4,249
Sydney All Ordinaries	2,699	2,616
Paris CAC-40	2,893	2,998

The second event is the Serbian war, the first war in Europe since 1945 where NATO was directly involved. It is worth looking at the steady rise of world markets from when war was first mooted through the first bombings of Belgrade which started in April and continued to 24 June 1999.

	Start of Serbian war	April 1999	24 June 1999
Dow Jones	9,340	10,789	10,522
London FT-SE 100	6,175	6,552	6,496
Nikkei	14,375	16,701	17,290
Frankfurt DAX	4,911	5,360	5,468
Paris CAC	4,092	4,490	4,545
Hang Seng	9,858	13,333	14,004

I also include here two stock markets local to the conflict:

Vienna	1,172	1,282	1,326
Athens	3,373	3,523	3,950

There were no large-scale losses even though Europe was entering a period of instability as a result of the most intense fighting in Europe since 1945.

Greece, paradoxically the exchange closest to the hostilities, actually enjoyed a huge rise in the period during the war.

The bombing of the Chinese Embassy in Belgrade did not lead to any dramatic changes in stock-market prices either. The Serbian war did not even send investors scurrying for gold as past history suggested it might. This 'failure' may well have signalled the end of gold as a significant market.

The end of the war did not provoke any rise on the stock markets either. The victory of the British in the Falklands War, by contrast, led to a rise on the London Stock Market.

The renewed semi-war between Israel and the Palestinian 'Authority' does not seem to have had much effect on the Tel Aviv stock market either.

The conclusion would seem to be that markets are more focused on the economy than in the past.

Economic newsflow

The most significant stories since 1997 were, it could be argued:

▓ the crisis in the tiger economies, like Malaysia and Indonesia;
▓ fears that the Japanese banking system would collapse;

The herd instinct, cartoon by Tony Judanath for *Psychology News* No. 12.

- the Russian default on debt in August 1998;
- in Britain the reduction of interest rates from May 1997;
- in the USA the continuing low interest rates environment;
- the collapse of confidence in high-tech stocks;
- sudden fears that the American boom was coming to an end.

Economic news does matter. Stock markets react far more to economic than to political headlines. For example, the Russian default on debt in August 1998 triggered a fall of 4.2 per cent on Wall Street and 5 per cent in London.

Perhaps even more surprising, markets reacted more strongly to news of the resignation of the governor of the central bank of Brazil and the devaluation of the Brazilian cruzeiro than to the start of NATO bombing in Kosovo.

On 13 January 1999, when Brazil devalued its currency, the stock market in London registered its biggest ever points fall. It fell by 282 points. In percentage terms this was a fall of 4.7 per cent, less than the falls on Black Monday and Black Tuesday in 1987 when the market fell by 11 per cent and 12 per cent, but still extremely dramatic. The Dow Jones fell 345 points over the 2 days after the Brazilian resignation. The Paris stock market fell by 5.8 per cent. Trading stopped in Amsterdam. In Madrid, which has close links with Brazil, the market fell by 8.2 per cent.

In other words, economic events in a country whose economy ranks around 20th in the developed world had much more of an impact on world share prices than the first war in Europe for 50 years.

Many market professionals acknowledge the primacy of economic news and see interest rates as the most important factor in pricing shares, but the suggestion that political news has so small an effect is perhaps a little surprising. One could joke that stock exchanges should stop subscribing to the news services.

It may be that the lack of impact of political news is the result of information overload. Analysts pay much less attention to political news because they already have to cope with so many, and often conflicting, economic stories and indicators. They focus on the economy and filter out what seems less immediately relevant – even what is happening in the world.

Case histories

Body Shop – the pleasure principle shares

The first two shares in my list are very much the creation of talented, memorable women. Both companies have been through difficult times, but have benefited from surprising loyalty from financial institutions – loyalty that doesn't seem that much related to financial performance or promise.

Anita Roddick became a household name in the 1980s. Friends who put up the money for the first Body Shop became millionaires. The company revolutionized the beauty business making good, sensual cosmetics for a low price and taking an interesting ethical stance on many world issues. The Roddicks have more of the hippies-made-good in them than most other entrepreneurs. Their business retails pleasure and has some principle.

Body Shop was floated in 1984. In the 1990s, however, Body Shop started to find business tougher. Anita Roddick came in for criticism. She was seen as a bit of an egoist. A *Dispatches* programme on Channel 4 in 1992 attacked the company and, though eventually the Body Shop sued Channel 4 and won, there was a lot of negative coverage – and stories which claimed that Roddicks were hypocritical.

Trading in the late 1990s was much less good. The Body Shop tried to expand its franchises into America, but its shops there did not fare well. A number of the franchises criticized the company. Commentators noted that all too often the skills to start a company were not the skills to manage it later. Vision had to be replaced by management.

The 1998 accounts made interesting reading in the light of these criticisms. The frontispiece had a picture of Anita Roddick talking to a man who is the image of a lounge lizard. He asks what a nice woman like here is doing in a joint like this. She replies that she owns it. It's a nice witty vignette.

In her statement as co-chair, Roddick notes: 'if anyone has managed to sort out the difference between stress and enthusiasm they haven't told me.' She added the company was taking risks again by backing five hemp products. 'Demystifying hemp and championing hemp farmers all over the globe while trying to rid the world of dry skin is *fun*,' she grins.

The annual report fizzes over with good presentational ideas – pictures with cartoon bubbles, pages that raise human rights issues and so on – but what I find most interesting is that it uses images that clearly attempt to create and evoke emotional associations.

One double-page spread trumpets how SMELL AND TOUCH (their caps) affect our sense of well-being. The dominant image is of a willowy girl throwing her arms up. A purple aura surrounds her body. Use Body Shop material and you will be not just sensuous but also spiritual. Roddick also promotes Ruby, a plump Rubenesque figure who fronts the Body Shop's Self-Esteem campaign. Fat is also beautiful. Do not obsess about thin, it says. 'Ruby's prize-winning face and figure are the dawn of a new consciousness in the beauty business,' the report adds, losing its cheekiness and lapsing into marketese.

Despite the clever presentation the financial figures remain flat. Earnings per share were 11.8p in 1998, a small increase of 0.4p a share over 1997. In 1995 they had been 11.5p per share. Gordon Roddick, co-chair, explains 'the profit growth we envisaged earlier was beyond our reach.' He blamed the fact that sales in the UK were 'not as strong as we expected' on problems in the States and fallout from the Asian economic crisis.

Things did not get better. In January 1999 Body Shop issued a profits warning. The company had, like many British retailers, had a very poor Christmas in 1998. The *Investors Chronicle* (April 1999) noted the company had somehow managed to make a loss in the booming American market. Profits fell to £3.4 million, on a turnover of £304 million, but there were exceptional items of £21 million.

Some commentators also snipe at the company's high moral and political tone. It is true that its cosmetics aren't tested on animals, and that the company campaigns for the Third World and the environment, but does anyone actually need peppermint oil for their feet or aromatherapy? Wouldn't the truly enlightened stance be to get out of the cosmetics business altogether for all it peddles is 'unnecessary luxury' (*Investors Chronicle*, April 1999).

Yet the market continues to value the company's stock on an extraordinarily high price/earnings ratio (PER). Body Shop were on 18 June 1999 trading at 114p on a PER of 52.4. This was the highest PER for general retailers in the UK. It did so both before and after the appointment of a new Chief Executive Officer who was not a Roddick. By October the share price had moved up to 118p, though, as financial performance had improved, the PER was now a mere 37.

Just before Christmas 2000, Body Shop was trading around 125p. It then issued a profits warning and shares fell to 95p and were still trading at a premium to other retailers, but still at a PER of 37.

If you compare Body Shop's PER with those of other retailers what do you find? The PERs of other leading retailers are as follows:

	June 1999	October 1999
Dixons	34	28.9
W.H. Smith	26	17
Boots	20.6	15
Great Universal Stores	15.5	15.3
Body Shop	52.4	37

Body Shop's high PER is astonishingly close to technology wonder shares like Vodafone. 'Wonder' shares like Pearsons – also now headed by a dynamic woman – are where you have to look for a comparable price/earnings performance. The answer for Boots is surely to emphasize the perfumes and get a woman CEO.

One reason may simply be that Anita Roddick continues to mesmerize investors and to hold out hope that she and her husband will find a new formula that matches the zeitgeist and make tremendous profits. Body Shop is a share with highly emotional associations, almost a wet dream of a share and the number crunchers of the City are seduced. Seduced, without knowing it, by the more subtle associations involved – associations of sensuality, sexuality and fun. The Body Shop markets pleasure. If you're guilty because you've been unfaithful to your wife you bring her Chanel. But if you want to frolic you use Roddick's massage oils.

There's one extra factor. Psychologists know smells are specially effective in triggering memories. Body Shop are at some level aware of the financial value of these smell associations, but I'd argue that no explanation for their stubbornly high PER can afford to ignore the pleasurable associations it evokes.

Brokers' recommendations: few made either to buy or sell.

Sentiment factors: Anita Roddick, love her or hate her; memories of tremendous success and hope that the once wonderful perform-ance of the shares will be repeated. Body Shop products as smells evoke memories very effectively, triggering memories both erotic and financial.

Enthusiasm quotient: nothing technological but Roddicks do whip up a little excitement.

Laura Ashley – designs for living

Laura Ashley, even though its share price has fallen steeply, would almost certainly be among the penny shares if it were not for the loyalty – almost the sentimental attachment – of one of the heads of that most unsentimental institution Goldman Sachs.

In the 1970s and 1980s Laura Ashley was a very chic designer. The cheerful clothes and home furnishings she created were in demand in Britain, the States and even Japan. Her designs represented a certain very English prettiness. The company benefited from Brit-ain's growing reputation as a centre of design, a reputation first established in the 1960s as part of swinging London. At first, its very sweet designs could almost be said to have a subtle irony, creating an instant English heritage image.

By the early 1990s Laura Ashley was no longer chic. The design concept did not change much. Commentators felt the company seemed to lose its way creatively. There had been other problems because the chief executive, Sir Bernard Ashley, got a less than glowing press. Sir Bernard was Laura Ashley's husband. *The Times* (29 April 1999) blamed 'the irascible Sir Bernard' for not being able to accept that Laura Ashley stopped being a family business the day it was floated.

The problems were reflected in the share price. In 1994 it was in the 100p range. Then it went up to around 200p in 1996 when profits were around £10 million. Profits were £16 million in 1997 when the shares still traded at around 200p. The company then got into difficulties. Its ranges looked too much heritage and too little cutting edge. Losses for 1998 were over £49 million.

Laura Ashley was never a large company. Nevertheless, the shares have benefited from surprising loyalty. When the profits slumped, and they did slump most after the death of Laura Ashley, Goldman Sachs's John Thornton found a Malaysian company that was willing to put in £25 million.

In October 1998 Laura Ashley closed five large-format stores in the States and announced the sale of a further five stores. The shares were down to 14p from a high during the year of 58p.

From the start Thornton seems to have been personally enthusiastic though some of his critics argue he made an initial misjudgement, but at least had the decency not to bale out. *The Times* noted Laura Ashley was still being saved by John Thornton 'keeping the old girl alive.'

The Malaysian company who Thornton had persuaded to rescue Laura Ashley were now being asked to provide a further £25 million so that the gingham shirts, skirts and tablecloths could continue. *The Times* asked what Mr Thornton 'saw in it'. Having asked the question, *The Times* failed to answer it.

The Times noted that Thornton's strategy was to take the company private so the owners would be able to conceal 'further indignities'. If that were so, of course, the lower the shares went the cheaper the eventual reprivatization.

The Times' negative assessment did not have that much impact on the share price. By 18 June 1999 with a rights issue due the shares were down to 12.25p. They rallied to 13p. By October the shares had risen to 17p – in fact a 25 per cent rise. By 2001 the situation had stabilized with the shares being worth 18p on 22 January. The shares then rose up to 26p as the company's recovery started to bear fruit. It even paid a dividend.

Given its many difficulties, we have to marvel at the survival of Laura Ashley.

Brokers' recommendations: few.
Sentiment factors: affection for a very English design, loyalty.

Vodafone – the miracle of mobile phones

Mobile phones don't have obvious emotional associations and if they were one of the wonder stocks of the 1996–2000 period it was largely because their technology aroused enormous enthusiasm. Even better the technology is not complicated. Everyone can understand it – and in the wake of biotechnology problems that probably helped the price. There is suspicion of high-tech shares whose technology most people can't understand.

Vodafone was floated on the stock market in 1995. Vodafone benefited from the fact that the mobile phone sector became fashionable after 1996 when it seemed mobile phones were becoming an indispensable tool of modern life. The company established itself as a market leader. Vodafone is a dry share. Mobile phones don't yet provoke many associations.

In October 1998 brokers ABN Amro recommended buying. By November the price had risen to 846p and there were more buy recommendations even though the PER was then 46.

On 1 January 1999 Vodafone stood at 975p. By the spring of 1999 its performance had been so strong many brokers were recommending investors to sell BT shares and use the money to buy Vodafone shares. On 30 April, the share price went up 12p to 1151p because it was seen as an Internet stock.

On 6 June 1999, the *Observer* advised people to watch for Vodafone which was expected to report profits of between £872 million and £916 million on the following Tuesday. Nevertheless, brokers noted the share price was making hard work of breaking above the 1,250p barrier.

Later in the month Vodafone passed that barrier. It stood at 1,308p on 18 June. The stock was trading at a PER of 69.4 as opposed to Cable and Wireless which was trading on a ratio of about 26 and JWE Telecom on 18.

The takeover of Airtouch catapulted Vodafone further up the FT-SE 100 Index. By October 1999 it was the second largest share on the London Stock Exchange, just after BP Amoco. It was trading on a PER of 72.4. The shares were then split. But the main fear was that the market would not grow as fast. In 2000, it became the largest UK's share with BP second; since then they have swapped places.

The most interesting aspect of Vodafone's rise is that enthusiasm was strong enough to counter fears that mobile-phone users are often bad credit risks and the health scare. In the spring and summer of 1999 a number of shock horror stories suggested mobile phones might leak radiation which might cause brain damage. Initially the market shrugged off the lawsuit risk and bad publicity. But then aggressive lawyers started looking for clients who used mobile phones and developed brain damage.

When biotechnology companies got press that highlighted medical risks their prices were badly affected. Analysts largely ignored these negative factors with Vodafone. The *Sunday Times* (20 June 1999) argued there was 'still mileage left in the shares.' Vodafone hit 342p but has since slipped back.

At the end of 2000, however, American lawyers announced the launch of brain cancer litigation, not directly against Vodafone but against mobile-phone companies. This could be as costly to mobile phone companies as lawsuits against tobacco companies. Yet the radiation story doesn't seem to have affected the price of shares as much as the poor performance of Nokia and other manufacturers like Motorola and Ericsson who announced lower than expected sales. The fear is that people will not need all the fancy new services mobile phones will offer. By May 2001 Vodafone had fallen in price to around 200 and was trading on a PER of 54.

The sheer size of Vodafone offered some protection but smaller telecom companies like Kingston Communications collapsed dramatically from over £10 to under £1.40.

Brokers' recommendations: consistently right in recommending them.
Sentiment factors: nil.
Enthusiasm quotient: high because of the growing market for mobile phones and links with the Internet.

The next two shares have long been at the heart of FT-SE 100 Index. They have deep history. The fate of both suggests that a company with strong associations can manage to hang on to a surprisingly strong PER despite the kind of press which would get a play closed in the West End very quickly. Some shares are loved – and those who speak against them can feel as if they're betraying a family friend.

Sainsbury's – three for the price of two usually

Sainsbury's, the Victorian grocers, turned itself into a chain of supermarkets in the 1960s and 1970s. In those decades Sainsbury's was the innovative market leader, the shop for the middle class. It was only in the 1990s that it was overtaken by Tesco. Tesco has been judged the more dynamic management for over 5 years now. It introduced the first loyalty card, for example. Nevertheless, Sainsbury's had – and has – an image as reliable and quite classy.

Sainsbury's is an unusual company as 35 per cent of the shares are still owned by members of the family. Pundits have often complained it doesn't have to respond to 'market disciplines' as a result.

Sainsbury's real troubles started in the late 1990s when there was a general feeling that it had lost its way. The long battle with Tesco was turning into a defeat.

Nevertheless, in August 1998, Charterhouse Tilney recommended holding. They sensed a change of culture and pointed out Sainsbury's banking operations were doing well. On 25 September 1998, when the shares were at 567p, Charles Stanley also recommended holding.

Sell recommendations only came 2 months later. By November Williams de Broe and Peel Hunt recommended selling. In December

Charterhouse Tilney changed their advice when the shares were at 528p. Some 2 weeks later, when the shares stood af 476p, SG Securities recommended selling. By the start of 1999 the shares were at 480p.

After that the shares continued to slide but, as we shall see, in terms of PER, Sainsbury's still outperforms all other supermarket chains bar Tesco. Given the depth of Sainsbury's problems for most of the period 1998–2000 that is surprising.

One way to highlight Sainsbury's difficulties is to compare its recent advertising campaign (late 1998, early 1999) starring John Cleese with Tesco's long-running ads starring Prunella Scales.

Tesco used Prunella Scales as a fussy, irritating but cost conscious middle aged shopper. Prunella Scales is well known for her role as John Cleese's wife in the classic comedy *Fawlty Towers*. Sainsbury's then decided to hire John Cleese to front its ads. But where Tesco had given Prunella Scales a totally different personality from her role in *Fawlty Towers*, John Cleese was stuck with an older version of his neurotic over-the-top persona from *Fawlty Towers*.

Cleese blared through a megaphone the amazing deals on offer at Sainsbury's every week. Casting Cleese to run opposite Scales was bound to echo *Fawlty Towers*, a point Sainsbury's seems to have missed. The campaign not only had a copycat air because of the casting, but it also didn't work because quality has been an important part of Sainsbury's image. The chain never sold itself on cheap prices. Stores said many customers took the best bargains Cleese was megaphoning and then left, having bought little else.

To make matters worse many newspapers in late 1998 and early 1999 warned that most supermarket chains were not passing on the discounts they advertised to customers. The *Sunday Times* (6 June 1999), which ran a campaign on the subject, showed Sainsbury's sometimes did not honour 'three for the price of two' or 'buy one get one free' discounts. I had endless experience of this in my local Sainsbury's. I often complained to local managers when I found the checkout tills did not ring up the price of the goods marked on the shelf or that 'buy one get one free' didn't seem to register. You had to check your bill carefully to make sure the shop honoured its discount promises.

Sainsbury's well-publicized problems damaged the share value, but far less than we might have imagined. On 21 February the

Observer ran a long article arguing that, as profits waned, the Sainsbury family had less and less reason to hang on to their shares. It also argued that if there was a takeover the company would fetch £10 billion rather than the market value of £7 billion. The *Observer* even usefully produced a business plan for potential bidders. A buyer for £10 billion could sell Sainsbury's 13 vast Savacentres, the Shaw business in New England and the do-it-yourself operation, Homebase.

These three operations would fetch something like £3.5 billion so the true price would only be £6.5 billion. One broker Charles Stanley again showed itself a fan. It had recommended holding on at 476p. Now, with the shares 100p down at 376p, it recommended holding on again, even though the company had failed to deliver forecasts.

Prospects of a takeover helped the shares rise from 376p and by mid-May touched 430p.

On 15 May 1999, *The Times* reported Sainsbury's would spend more than £150 million to refurbish its head office. The project had yet to be announced to either the staff or the Stock Exchange. *The Times* hinted that, as Sainsbury's had decided to axe 300 head-office jobs, staff wouldn't be dancing with joy about the refurbishment.

The share price fell again and by 6 June it was at 400.5p.

On 6 June 1999 the *Sunday Times*'s business section reported that Sainsbury's was starting a makeover of 413 of its stores. There would be new plastic bags, new signs all over shops and a new motto 'making life taste better'.

Early in June Sainsbury's also announced it would sell books, clothes and compact discs and at the same it planned to sack 1,650 staff. 'These initiatives do not strike me as a way to beat the competition,' said one analyst.

Sceptical commentators pointed out this was the third time in 3 years that Sainsbury's had overhauled its advertising. Was there a crisis of identity? Sainsbury's marketing gurus wrestled with the issue. In the past Sainsbury's had seemed somewhat aloof; today Sainsbury's needed to be more engaging. The latest ad to go with the bags and new slogan would star a sulky child. This lucky kid wasn't going to have John Cleese's foghorn in its ear about low prices. To appease her child, mum would buy it a gingerbread man. The child's face lights up. Happiness is shopping in a caring, not aloof supermarket. And – the cleverness disarms – in the ad the checkout registers 'peace offering 35p'. The message: Sainsbury's cares and is competitive on price.

The *Sunday Times* sniped the 'spirit of glasnost sounds spookily similar to that sweeping through Marks & Spencer, another leading retailer in troubled times.' Stock market analysts were sceptical about whether Sainsbury's culture could really deliver change.

The *Sunday Times* recommended SELL and pointed out that the only hope for Sainsbury's was to be taken over by Wal Mart. The Sainsbury's price stayed in the 400p range, however.

The next dramatic fall came when the Asda–Wal Mart link up was announced. Sainsbury's went down to 368p, but then rallied to 380p even though the Asda–Wal Mart merger meant that Sainsbury's now had far tougher competition to face. That left the price just 4p higher than in February when Charles Stanley said it was worth holding on as recovery prospects were good.

On 18 June 1999, some 3 days after the announcement of the Asda–Wal Mart merger, Sainsbury's was trading on a PER of 14.4. By 27 October the PER was down to 13.3. They held on to this even after a BBC programme which followed their chief executive working a few days on the floor. It became clear he had little idea of the problems his staff were having to deal with daily, including expensive new tills which didn't work properly and reduced stickers placed on items which caused tremendous delays because the lower prices couldn't be read. The Sainsbury family, however, the *Guardian* noted, promoted the chief executive to think great thoughts. On 1 November 1999, the *Guardian* compared the problems of Sainsbury's with those of the House of Windsor, an institution that certainly arouses emotional associations.

In 2000 a new Chief Executive, Peter Davis who had previously run the Prudential was appointed. Sainsbury's was trying to expand into new areas in their shops. At London Colney, for example, where they share a site with M&S, Sainsbury's was trying to learn how to sell more clothes. The local M&S manager confided they had a lot to learn about displaying clothes attractively! By May 2001, even though Tesco remained very much the market leader, Sainsbury's price had recovered to 400p and they were trading on a PER of 22.8.

My potted tale of Sainsbury's suggests that a retailer in difficulties, wriggling this way and that, on the receiving end of a highly critical press and now facing competition from an aggressive chain with American cutting-edge buying techniques, can still get a surprising numbers of brokers to recommend hanging on.

Perhaps even more astonishingly Sainsbury's was outperforming a number of its competitors in terms of its PER.

The comparable PER figures for the larger supermarket chains were:

	18 June 2000	27 October 2000	9 May 2001
Budgen's	11.5	11.1	11.8
Somerfield	8.9	4.3	6.7
Safeway	10.4	8.3	17.7
Tesco	18.6	20.4	21.3
Sainsbury's	14.4	13.3	22.8

It can be argued that the resistance of Sainsbury's to bad press and poor financial figures represents a mixture of loyalty and 'clinging on' because the company evokes associations – today's adults and analysts shopped there as children, for example – and those emotional associations act as a buffer. They also mean that when there is some sign of improved management the shares respond very well.

Sentiment factors: unconscious positive attitudes to food, memories of visiting shops as children as part of family life, warm associations.

Marks & Spencer

Like Sainsbury's, Marks & Spencer is a familiar shop and an old company which millions of Britons have invested in. It was famed for its good staff relations and reliability. It has been estimated that half the population wear M&S knickers.

Two developments in the late 1980s affected the company for the next decade. First, it bought Brooks Brothers, the high-class American clothes manufacturers, and paid $750 million, far too high a price according to analysts. This was the first of a number of foreign adventures that went wrong.

More positively in the late 1980s and early 1990s, M&S put itself on the cutting edge of food retailing. The purveyors of dull knickers to the nation pioneered packaging extremely classy foods; the thinking was that middle England was more willing to play with, and pay for, exotic grub than exotic sex. M&S became extremely successful food retailers.

By the late 1990s, however, M&S was in difficulties. It seemed to have lost the knack of understanding British middle-class taste. Its clothes seemed dull. Aggressive competitors like Next were luring customers away. M&S had to have a sale because it was stuck with so many of the clothes bought for Christmas 1998 which could simply not shift.

Even more than Sainsbury's, however, brokers recommended M&S. In 1998 M&S hit 563p. In July, when it was down to 530p, Flemings recommended it as a buy because expansion plans looked good. In August the shares were down to 501 when Charterhouse Tilney recommended M&S as a buy. On 4 September, Sutherlands recommended it as a long-term buy. Even after the *Investors Chronicle* starred it as a sell on 18 September, many brokers remained surprisingly positive. On 2 October Morgans recommended holding on.

In the week 23–30 October 1998, M&S shares were trading at 435p. Williams de Broe recommended buying as did Sutherlands. A month later with the shares at much the same price, Sutherlands recommended selling while BT Alex Brown, Butterfield Securities and Morgan Stanley recommended holding. Peel Hunt said the shares wouldn't fall below 400p and recommended buying. So did Williams de Broe. On 11 December Sutherlands recommended selling at 400p.

It is all too clear that the brokers were in some way convinced M&S would recover. They were proved wrong.

In January 1999, after a series of boardroom rows, M&S hit $333\frac{1}{4}$p, a 5 year low. In February Killik & Co. noted Marks had its own specific problems including a very centralized business culture and misjudgements of the economy. At 337p Killik & Co. thought 'the new management still has a lot to prove – too early to buy.'

On 25 February 1999, M&S went in for the 'cold-blooded axeing' of three directors, ruthlessness the press didn't think the company capable of. Until recently, newspapers noted, Lord Sieff would regularly drop in for lunch at M&S headquarters – and lunch was haute cuisine, served by a butler who knew his Sancerre from his Chablis.

The Times noted that, if 31 of the top 125 jobs could be 'axed', M&S must be truly bloated with bureaucracy.

The Times also reported that M&S faced an unusual problem. The lease for its head office building had been negotiated with such skill (by the old buccaneers who ran the firm in the 1950s) it cost hardly more than a peppercorn rent. So M&S was trapped in its sprawling head office and couldn't afford to move or to decentralize.

The Times (25 February 1999) praised the new chief executive, Peter Salsbury, for deciding he would concentrate on the British trouble spots. It added that, despite this unusual willingness to break with the past, the chain was not proving any better at judging the taste of customers.

On 5 March 1999, after a sale to shift all the unsold Christmas goods, the price was at 399p and Paribas recommended selling.

Despite James Benfield, M&S's marketing director, outlining a number of bright ideas, broker West LB Panmure issued a sell circular. Panmure thought it was going to be particularly painful for M&S to become competitive especially in the once glorious food division. The brokers floated the idea that Safeway or Asda could take over the M&S food division as it was small enough to stop the Monopolies Commission getting involved. Nevertheless, Panmure recommended selling. The effect on the share price was to put the shares back to 371p.

Then rumours helped the share price. Warren Buffett announced his intention to buy into a British blue-chip company. Given his taste for fundamental value, M&S seemed a likely candidate. On 30 April talk of a 'dream merger' between Tesco and M&S also did the rounds. These two factors pushed the shares up to 430p. By 26 April they were at 454p because of continuing merger hopes.

Quickly, however, scepticism set in. There was no evidence that Buffett had built up a 3 per cent stake in the company or that he was planning to – and no sign of a merger.

On 14 May 1999, the *Investors Chronicle* noted M&S had decided it had to make a return on capital of at least 9.7 per cent. The journal was critical of the directors. In 1991 they had been given share options to exercise if the price was over 225p. The *Investors Chronicle* calculated that, with the shares just over 400p, you could argue that 150p of the rise since 1991 was due to the long bull market. The contribution of the directors over 8 years could be said to be worth a princely 25p per share. They were hardly, the *Investors Chronicle* blasted, worth their share perks.

On 28 May 1999, Deutsche Bank said M&S shares 'underperform'. The Bank insisted the food sector was weak. M&S also cut back on its recruiting and wrote to hundreds of graduates who had been promised jobs to tell them 'sorry' but they wouldn't be hired.

By late May 1999 commentators were also drawing interesting comparisons between M&S and Sainsbury's. Marks came out of this better. At least customers still visited its shops even if they didn't buy. Was this a question of loyalty or the result of the fact that people window shop for clothes but no one window shops between supermarkets?

At the end of May 1999 M&S had risen to 394p. On 6 June when the *Sunday Times* analysed 10 popular shares it was much more bullish about M&S than Sainsbury's. Yet criticisms of both groups were oddly similar. 'The knicker elastic is looking frayed at Marks & Sparks. It is being beaten hands down by other shops on virtually every product it sells. It needs to fight hard to regain its position as the shop for middle England,' concluded James Urquhart Stewart of Barclays Stockbrokers.

Nevertheless, the *Sunday Times* recommended BUY. It detected more willingness to change than at Sainsbury's. It was a psychological judgement about the psychology of an organization's attitude to change that swayed the *Sunday Times*.

Most brokers agreed with this assessment. They also argued there was more chance of M&S selling its food division without causing problems in terms of a reference to the Monopolies Commission.

Hilary Cook, director of research for Barclays Stockbrokers and, in effect, the person who recommends what shares Barclays unit trusts should buy and sell told me she had decided to sell M&S shares in 1999. 'I felt that they had lost the plot.' She told me she was nervous about this because many of their investors were middle-aged women who had probably shopped at M&S all their lives. 'I expected many cries of protest from investors, many of whom were loyal M&S customers, but the protests never came.'

On 16 June 1999, when the acquisition of Asda by the US giant Wal Mart was announced, the share price went down again and by 21 June M&S was at 359p on a PER of 24.2.

It's worth comparing M&S PER with that of other shops. In the general retailers sector the following had higher PERs:

The Body Shop	52.4
Allied Carpets	37.6
Dixons	34.0
Wyevale (the garden centre operators)	27.6
W.H. Smith	26.0

Shops in direct competition with M&S, like Next, the French Connection and Moss Bros, were all trading on lower PERs than M&S even though most were doing better in attracting consumers and persuading them to buy.

In the 3 months after the Wal Mart buyout – and in the face of a continuously bad press – M&S's share price fell to under 300p, but it was still trading on a more than respectable PER.

On 27 October 1999 these were the comparisons:

M&S	18.4
Moss Bros	12.1
JJB Sports	16.4
Next	16.7
Storehouse	4.2

I have included JJB Sports because it has been a stock consistently backed by Jim Slater – yet it doesn't manage as good a PER as M&S.

On 27 October 1999, Richard Ratner of Seymour Price said that M&S 'is positioning itself as a market retailer ... I would not be unhappy to buy the stock at this price.' I find the double negative interesting; it evokes English emotional repression so beautifully and yet the emotional tie to M&S still seems there.

The year 2000 was a truly bad one for M&S. There were continuing tales of disappointing sales; the share price went below 300p.

M&S appointed a new chairman, Luc van der Velde, and started a controversial advertising campaign with a naked woman who screamed that, as she was size 16, she was normal. The company also developed so-called concept stores. One of their managers told me these were supposed to 'lead the customer' from one story to another and make them come back for more buying opportunities.

The share price kept on falling, going as low as 178p. By January 2001 it had recovered to 199.5p even though Christmas trading was poor. It is staggering, however, that the day when its results were announced and faced with a universally bad press, shares in M&S actually posted a rise from 199p to 206p. The next day the shares rose to 221p. The *Independent* could not bring itself to attribute such resistance to emotional factors, but said that Americans were buying into the stock because it was cheap as the dollar was high against sterling. That's true, of course, of every stock quoted in pounds.

From the point of view of the wet share/dry share analysis the interesting thing is that, despite thousands of negative articles and years of poor sales figures, the shares were trading on 9 May 2001 at 269p on a PER of 22.7.

This put them after a 5 year decline still well above Kingfisher at 11.3 or Great Universal Stores on around 14 or Boots on around 12. Who says investors don't have unconscious sentiments?

Sentiment factors: considerable and complex. Very similar to Sainsbury's but in addition unconscious associations with warm, if not exotic, sex, delicious sweets and food and the kind of family expedition that is often warm.
Enthusiasm quotient: nil.

Allied Carpets –
no accounting for carpets

Allied Carpets was is a well-established high-street chain. It spent a good deal on advertising in the 1980s and 1990s. It offered customers perfectly good carpets, floor coverings and some basic items of furniture at lowish prices. One of its main rivals is Lord Harris' Carpetright.

The story of Allied is peculiar. It never enjoyed the kind of loyalty customers gave to Sainsbury's and M&S. But Allied was a presence in the high street offering reasonably priced carpets. Not the cheapest but good value.

Allied developed very serious problems in 1998, however, when some unusual accountancy practices were revealed. Orders were logged in as sold before they really had been delivered. The directors involved were made to resign, but got generous pay-offs. The rules at Allied seem 'to have been such that an articled clerk might have been confused', *The Times* (29 April 1999) sniped. A £2 million black hole in Allied's accounts was exposed.

In August 1998 as the scandal became clear the price of Allied plunged to 53p. The board vowed 'the rebuilding starts today'. The shares slumped, however. In September 1998 there were hopes of a merger and the shares rose to 66p. But they then fell back again.

On 29 April 1999 *The Times* reported that Julian Lee was not resigning as chair of Allied Carpets. Lee became chairman of Allied Carpets when it came to the market in 1996. *The Times* highlighted the fact that the prospectus was signed off by Arthur Andersen, a company Lee used to work for.

On 29 April 1999 Allied stood at 39p. The *Sunday Times* (21 February 1999) suggested that Mr Lee who had seen a previous firm go broke might like to resign. Lord Harris' Carpetright was taking business away in two ways. First, he had bought 27 shops from Allied. Second, on the high street Carpetright was winning customers from Allied. Analysts believed that the new Allied shops would help push Carpetright's profits up from £22 million to £31 million next year.

Allied did go down especially when it was forced again to issue a profits warning. By 15 June 1999, the shares were down at 29p. From this point, however, the shares started to climb for no discernible reason.

By 18 June 1999 Allied Carpets was back to $33\frac{1}{2}$p. On Monday 21 June, it was up to 37.5p. The shares had increased in value by 25 per cent in just over a week and were trading on a PER of 42. The shares were low in absolute terms, but the company's position in the PER league of general retailers needs explaining.

Comparison of share price and PER among general retailers on 21 June 1999:

	Share price	PER
Allied Carpets	37.5p	42
MFI	37p	21.9
Courts Furnishings	402p	18
Carpetright	373p	17.6
Wickes	385p	12.2

There is no reason why Allied should have done so much better in PER terms than the other retailers when it had received such a critical press. Some analysts suggested that in mid-1999 with the housing boom more carpets would be needed. But why get them from Allied? One answer is that people saw it as a recovery situation or a takeover target. There is another possibility. MFI, Courts and Carpetright, however, do advertise very much on the basis of their low prices and discounts, while Allied emphasizes something more of a family atmosphere. I suggested in June 1999 that this, combined with the recovery potential, explained its valuation.

Allied subsequently zoomed up to 99p as a result of takeover interest. It was then taken over. I have included it as it was an interesting case published in the 2000 edition of *Bears and Bulls*.

Sentiment factors: house, family.
Enthusiasm quotient: none except as a recovery stock.

Manchester United Football Club – shares for fans

The bizarre relationship between success, loyalty and share price is also illustrated if you look at the price of soccer clubs. In Britain those floated include Tottenham Hotspur, Newcastle United and Sunderland. Sunderland won promotion back to the Premiership in May 1999 and promptly lost 12p to 472p. Even historic honours don't seem to give football club shares the chance to score.

Manchester United pulled off a unique treble in May 1999 winning the Premiership, the FA Cup and the European Championship. The following year it was able to market itself more aggressively than ever before. The Club has its own television station. Manchester United is one of the most famous football clubs in the world with supporters from Japan to Tierra del Fuego. In marketing speak the brand is worldwide.

Yet so far, despite all these enthusiasms and successes, the share price is still pedestrian – more like the England team than Manchester United.

In May 1999 after winning the treble Manchester United's share price rose to just over 195p. It then doldrummed down to 189p, just 2.5p above its low for the year. The PER was 29.5, significantly higher than that of Charlton Athletic (relegated from the Premiership, PER of 18.7) but way below that of Newcastle United trading on 34.4 and Chelsea trading on a PER of over 50. By 27 October 1999, when Manchester United had lost a number of critical games, the PER had improved to 32.8.

By January 2001, the price had not improved hugely. It was at 217p. As the club failed in Europe in 2001, the price retreated to 177p on a PER of 28.1.

The question we long to ask is why Manchester United, who have far more possibilities of doing interesting international deals and who have millions of eager fans, should remain on a relatively conservative PER in today's market conditions.

One explanation may be that football club shares are seen as a hobby. Body Shop, Marks & Spencer, Sainsbury's and Laura Ashley are clearly businesses which evoke loyalties and passions. Manchester United is a passion which has become a business. We would have no difficulty evoking all kinds of passionate associations, but there is an underlying perception that soccer is not true commerce. The football net is very different from the Internet.

Sentiment factors: dedication of fans, success,
Enthusiasm quotient: low in financial terms because of the perception that soccer is not really a business.

Football club shares have suffered because they became mildly fashionable at the time the biotechnology boom was fading and hard questions were being asked about shares which soared upwards for irrational reasons.

British Biotech – a germ of an idea

British Biotech was floated in 1992. It was only in 1994 that the share price started to move dramatically. Like all biotechnology firms its lure was that its research would hit on some sort of miracle drug which would create enormous profits. British Biotech were said to be working on a cancer drug. By the middle of 1996 the shares had zoomed to 330p. Their market capitalization was in the region of £2 billion and it was threatening to enter the Footsie 100.

Such flashy figures only made sense if the company could sell something like £1 billion of medicines by 2004 and make profits of £80 million on that.

At the time the company was posting losses of £25 million a year and it still had it all to do in research and development to bring drugs to the market. In the middle of 1997 the shares were still high fetching 252p, however.

Then scepticism set in. The shares fell steeply during the last 6 months of 1997 as the press got wind of real problems in proving that some of their drugs worked. The profile was typical of dry shares in trouble. With no loyalty to fall back on, the poor newsflow damaged the share price.

In July 1998 the shares were down to 36p having lost 200p in about 6 months. Worse was to come. In February 1999 one of British Biotech's drugs, Marimastat, failed to clear its first regulatory hurdle in the pancreatic cancer. *Sunday Business* (21 February 1999) predicted there was more trouble on the way and advised selling at 22p. The trouble was a dispute with its director of research.

On 25 March 1999 the *Evening Standard* reported 'the troubled group' British Biotech was ending work on Zacutex, a treatment for acute pancreaitis. A study showed no significant difference between using the drug and using a placebo. The development of Zacutex had cost £30 million. Biotech announced its chief medical officer Peter Jensen was leaving. The company would also axe 60 of its 350 employees and focus its research on so-called metalloenzyme inhibitors.

The price on 15 June 1999 was 16p and seemed to be heading up again very marginally. On 18 June it gained 2.75p to stand at 19p. By October 27 the shares had risen by 50 per cent to 29.5.

British Biotech is not a household name and that has made its fall steeper. It is a dry share and has no particularly positive associations. It suffered too when it was censured in July 1999 by the Stock Exchange. But it's interesting too that the sector has done poorly at a time when there have been many anxieties raised about genetically engineered foods. British Biotech are in a sector which promised much, largely has failed to deliver its promises and also has vague associations with what the tabloids call 'Frankenstein foods' even though the company is developing drugs, not foods.

The failure of British Biotech to deliver the once promised profits meant that in January 2001 it was trading at around 21p. In March the share dipped further but then recovered to 23p in May 2001. The share was the opposite of Urquhart's 'ten banger'; it was a 'ten loser' having declined by 1,000 per cent since its highs – a fate that warns some e-xciting shares may languish in the lows for years.

Sentiment factors: increasingly negative due to fears aroused by cloning, genetic foods.

Enthusiasm quotient: destroyed due to poor record of converting good research ideas into proper medicines.

As a share which was always 'dry' British Biotech had little emotional support when conditions turned sour.

Amazon.com

Internet stocks were the hit at the end of the 1990s as e-commerce became a buzz word and investors were intrigued by an equity that had www attached to its name.

Amazon boasts it is the largest bookshop in the world. It was started in 1995. When the shares were first floated on the stock market the price was $15.

On 2 January 1998, Amazon was quoted at $24. By the end of the year it was close to $105. As the New York market rose steeply in the spring of 1999 Amazon reached $221 but it fell back to $119 in the last week of May. From October 1998 to October 1999, the price had still risen 352 per cent.

Other signs that Internet enthusiasm was failing came when Barnes and Noble, America's biggest bookstore, floated its online unit. The shares rose by only 27 per cent on the first day of trading. The *Sunday Times* (30 May 1999) called this 'disappointing' by comparison with previous Internet flotations.

Edmond Warner in *Sunday Business* (14 February 1999) looked at Amazon as part of a review of the Internet phenomenon. Warner warned the rise of Internet stocks were part of a 'general bubble'. He recalled living in Taiwan in 1989 when the Taiwan stock market had 'septupled' in 2 years. Housewives and taxi drivers had given up their day jobs to play the market full time. The broking office looked like a bookie's office, he said with 'a cross-section of society in a variety of states of repose'. A year later the Taiwan stock market had lost 75 per cent of its value. Warner hoped the taxi drivers still had day jobs to go back too. The Internet frenzy reminded him of this.

Other pundits took the opposite view and argued that Internet stocks have more resistance than biotechnology stocks did. I would suggest that this is partly because the technology is understandable. We can understand the potential of e-commerce more easily than the potential of monoamine inhibitor genetic sites.

In May 1999 Keith Benjamin of Banc Boston Robertson argued that many investors had been frightened off the Internet, but he predicted top-quality results for large companies like Amazon and Yahoo and that those who panicked would regret it.

There are logical reasons why Internet stocks should arouse even more enthusiasm than biotechnology stocks once did. The negative factors are less obvious. First, Internet companies do not face the regulatory hurdles drug and biotech companies face so there is much less of a time gap between having an idea, implementing it and reaping profits from it. Second, unlike British Biotech and other biotechnology stocks, Amazon has become a household name and has attracted huge interest among investors. Yet Amazon's boss Jeff Bezos famously warned small investors that his company was not necessarily a stock for them. As their price in May 2001 is $16.92, I can only admire his honesty. Lastminute.com in the UK has not done its investors many favours either. On 6 May 2001 the stock fell 7.5% as profit-takers (who had bought at 44p) took modest profits when it 'soared' and 'roared' back to 56p.

In March 1999 six companies were selected for classification as Internet companies by the *International Herald Tribune* (6–7 March 1999) who sniped that investors looking for pure Internet companies would do better to look at Canada. By May 2001 it is clear that Internet businesses will now have to deliver real results, not promises. As dry shares, they will fall hard if they don't deliver the profits.

Brokers' recommendation: One useful piece of information is that American research on Amazon was very positive: 71 per cent said buy, 19 per cent hold and 10 per cent sell in December 1998. Even this is a kind of basic analysis of sentimental that is usually missing in Britain.
Sentiment factors: nil.
Enthusiasm quotient: high, due to the Internet.

Baltimore Technologies

Baltimore was one of the stars of the high-tech stocks. It makes security systems for the Web and is therefore very different from e-businesses like lastminute.com or letsbuyit.com which depend on expensive marketing to attract consumers.

A number of brokerage houses like Killik & Co. began to recommend Baltimore when it zoomed up from an offer price of £10 a share in 1998 to £29 in the autumn of 1999. Then the company became a truly hot stock and, in the space of 6 months, it advanced to over £140. One reason for this was that the company was producing a real product and posted a small profit.

There were some brokers who were worried that Baltimore had gone too high and recommended taking profits when the price had surged to over £100 a share. But many kept on insisting it would go ever upwards. Baltimore's market capitalization was so large that it became one of the FT-SE 100 shares in the spring of 2000. The shares were split so that 1 share of £140 became 100 shares at £14. But then a retreat started as the anxieties about high-tech shares mounted. As one of the smallest players in the FT-SE 100 Baltimore did not profit that much from being in the Index when times became hard. Tracker funds clearly did not buy that much of the stock.

In December 2000 the stock fell to its lowest price of 258p. By then it was no longer in the FT-SE 100. Then it recovered as the feeling grew that it had been over-sold and that some high-tech shares might have a better future than e-shares. But then it issued a profit warning and in line with my theory of 'dry' stocks it fell down to 61p. It hit 92p in May again and declined again after poor results.

Brokers' recommendations: many still love the stock, but essentially dry.
Sentiment factors: some loyalty.

BP Amoco

BP Amoco is the largest share in the Footsie 100. In the 12 months to June 1999 it achieved two huge takeovers. BP took over Amoco in August 1998 some months after it had taken over Atlantic Richfield, a $20 billion company which felt it was too small to compete in the global oil market.

The takeovers were partly a solution to the problems the oil industry faced in 1998. Like Exxon and Royal Dutch Shell, BP needed to find new sources of oil. In the early 1990s oil companies 'chased volume' but getting oil out of new sites like the Caspian Sea, the Gulf of Mexico and West Africa was expensive. Broker BT Alex Brown noted that, while production of oil had increased by 10 per cent in 1997, reserves had stayed the same – at 12 years supply.

Some projects like BP's Foinaven faced delays; other explorations were proving far more expensive than budgeted. BP also faced problems in Colombia, once touted as a prize new oil province, and now problematic with bandits, drug barons and a less than admirable government.

The cheapness of oil in 1998 and early 1999 made the situation worse. The price of Brent Crude hovered around $10 to $12 a barrel. Calculations by analysts Wood Mackenzie suggested that 24 per cent of the world's oil deposits needed an oil price of $15 per barrel to get a return on capital of 15 per cent.

BP then went for Amoco and succeeded. The merger offered BP a bigger share of the US market and eventual savings of $2 billion with the loss of 10,000 jobs. The purchase of Arco offered BP better sites for oil and gas in Alaska.

In July 1998 J.P. Morgan advised buying BP, as they then were, when the price was 814p. A month later the shares were down to 790p. When the merger with Amoco was announced the price of the shares steadied at 810p. Many, but not all, brokers welcomed the deal. Merrill Lynch upgraded BP to buy from accumulate. Flemings were generally bullish about the merger. But there were dissenting voices. Charles Stanley recommended selling BP at 810p while SG Securities were cautious. The shares did not move much. They were 816p in September when there was another positive recommendation.

It was only slowly that the market realized one implication of BP Amoco's position as top share in the Footsie 100. The tracker funds needed large quantities of BP Amoco. In February Killik & Co. recommended buying at 872p because trackers were still underweight. Killik's recommendation contradicted brokers Charles Stanley who said the outlook for oil shares was gloomy with the long-term oil price likely to stay around $10 to $12.

The fact that trackers needed the shares pushed the price steadily upwards. On 13 May, BP Amoco stood at 1,089p despite continuing worries about low prices for Brent Crude. By 21 June, the shares were at 1,179p, a rise of 39 per cent since the Amoco merger. It was then trading on a PER of 54.5. On 4 October the stock was split and went even higher.

Looking back on the first 6 months of 1999, the equities strategy team at Salomon Barney Smith argued oil shares benefited in general as telecoms, life assurance, electronics and other wonder stocks of 1998 either slowed down or went into reverse. Oil and gas as a sector rose by 18 per cent. BP Amoco did better than the sector average. Big is beautiful in the time of the tracker funds. In 2000 and early 2001, the shares traded between 550 and 600 mainly on a PER of 16, solid but not phenomenal.

Sentiment factors: negative associations, due to environmental problems linked to the oil industry.

Enthusiasm quotient: some, due to the economic effects of the mergers.

Barclays Bank

The banking industry has changed radically over the last 10 years with cutbacks in branches, the growth of telephone banking and the virtual disappearance of the bank manager. Banks have benefited enormously from technological changes. Yet no one loves banks.

Consumers complain about poor service, inflated charges and mistakes. Increasingly, banks try to sell customers additional products; they trade on the bank manager making you feel guilty even though he has now become a long-distance voice. Millions feel residual anxiety. Upset the bank manager, the voice on the telephone, and next time you need to borrow money the voice will leave you swinging in the wind.

Studies of the relationship between banks and customers suggest that banks in the past liked to make customers as dependent as possible. The bank manager was the father figure. Obviously that's changed, but attitudes to Barclays' problem suggest there may be some of these feelings remaining. When the bank hit problems the shares suffered more than finances warranted.

In January 1998 the bank stood at 1,800p having recently appointed Martin Taylor as its chief executive.

More than most banks Barclays lent to Russia. When, in August 1998, Russia announced that it was defaulting on its debt Barclays fell drastically to just over 824p.

Barclays' exposure to Russia was, in fact, not that great – around £250 million. Martin Taylor had seen that the retail bank was the best performing part of Barclays and so he started reporting the bank's profits in two separate sections – to emphasize how well the retail operations were doing. The losses in Russia did not dent those profits much, but they were seen as somehow symbolic. Certainly they offered bears – and perhaps investors terminally irritated with banks – the chance to punish the bank by driving the share price down.

Through late August and September 1998 Barclays did not recover that much. By the end of September its price was down round 900p.

An apparent disaster then helped push the shares back up. In November Taylor resigned suddenly. The impact on the shares was largely positive. Most of the financial press argued that he had his critics.

After a prolonged search for a new chief executive the bank appointed Mike O'Neill. O'Neill was supposed to be one of America's toughest bankers, but, on the very day he started work, he resigned for health reasons. His doctors warned him that he might die if he took on the stresses of the Barclays' job.

The vacuum allowed bidders to hover. Pundits argued Barclays might be targeted by a smaller bank, such as the Royal Bank of Scotland. On 5 May 1999 Sir George Mathewson, chief executive of the Royal Bank, said that if Britain did not create large national banks it would leave the door open for European banks to take over domestic operations. The Royal Bank sensed insecurity, an empire without a king – to lose one chief executive might be strategy; to lose a second would suggest carelessness – and so sniffed around Barclays.

Ironically, not having a chief executive helped Barclays' share price. The chairman Sir Peter Middleton took on the role of acting chief executive. Within a few weeks he was cutting 7,500 jobs, much to the City's delight – macho management being in favour.

In May 1999 Barclays reached a high of 2,052p. The shares slipped back to 1,852p by 6 June. Still the shares were worth twice what they had been worth at the time of the Russian default. Some 2 weeks later and without a chief executive, the shares had risen to 1,981p. Salomon Smith Barney raised its judgement to 'outperform' from 'neutral' and Dresdner Kleinwort Benson marked it 'buy'.

The year 2000 did not see much change in the fortunes of the bank and in January 2001 the shares stood at 2,100p. In May they stood at 2,227p.

In 1999 I wondered whether Barclays was doing so well *because* it had no chief executive. In terms of management theory this makes little sense even though Middleton did not let the bank drift. What is striking about Barclays' performance though is the steep fall in the late summer of 1998. Bank shares have one special emotional ingredient – fear. It was this fear, almost panic, that sent the shares down. The arrival of a new chief executive has not drastically affected the share's value once the panic was over!

Sentiment factors: mainly fear in the event of any major threat of a banking collapse and a small dose of guilt/anger towards the now invisible bank manager.

Enthusiasm quotient: considerable, every new technology means a smaller payroll and insecurity for bank staff.

ARM Holdings

ARM Holdings started in Cambridge in 1990 under the name Advanced Risc Machines. Risc has nothing to do with risk; it stands for 'reduced instruction set computing'. The company was originally an alliance between Acorn, the British computer company that had made the BBC Microprocessor, and America's Apple and VLSI.

One of Acorn's founders, Hermann Hauser, wanted to design Risc chips which were cheaper and more efficient than other chips. Robin Saxby, now the chairman of ARM, believes he was given the job because, when he was asked at his interview how he could turn Acorn's chip into a global standard, he replied that if ARM were to become a global company it had to have a global presence from the beginning.

Saxby decided not to be a manufacturer but a designer. He would make ARM global by developing partnerships which used ARM's intellectual property. The company would design high-performance low-cost chips, but wouldn't make them. It would sell licences to others to make the chips and use them in electronic goods. ARM's clients include Hewlett Packard, IBM and Philips and its chips can be found in mobile phones, laptop and palmtop computers. ARM likes to say it is a chipless chip company.

From 1994 to 1997, while the company was still private, it achieved a compound growth rate in sales of 87 per cent.

In 1998 profits rose from £4.5 million to £9.4 million on sales which were 59 per cent up at £42.3 million. Unlike Amazon, therefore, ARM has actually made profits. When it went public in April 1998 ARM was valued at £264 million. Acorn owned 24 per cent of the company. In June the company was trading at 187p.

Throughout 1998, backed by certain brokers like Killik & Co., ARM rose steeply.

In April 1999 Acorn was broken up and disappeared from the stock market. ARM fell steeply, when the deal was announced, to 665p, but 2 months later it had risen further to 682p.

On 24 June 1999 ARM announced a further deal in which it sold a new chip to Lucent Technologies. The shares rose to 770p. There were rumours too of further deals with Motorola and Texas Utilities. It was now in the FT-SE 250 and trading on a PER of 299!

In 2001 ARM suffered from the tech stock falls and retreated from a high of 965p to 221p. Since then it has recovered to trade at 390p but is now comfortably in the FT-SE 100.

ARM has obviously been something of a wonder stock, but, unlike many other wonder stocks, it has delivered some profits to its investors. The interesting comparison is with British Biotech which at its peak was valued at £2 billion.

Sentiment factors: nil, in fact even slightly negative since the company has been implicated in the demise of Acorn which many people remember fondly because of the BBC microprocessor.

Enthusiasm quotient: huge because the technology ARM produces is innovative and their global strategy is clearly working.

Conclusions – wet shares, dry shares and new enthusiasms

I would suggest that in the case of six 'dry' shares – BP Amoco, Vodafone, ARM, Amazon.com, Baltimore Technologies, British Biotech – there is a clear and fairly rational link between the expectations the technology arouses and the value of the shares. These shares can trade at phenomenal PERs because, as in four of the cases studied here, they are opening up markets with huge potentials. The only 'wet' share in my list which was ever comparable was Body Shop and its PER remains high. But if there are problems, the shares fall steeply with no buffers.

The six wet shares, with their much more emotional associations – Sainsbury's, Marks & Spencer, Body Shop, Allied Carpets, Laura Ashley and Manchester United – arouse strong feelings and loyalties, conscious and unconscious. I'd argue my analysis of the flow of both share prices and brokers recommendations shows that 'sentiment' here involves a lot of clinging to the companies. They attract emotional support which can outweigh financial realities.

Manchester United is the oddity here trading at a lower PER than far less successful football clubs. Had I been looking at Newcastle United or Sunderland, however, I would have found a situation similar to the other 'wet' shares – a PER being held high despite less than wonderful performances at the cash register.

Barclays Bank is a share which is neither wet nor dry simply because millions have experience of banks (like my fictional Middlesex Railways) and yet the banks' retail sections have made extensive use of new technologies.

I suggest investors should think about the psychology of any share before they buy and, in particular, examine whether they continually find they're thinking of selling, but can never quite bring themselves to do it. A certain reluctance always turns up.

I want to add a final point.

Brokers' recommendations – and principles of scaling

One problem about arriving at measures of expectation is that every broker seems to frame their recommendations a little differently. Many follow the rule of the five-point scale which is widely used in psychometric testing to determine attitudes and feelings:

- buy;
- weak buy;
- hold;
- weak sell;
- sell.

Sometimes 'good value' is used as a weak buy.

The five-point scale has its pitfalls because it is a little crude. Some brokers have different points using:

■ accumulate;
■ high enough;
■ and strong buy

for emphasis. There is no standard, however, which makes it very difficult to compile figures which quantify properly attitudes towards a particular share.

Psychologists suggest that it is better to have a seven- or a nine-point scale if you want to judge the strength of feelings or attitudes. (I know I haven't always used that advice myself.)

In terms of recommendations for shares that would mean a nine-point scale as follows:

■ strong buy;
■ buy;
■ accumulate;
■ weak buy;
■ hold;
■ high enough;
■ think about selling;
■ weak sell;
■ sell.

It would make it possible to have much better economic and psychological data about shares if brokers agreed to frame their recommendations on such a nine-point scale. They've got numerate staff. Surely that's not impossible.

ten

Faith, fraud and financial IQ

Last words of wisdom are never easy. I have argued throughout that it is too simple to claim that market psychology is just a matter of greed, fear and the herd instinct. The market is a far more complex beast. Brokers – perhaps British ones especially – like to quote that formula partly because most come from a background and culture where psychology is treated with suspicion and introspection is for wimps. Throughout I have referred to cases of bizarre and sometimes disturbed behaviour in the financial community. The most obvious examples are the highly publicized case of Peter Young, the broker who when charged with fraud came to court dressed as a woman, and the firm of Turnell & Tokyo, which made one of its brokers dress up as a Nazi. The broker involved was Jewish. The firm argued that, while it might have been a joke that had gone too far, it was clearly a joke. It wouldn't have been much fun otherwise. Many women City workers have also complained bitterly of sexual harassment. One way of seeing such incidents is as symptoms of stress where brokers and others are under extreme pressure.

For investors the underlying question is: 'Are these cases the tip of the iceberg and should we entrust money to such stressed-out brains?'

Though I set out the investigate the psychology of the market, nothing led me to expect some of my findings – and a number are frankly psychological. First, it is clear that equities are not just impersonal objects or certificates; we place emotional value on them. Second, unconscious factors and attitudes seem to affect our financial behaviour. I am not a Freudian, but I am struck by the power of his analysis of slang relating to money and shares.

What is perhaps most surprising is that the powerful emotional associations evoked by some shares – see the distinction made in Chapter 9 between wet and dry shares – is reflected in the price/earning ratio (PER), which is a sober fraction. And the 'wetness' of shares seems to relate to their price movements.

At the beginning of 2001 the market is more bearish than it has been since 1987. This distinction between wet and dry shares may be very useful when dealing with such a market – especially when, as Hugh Priestley and Andrew Smithers both pointed out, 'youngish' brokers have had no experience of bear markets. In this context, a sense of the 'wetness' of shares may be very useful.

As I finished writing this book shares in Marks & Spencer bounced back upwards. The signing up of design guru George Davies who had founded Next made the shares leap 10 per cent in early 2001. On 3 February 2001 they were trading on a PER of 29.2 and at 240p. This was just 10p down on their price on 8 December 1999. Despite a very poor year and disastrous Christmas trading, just the merest glimmer of hope made this supremely wet share move up sharply.

I was left with three other final impressions. First, almost no analysts talked about the growth of ethical investing, an interesting field since many people want to invest well and yet do not want their savings to finance certain kinds of companies. Second, many management consultants would be surprised at the relatively narrow criteria used by financial analysts to evaluate companies. The assumption seems to be that they shouldn't bother too much about staff morale or how customers see a company. The bottom line is the bottom. There are exceptions. The well-known brokers Schröders started an advertising campaign in 2001 which stressed that they look at the people behind the bottom line and the whole tone of the ad is to persuade the investor that savvy Schröders are privy to special information. Their staff made over 2,000 visits to companies. In fact, most such presentations are on offer to all analysts in the City, so the Schröders team would not usually be seeing something others are not.

Third, there is the growing question of fraud – a subject which is not reported perhaps as much as it should be. For the press, financial advertising is lucrative. I am not suggesting this affects stories or that newspapers and magazines suppress some stories, but the message of nearly all financial journalism is that it is sensible to invest. People have to save – especially for their retirement – they need to do something with their money. The financial pages essentially suggest the only option is to choose what suits you best between shares or unit trusts or pension schemes linked to shares.

Yet the last few years have seen as much fraud and mismanagement as ever before where, as ever, poor saps and greedy saps have been conned and fleeced. I have discussed cases like that of Hugh Eaves, the City Slickers accusations, Peter Young and the mighty Equitable Life. There are now allegations in the US that certain investors got preferential treatment at floats of new shares in return for paying bribes. All this reinforces my feeling that investors can use psychology in that most traditional of ways – to empower themselves and not to let experts overawe them. The City must do better than blare: 'We know about money – you don't. So give us your cash.'

My interviews with market professionals show, in fact, how different their approaches to investment are. Most spoke of their successes; few spoke of their failures, a very understandable stance in an industry where experts have to sell their services. But investors have to realize that brokers do not have all the answers. It is important for any investor to have the confidence to approach brokers and ask them critical questions. One way to that confidence is to be well informed and to have a sense of our own financial IQ.

And we might ask why investors should be brimming with confidence in City experts, given the poor average performance of funds. Only Hugh Priestley of Rathbone confronted the hard question for brokers, traders and analysts. Why is their record so poor? Priestley went on to contend, in the face of much evidence, that active management can still outperform tracker funds. Before being convinced of the brilliant record of any broker, ask searching questions.

I want to return briefly to Hilton's (1998) paper. He argues that the City has much to learn from psychology in terms of how to market itself. Institutions should do more research into how they present themselves and their products. One of the points he stresses illustrates the risks and benefits. He notes investors seem very attracted by investment products that limit losses or, indeed, appear to limit losses. My own reading of financial advertising suggests, however, that, as ever, the small print and the charges matter. One thing is certain. Financial institutions will not be offering guarantees to investors to limit losses if they can't make money out of it. Loss leaders don't exist in the City.

Don't let me press you to invest . . .

More than in the 1990s, the recent falls have made it obvious to investors that shares can go down as well as up. Yet how did the press – and financial analysts – play this at the end of 2000?

First, the figures. In 2000 the NASDAQ Index fell 39.3 per cent and it ended the year 54 per cent below its high. But that did not make many analysts and commentators pause or feel shame. At the start of January 2001, for example, the *International Herald Tribune* (8 January 2001) rounded up the opinions of leading American analysts. Few were that pessimistic. The smart investor would not let gloom go too far, analysts purred reassuringly. I pick out two typical comments. Brokers Stolper & Co of San Diego accepted that shares had fallen and tech shares no longer were an instant road to riches but 'most of the pain is behind us'. Ivy Management said 'it would be a tremendous mistake to get out now.' A number of analysts suggested that we had been seeing not the start of a bear market – Wall Street fell less than 50 per cent from its high in 1929 – but the rater more reassuring process of a 'correction' in the market.

The headline for the *International Herald Tribune* piece suggested analysts were rediscovering the sober principles of Benjamin Graham. 'Burst in Tech Bubble teaches investors to find value' ran the headline, but actually value did not mean value in any conventional sense. Analysts confidently told the *International Herald Tribune* that the smart investor should not be defeatist. Accentuate the positive, eliminate the negative seemed to be the fund of their wisdom. Trust us and the good times will soon be back.

In a similar piece at the start of January *USA Today* noted that 11 of 50 companies on its e-consumer Internet index were trading at less than $2 a share. These companies had all been high-flyers who turned out never to make a buck. Yet Marc Andersen co-founder of Netscape, told *USA Today* that 'despite the bear market and the continued bloodshed, this will be remembered as a time when great e-businesses were built.' Some 3 weeks later Amazon did report better than expected figures, but in Britain more firms were going bankrupt than at any time since 1995 and brokers Charles Schwab were instructing employees to take a number of extra days off so there would not have to be lay-offs.

It is not just institutions who find it hard to admit the financial failures of 2000 and early 2001. David Stevenson writes a column detailing his experiences as a member of an investment club. He admitted in January 2001 that his club had quite a few stocks that had fallen by 60 per cent, though, he boasted, they had none that had fallen 99 per cent. He added that the feeling was that there were many shares which had now sunk to bargain basement prices. The club's new strategy was to look for technology shares which had fallen too far. One stock they now favoured was New Media Spark on which they had already taken a loss; still they thought they should buy more shares as the price was now very very low. There was no sense in an investment club having 40 per cent of its capital in cash. (In fact, if the club had bought euros or French francs, rather than be obsessed with shares, they would have seen a rise of about 12 per cent between late November 2000 and February 2001). Accentuate the positive indeed.

An interesting twist to this 'resist the gloom scenario' came in a statement from Paul Killik of Killik & Co. He started by saying investors were confused but he suggested that the conservative swing to safe shares like banking and housing was misguided. These shares were now overvalued. Like David Stevenson, Killik suggested there were technology shares out there which were still cheap.

Given the enormous fall in the NASDAQ, not to mention growing anxieties of slowing growth in mobile phones and radiation problems, this seems true optimism. Shares that Killiks had backed in 2000 included Eidos, the Money Channel and Kingston Communication. I do not mean to single out these brokers for criticism incidentally because virtually no brokers adopted the catastrophic pessimism position and got out of equities as Buffett had done before the bear market of 1973/74. (Even Buffett did not this time.) But the long bull market of the 1990s made optimism a habit, almost a reflex that was hard to drop.

'Buyer, beware' remains a good motto in dealing with investments.

I have stressed that this is not a book about share tipping, but I think I have shown it is important for investors to be self-aware, to understand their own attitudes to risk and to use their money in accordance with that self-awareness and understanding. Feeling comfortable is vital. That is why readers should take note of the results to the questionnaires on information and risk on pages 97 and 151. It is also wise to be aware of cognitive dissonance and to seek out, quite deliberately, information which may contradict your hunches and favourite ideas about shares. All this means making the effort to master the inevitable mathematics involved in assessing shares, and not succumbing to information overload or burnout.

If you are faced with information overload do not complain or avoid it, but rather accept it as a problem for you. Then, start to find ways of dealing with your own tendencies to skip uncomfortable or disturbing information. You can solve – and resolve – the problems it causes you.

Finally, remember you have choices. Never feel you have to do something now. If the history of financial markets shows anything it is that opportunities to make money are always there – every day of the week. Invest to your own rhythm and timing.

Glossary

As this book explores both psychological and financial ideas, it seemed useful to include a glossary, since few specialists in investment will be familiar with psychological terms and psychologists are unlikely to be familiar with all the financial terms. (We are left with admiration for Dr Johnson, who wrote the first English dictionary.)

active fund management: funds where analysts pick shares to buy and sell on the basis of their research and intuition – the opposite of tracker funds.

advisory clients: accounts where only the client can authorize the buying and selling of shares. The broker consults and advises but does not have a mandate to buy and sell as he sees best.

AIM market: alternative investment market – the smallest of the London stock exchanges.

anal personality: a Freudian personality who tends to hoard faeces as a child and becomes an adult who is obsessed with money.

behaviourism: a theory first developed by John B. Watson, which holds that observation of and experimentation on external behaviour is the only valid method for psychology. It has implications for understanding how we invest.

blue buttons: junior members on the stock market in the 19th century wore jackets with blue buttons.

brokers' recommendations: brokers put out circulars to their clients on a regular basis and in these they recommend shares to buy, hold or sell.

bubble: according to Dr Johnson, who was close in time to the South Sea Bubble, the term came to mean unwise and greedy financial speculation.

buy options: these secure the right to buy a share at a fixed price within a defined period. Far from being modern financial instruments, they were known and used in London before 1700 and sometimes known as a privilege.

Cadbury proposals: proposals on how directors should behave and be paid, which were set out by a committee chaired by Adrian Cadbury.

capitalization: if a company has 1 million shares and their price today is £2.5, its market capitalization will be £2.5 million. The market capitalization of a company fluctuates constantly in relation to its share price.

chartists: investment advisers who are not influenced by the underlying value of the companies, but who buy and sell according to share movements which they chart. Extel provide a chart of recent price movements in every share as part of their information package.

Chicago Futures market: the first official futures market set up in 1851.

Chinese walls: large companies separate different operations so that there cannot be accusations of insider or privileged trading.

cognitive dissonance: a theory which holds that it is psychologically uncomfortable to hold two contradictory beliefs and that human beings act to reduce this dissonance. Investors may, for example, seek out positive information about a share they think they should sell in order to persuade themselves to hold on to it.

commodities: there are markets in physical commodities such as copper, coffee and oil as well as in shares. Futures dealing started in such commodities.

computer modelling: a controversial area, in both psychology and investment. Computer enthusiasts claim to have powerful models of both how the brain works and how financial markets work. The argument centres on whether these are just or whether they can usefully predict market movements.

contrarian: someone whose investment strategy runs counter to current orthodoxy.

Consols: the earliest British government security. Consols stands for consolidated loan.

control group: a group used for comparison with an experimental group.

convertible bonds: bonds issued by a company which allow holders to convert some of their holdings into shares.

covering the dividend: the profits of a company should cover the dividend it intends to pay to shareholders.

day trading: the new form of Internet and electronic trading becoming popular in the United States. Day traders close their positions at the end of each day and hope to have made a profit. Typically day traders hope to make small profits on many traders.

debt/equity ratio: if a company has more debt than its equity is valued at, the debt/equity ratio is negative and many analysts would counsel against investing in such a share.

derivatives: are financial products whose value is derived from something else. Nick Leeson traded in derivatives, in the value of the Nikkei 225 Index, which itself derived its value from the price of shares on the Tokyo Stock Exchange. Options are also derivatives.

discretionary clients: are clients who give a broker a mandate allowing him or her to deal on their account. The broker has discretion to buy or sell within that mandate.

dividends: are a part of the profit made by a company which is paid to shareholders usually twice a year.

Dow Jones: the main index used on Wall Street. It recently started to include Microsoft, explaining that it had taken many years to do so because the main Dow Jones Index includes only shares that have at least a 20-year history. (No fly by night firms please, however large.)

e-trading: trading done on the Internet.

earnings per share: one key tool of stock analysis is to divide the total profits of a company by the number of shares issued to arrive at earnings per share.

equities: shares or stocks.

extroversion: a personality trait on the continuum of extroversion–introversion. Those who score high in extroversion tend to be sociable and sensation-seeking. They will tend to be more comfortable with taking risks than those who score lower.

Financial Services Authority: the British regulatory authority that supervises most dealing in financial services. Its current chairman Howard Davies was recently Deputy Governor of the Bank of England.

free association: a technique used by Freud to analyse patients. He would ask them to think of the first thing that came into their mind and then ask what next. He hoped thereby to understand the structure of a patient's thought and defences.

FT-SE 100 Index: the main index used on the London stock market. It lists the 100 biggest shares by market capitalization. It replaced the FT 30 shares index in 1986. There are a number of other indices, including the FT-SE 250, which includes the next 250 largest shares. There is also a FT-SE 350, or small capitalization index, and an FT Fledgling Index.

futures: trading in commodities has since the 19th century included buying the right to acquire goods at a set price at a future date.

futures market: markets that deal in options and derivatives.

growth stocks: shares which have potential for rapid growth.

herd instinct: conformity. Many analysts believe this is a key factor in explaining investor behaviour.

information overload: the problem of having too much information to handle, which can lead to stress and poor decision-making.

information theory: a psychological theory which sees human beings essentially as information-processing entities. Our brain is a channel for handling information.

insider trading: using privileged information to buy or sell shares for one's advantage. It used to be routine practice on Wall Street before the crash of 1929 when powerful investors were offered shares often earlier and at a better price than ordinary investors. The practice is now illegal. Novelist Jeffrey Archer was famously accused of insider trading when he bought shares in a television company on whose board his wife sat. Nothing was conclusively proved against him.

introspection: thinking about oneself. In the early 20th century it was used as an investigative technique but thinking about how we think turns out not to be that fruitful a scientific method because individual differences are so great. Yet it remains a useful method of being aware of our feelings, strengths and weaknesses.

introversion: a personality trait that is the opposite of extroversion. Typically those who score high on introversion are quiet, anxious, meticulous and afraid to make mistakes.

investment trusts: companies whose only assets are the shares they hold in other companies.

IQ: intelligence quotient, the most used measure of intelligence, which comes from dividing mental age by chronological age.

jobbers: pre-1987 it was jobbers who made the market in particular shares. Jobbers could only deal with stockbrokers.

joynt stocks: an early name for companies.

junk bonds: bonds issued by companies at a high rate of interest, usually because the company is at some risk. They have been used to finance some spectacular takeovers since the 1980s.

liquidity premium: the extra investors will pay for a bond that is very easy to trade because its history suggests buyers will never be too hard to find.

locus of control: a psychological theory that distinguishes between individuals who have an inner locus of control and see themselves as being in control and being responsible and those with an external locus of control who blame others and the outside world for their failures.

magical thinking: irrational and often over-optimistic thinking.

margin: trading on the margin means that investors do not have to put down the whole price of a stock – merely 10 or 50 per cent. It was argued that this was one of the causes of the 1929 Wall Street Crash.

margin call: if the price of a stock goes down brokers will call on clients for more funds to maintain their margin.

momentum trader: a trader who buys shares that are going up and sells shares that are going down. He or she goes with the momentum.

nAch: need for achievement – a technical term used by David McClelland in his theory of motivation. Those with a high nAch are more likely to become successful entrepreneurs.

NASDAQ: originally the alternative American Stock Exchange, which dealt in smaller shares, but now some of those it lists such as Microsoft have become giants. Over 5,000 stocks are listed.

Nikkei 225: the main index of the Tokyo Stock Exchange.

noise trader: a trader who responds to gossip and rumours in the market. Some analysts also see those who are momentum traders as noise traders.

options: options buy the right to buy or sell shares in the future at a set price. They are perhaps the original derivative because their value is derived from the share price.

overweight: in the latest jargon brokers often recommend a portfolio being overweight in particular shares such as oils or telecoms because they think these will rise more than the rest of the market.

penny shares: shares that trade for tiny amounts – often a penny.

pension funds: these are among the largest and most influential investors in the UK.

price/earnings growth ratio: is one the key ideas in Jim Slater's *Beyond the Zulu Principle*. He argues that the relationship between the price/earnings ratio (PER) and the expected rate of growth in earnings per share is an excellent clue to the prospects of a company. The price/earnings growth ratio is calculated as follows. If a company has a PER of 12 and it is growing at 12 per cent a year the price/earnings growth ratio is 12/12 or 1. If the company is growing at 24 per cent the price/earnings growth ratio is 12/24 or 0.5.

price/earnings ratio (PER): the price of a share divided by the earnings per share. So if a share is at 100p and the earnings per share are 10p, the PER will be 10.

probability blindness: is a form of irrational thinking where people do not calculate the often complex true probability of events.

profit forecasts: are forecasts issued by companies and brokers which attempt to estimate future profits. Profit warnings are SOS messages sent out by companies to indicate that they will not meet their targets.

psychoanalytic theories: theories developed by Sigmund Freud which focus on the different psychosexual stages – oral, anal, genital, latency – which children grow through. Freud always maintained there were links between these psychosexual stages and personality development – hence his concept of the anally retentive person.

psychosexual development: according to Freud, babies and infants move through times when they get satisfaction from different areas of the body. The mouth is the orifice in the oral stage. Then, with the emphasis on toilet training, infants go through an anal stage. Then comes a genital phase.

rational economic man: shorthand for theoretical approaches to economics which claim that human beings calculate advantage and risk unemotionally.

regression to the mean: a term used in statistics meaning the tendency for the value of a variable as predicted from a regression equation to be closer to the mean than it should be. For example, while very tall and very short parents have children who take after them, regression to the mean determines that children are usually closer to the average height of the whole population than the height of their parents.

repression: a psychoanalytic term for when memories and ideas are kept out of consciousness.

risk premium: an important theoretical concept. Equities are supposed to be riskier than bonds. To compensate for that risk they should offer more potential reward – and that extra is the risk premium.

selling short: the strategy of selling a share or currency that you do not own in the hope that by the time you have to deliver it its price will be far lower. George Soros did this with sterling in 1992. (Given what we have learned about psychoanalytic theories linking money and toilets, we can only be struck by the expression 'being caught short' – it seems to apply to both stock markets and defecation.)

syllogism: a logical puzzle where you have to deduce a conclusion from two premises. 'All men are mortal. Socrates is a man. Therefore Socrates is mortal' is perhaps the most famous.

tracker funds: funds which invest in shares in an index and which usually invest in particular shares in a precise ratio to the weight of that share in the index. FT-SE 100 tracker funds, for example, have to hold about 8 per cent of BP Amoco because its market capitalization represents 8 per cent of all the shares in the FT-SE 100.

trading on the margin: in the UK you usually have to pay for your shares in full: in America, you can put down only part 'the margin' and brokers lend you the balance. But if the price of a stock goes down, they can ask for more funds.

underweight: the reverse of overweight. Brokers will recommend being underweight in a particular sector if they think it will perform badly.

References

Abraham, K. (1979) *Selected Papers*, Maresfield Reprints.

Adler, A. (1929) *The Theory and Practice of Individual Psychology*, Routledge and Kegan Paul.

Apter, M. (1992) *The Dangerous Edge: The Psychology of Excitement*, Free Press (*Playboy* interview with Donald Trump).

Asch, S. (1952) *Social Psychology*, Prentice.

Bannister, D. and F. Fransella (1977) *A Manual of Repertory Grid Techniques*, Academic Press.

Basic Skills Agency (1996) *International Standards of Numeracy* (report).

Basso, T. (1994) *Panic Proof Investing*, John Wiley.

Beckers, S. (1997) 'Manager skill and investment performance', *Journal of Portfolio Management*, **23**, 9–23.

Benos, A. (1999) 'Aggression and the survival of overconfident traders', *Journal of Financial Markets*, **1**, 353–385.

Bergler, E. (1985) *Money and Emotional Conflict*, International Universities Press.

Bergler, Edmund (1958) 'Are you a money neurotic?', *Harpers*, 94–95.

Black, T. (1980) paper given at *Symposium on the 21st Anniversary of Broadmoor's Psychology Department, London* (conference of the British Psychological Society).

Blanton, Smiley (1957) 'The hidden faces of money' in *Now or Never: The Promise of the Middle Years*, Prentice Hall.

Bornemann, F. (1976) *The Psychoanalysis of Money*, Urizen Press. This book has a long introduction by Bornemann and then a number of articles including *Sex in Volksmund* – some he approves of and some he mocks – by other authors. As the book is both useful and hard to find, it is worth noting that there is a copy in the University of London Library at Senate House.

Bowden, P. (1981) 'The fate of special hospital patients', *British Journal of Psychiatry*, **138**, 340–3554.

Burger, J.M. (1986) 'Desire for control and the illusion of control', *Journal of Research in Personality*, **20**, 66–76.

Burrough, B. and J. Helyar (1990) *The Barbarians at the Gate*, Arrow.

Byrne, Richard (1999) *Human Cognitive Evolution in the Descent of Man* (edited by Michael Corballis and Stephen Lea), Oxford University Press.

Cabot, W. (1998) 'Restrictive guidelines and pressure to outperform', *Financial Analysts Journal*, July/August, 5–8.

Carleton, W. T., C. Chen and T. Steiner (1998) 'Optimism biases among brokers' and non-brokerage firms' equity recommendations', *Financial Management*, 17–30.

Carswell, J. (1993) *The South Sea Bubble*, Alan Sutton.

Castro, A. and B. Lee (1999) 'The origin of dealings in joynt stock companies', *Journal of Economic History*, **58**, 320.

Chancellor, E. (1999) *The Devil Take the Hindmost*, Farrar, Straus and Giroux.

Chapman, C. (1988) *How the Stock Exchange Works*, Hutchinson.

Cohen, D. (1977) 'Leon Festinger interview', *Psychologists on Psychology*, Routledge and Kegan Paul.

Cohen, D. (1997) *Carl Rogers: A Critical Biography*, Constable.

Dremer, D. and M.A. Barry (1998) 'Forecasts by brokers', *Financial Analysts Journal*, **24**, 17–29.

Edwards, A.L. (1959) *Edwards Personal Preference Schedule*, The Psychological Corporation.

Eysenck, H.J. (1967) *The Biological Basis of Personality*, University of Chicago Press.

Eysenck, H.J. (1996) *Genius*, Cambridge University Press.

Fay, Stephen (1996) *The Collapse of Barings*, Richard Cohen Books.

Fenton O'Creevy, M., N. Nicholson, E. Soans and P. Willman (1998) *Individual and Contextual Influences on the Market Behaviour of Finance Professionals*, ESCR Conference Paper, September, London Business School research paper.

Ferenczi, S. (1930) 'The ontogenesis of interest in money', cited in E. Bornemann (1976).

Ferris, P. (1961) *The City*, Penguin.

Festinger, Leon (1957) *Theory of Cognitive Dissonance*, Row and Peterson.

Fisher, I. (1928) *Theory of Interest*, Macmillan.

Forrester, I. (1998) *Truth, Games, Lies, Money and Psychoanalysis*, Harvard University Press.

Freud, S. (1900) *The Interpretation of Dreams* (translated by James Strachey),

Hogarth Press; republished 1999 in a new translation by Joyce Crick, Oxford University Press.

Freud, S. (1905) *The Psychopathology of Everyday Life* (translated by James Strachey), Hogarth Press.

Freud, S. (1929) *The Future of an Illusion*, Hogarth Press.

Freud, S. (1979) 'The wolf man', *Case Histories*, No. 2, Penguin. An extensive literature on this case exists.

Fromm, Erich (1978) *To Have or to Be*, Jonathan Cape.

Furnham, A. and M. Argyle (1998) *The Psychology of Money*, Routledge.

Galbraith, J.K. (1933) *A Short History of Financial Euphoria*, Whittle, New York.

Galbraith, J.K. (1955) *The Great Crash*, Hamish Hamilton.

Gardiner, M. (1972) *The Wolf Man and Freud*, Hogarth Press.

Golding, E. (1980), paper read at *British Psychological Conference*, reported in *Psychology News*, 13.

Goldman Eisler, A. (1970) 'The anal personality', cited in P. Kline (1972) *Fact and Fantasy in Freudian Theory*, Methuen.

Graham, B. and David Dodd (1951) *Security Analysis* (3rd edition), McGraw Hill.

Gray, J. (1993) *The Psychology of Fear and Stress*, Cambridge University Press.

Greenberg, P. (1977) 'High risk sports', *Human Behaviour*, August.

Gudjudsson, G. (1995) *The Psychology of Investigations, Confessions and Testimony*, John Wiley.

Haugen, R. (1996) 'The effects of intrigue, liquidity, imprecision and bias on expected stock ratio', *Financial Analysts Journal*, **22**, 8–17.

Helzer, J. and L. Robins (1988), 'The prevalence of post-traumatic stress disorder', *New England Journal of Medicine*, **317**, 578–583.

Higgins, Hung N. (1998) 'Forecasting performance in seven countries', *Financial Analysts Journal*, May/June, 58–60.

Hilton, D. (1998), *Psychology and the City*, Center for the Study of Financial Innovation, paper no. 38.

Hinshley, M. (1998) 'How much is a tulip worth?', *Journal of Financial Analysis*, July/August, 11–15.

Hockey, I. (1970) 'Increased selectivity in noise', *Quarterly Journal of Experimental Psychology*, **22**, 37–42

Houghton, J. (1694) cited in E. V. Morgan and W. A. Thomas (1962) *A History of the Stock Exchange*, Elek.

Human Behaviour, August 1977, Survey of risk.

International Journal of Advertising and Marketing to Children (1999), **1**(1), Winthorp Publications.Johnson, Samuel (1905) *The Life of the English Poets*, Clarendon Press.

Julander, C.R. (1975) 'Sparande od effekter ur okad kunsop om in komstens anvanding', Doctoral dissertation, Stockholm School of Economics.

Kahn, H. and Cary Cooper (1993) *Stress in the Dealing Room*, Routledge & Kegan Paul.

Kahneman, D.E. (1998) 'Psychological biases and risk-taking in financial decisions', *IIR Seminar on Behavioural Finance, London, November.*

Kahneman, D.F. and A. Tversky (1979) 'Prospect theory: an analysis of decision under risk', *Econometrica*, **47**, 263–291.

Keynes, J. M. (1936) *The General Theory of Employment, Interest and Money*, Macmillan.

Kindelberger, C. (1994) *Money, Panic and Crashes*, John Wiley.

Klein, N. (2000), *No Logo*, Flamingo.

Kline, P. (1993) *Psychology Exposed*, Routledge.

Kline, P. (1972), *Fact and Fantasy in Freudian Theory*, Methuen.

Kogan, N. and M. Wallach (1964) *Risk Taking: A Study in Cognition and Personality*, Holt, Rinehart and Winston.

Kynaston, D. and W. Reader (1992) *A History of Phillips and Drew*, Phillips and Drew.

Lamont, Norman (1999) *In Office*, Little, Brown.

Langer, E. (1975) 'The illusion of control', *Journal of Personality and Social Psychology*, **32**, 311–328.

Leeson, Nick (1996) *Rogue Trader*, Warner.

Lenhoff, M. and S. Rubinsohn (1999) *Market Report*, April, Capel Cure Sharp.

Lewin, H.G. (1936) 'Railway mania and its aftermath', *Railway Gazette.*

Lewis, M. (1999), *New York Times* magazine, February.

Lewis, Michael (1990) *Liar's Poker*, Coronet.

Loffler, G. (1998) 'Biases in analysts' forecasts', *International Journal of Forecasting*, 261–275.

Lowenstein, R. (1995) *Buffett: The Making of an American Capitalist*, Random House.

Mackay, C. (1852) *History of Extraordinary Popular Delusions and the Madness of Crowds*, Office of the National Library.

Major, John (1999) *The Autobiography of John Major*, HarperCollins.

Mapstone, E. (1998) *Wars with Words*, Viking.

Maslow, A. (1973), *Further Research of Human Nature*, Penguin.

Matathia, I. and M. Salzman (1998) *Next*, Overlook Press.

McClelland, D. (1952) *The Achieving Society*, Princeton University Press.

McClelland, D. (1977) cited in Cohen, D. (1997) *Carl Rogers: A Critical Biography*, Constable.

McLynn, F. (1996) *Carl Gustav Jung*, Bantam.

Michie, R.C. (1981) *Money Markets and Mania*, Donald.

Miller, G. (1956) 'The magical number 7 plus or minus two', *Psychological Reviews*, **63**, 81–97.

Morris, Desmond (1965) *The Naked Ape*, Jonathan Cape.

Morton, F. (1966) *The Rothschilds*, Secker & Warburg.

Nagy, I. (1998) 'The motivation of investors', *Financial Analysts Journal*, May/June, 13–17.

Ormerod, P. (1997) *Butterfly Economics*, Faber & Faber.

Partridge, E. (1984) *A Dictionary of Slang*, Routledge.

Patel, A.B. (1997) *The Mind of a Trader*, Pitman Publishing.

Perl, J. (1999) 'Volatility in the oil markets', *Pipeline*, January.

Piatelli Palmarini, J. (1994) *Cognitive Illusions*, Harper Collins.

Pinnock Report (1975), HMSO.

Popper, Karl (1995) *The Open Society and Its Enemies*, Routledge (originally published 1945).

Rand, Nicholas and Maria Torok (1997) *Questions for Freud*, Harvard University Press.

Raskob, John (1929) 'Everyone ought to be rich', *Ladies Home Journal*, March.

Rever, D. (1999) cited in E.K. Wärneryd (1999) *The Psychology of Saving*, Edward Elgar Books.

Riviere, J. (1937) 'Hate greed', *The Inner World of Joan Rivière*, republished 1985 by Karnac.

Rogers, Carl (1965) *A History of Psychology in Autobiography* (edited by F. Boring and G. Lindzey), Appleton Crofts.

Rubinstein, H. (1981) 'Survey of attitudes', *Psychology Today*.

Ryle, G. (1949) *The Concept of Mind*, Hutchinson.

Sapolsky, R. (1996) 'Why stress is bad for the brain', *Science*, 749–750.

Sawyer, W.W. (1951) *Prelude to Mathematics*, Penguin.

Schachter, Stanley, Leon Festinger and H.W. Riecken (1964) *When Prophesy Fails*, Harper and Row.

Schama, S. (1994) *An Embarrassment of Riches*, Knopf.

Shiller, R. (2000), *Irrational Exuberance*, Princeton University Press.

Skinner, B. F. (1984) *Particulars of My Life*, Jonathan Cape.

Skinner, B.F. (1953) *Science and Human Behaviour*, Macmillan.

Slater, J. (1994) *The Zulu Principle*, Orion.

Slater, J. (1997) *Beyond the Zulu Principle*, Orion.

Soros, G. (1988) *The Alchemy of Finance*, Weidenfeld and Nicolson.

Soros, G. (1995) *Soros on Soros*, John Wiley.

Steptoe, A. (1999) *Genius in the Mind*, Cambridge University Press.

Storr, Anthony (1999) *The Dynamics of Creation*, Penguin.

Svebak, S. (1980) 'The significance of effort as well as serious minded and playful motivational states for task induced tonic physiological changes', Paper presented to British Psychological Society, London.

Tannen, D. (1997) *The Argument Culture*, Random House.

Toffler, A. (1970) *Future Shock*, Pan.

Train, J. (1986) *The Midas Touch*, Harper and Row.

Tversky, A. and D. F. Kahneman (1992) 'Advances in prospect theory', *Journal of Risk and Uncertainty*, **5**, 297–323.

Wärneryd, E.K. (1999) *The Psychology of Saving*, Edward Elgar Books.

Wahlund, R. (1991) 'Mental discounting and financial strategies', *Journal of Economic Psychology*, **17**, 709–730.

Walker, M. (1995) *The Psychology of Gambling*, Butterworth.

Wall Street Journal, 24 October 1929.

Walters, Michael (1995) *How to Make a Killing from Penny Shares*, Rushmere Wynne.

Wason P. and N.J. Johnson Laird (1972) *The Psychology of Reasoning*, Batsford.

Watson, John B. (1928) *NEA Magazine*.

Wharton, Edith. (1912) *The Custom of the Country*, Scribner.

Wilcox, J. (1998) 'Investing at the edge', *Journal of Portfolio Management*, Spring, 9–21.

Wolfe, T. (1979) *The Right Stuff*, Farrar, Straus and Giroux.

Womack, K. (1997) 'Do brokerage analysts' recommendations have value?', *Journal of Finance*, **96**, 137–167.

Zuckerman, M. (1991) *Psychobiology of Personality*, Cambridge University Press.

Index